Employment Opportunities in Education

How To Secure Your Career

JEANNE M. MACHADO
ROMANA E. REYNOLDS

THOMSON

DELMAR LEARNING   Australia Canada Mexico Singapore Spain United Kingdom United States

Employment Opportunities in Education: How to Secure Your Career
by Jeanne M. Machado, Romana E. Reynolds

Vice President, Career Education SBU:
Dawn Gerrain

Director of Editorial:
Sherry Gomoll

Acquisitions Editor:
Erin O'Connor

Developmental Editor:
Alexis Breen Ferraro

Technology Project Manager:
Sandy Charette

Editorial Assistant:
Stephanie Kelly

Director of Production:
Wendy A. Troeger

Production Manager:
J.P. Henkel

Production Editor:
Amber Leith

Production Assistant:
Angela Iula

Director of Marketing:
Wendy E. Mapstone

Channel Manager:
Kristin McNary

Marketing Coordinator:
David White

Composition:
Pre-Press Company, Inc.

Cover Design:
Ark Stein

Library of Congress Cataloging-in-Publication Data

Machado, Jeanne M.
  Employment opportunities in education how to secure your career / Jeanne M. Machado, Romana E. Reynolds.-- 1st ed.
     p. cm.
  Includes bibliographical references and index.
  ISBN 1-4180-0105-8
  1. Teaching--Vocational guidance--United States. I. Reynolds, Romana E. II. Title.

LB1775.2.M22 2006
370'.23'73--dc22

2005020672

NOTICE TO THE READER

Contents

Preface

Education majors learn the educational theories and research that underlie and support teacher actions. They know how children best learn, and are given firsthand experience when student teaching. Teacher training programs rarely have the time to prepare students to market their competencies and skills, or to alert students to the many varying and emerging areas and sectors of employment that exist. This text emphasizes career self-management and suggests a planned course of action to aid student's realization of their "dream" job. It can be thought of as a personal career coach.

With new federal and state emphasis and additional media recognition of the importance of children's early years and the need for highly qualified educators, the field has new hope for good positions in education, better working environments, and salaries equal to professional training and experience.

Students need to graduate from training programs understanding the realities of this field of work, with a knowledge of its laws, its rewards, and well-prepared to compete for the best positions. There is also a need for educators to advocate for themselves, children and families.

The text contains charts, lists, motivational pep talks, written exercises, photographs, Web sites, and lots of hints and tips. The materials provided give students every chance of success in job search techniques, interviews, and self-employment ventures.

It is hoped that through use of this text, new students of Education or those who are currently working, become savvy dedicated professionals able to skillfully guide their careers, find joy in their efforts, and achieve life/work balance.

Since few other texts like this have been written, the authors hope it fills a void. Hopefully, it may help stem the high rate of turnover that exists in the early childhood field. Because of the background of the authors, many parts of the text focus upon early education and elementary education, but middle school, secondary school, community college and university education is not slighted.

This text particularly suits individuals entering the field with early childhood classroom experiences or training.

Content of Chapters

Because this volume deals with employment, you will notice the terms *worker, childcare provider, employee,* and *caregiver,* may be used. The authors would prefer to use the terms *early childhood educator, professional,* or *preschool teacher* for those who work with children before kindergarten, and *teacher* or *educator* for those above pre-kindergarten level. When we are quoting from other sources, we use the terminology of that source.

Chapter 1 offers an accurate, realistic picture of employment in the field of education. States differ greatly. Early childhood education is covered in depth. It includes a discussion of wages and benefits, and legislation affecting educators.

Readers are asked to dream a little about a future career and to review their present skills. These exercises help formulate the possible steps to proceed toward career goals. These steps often include further training or experience.

Chapter 2 discusses why this is a good time to launch an education career. It alerts the reader to the many employment areas that characterize the field and to the support service businesses that have grown and flourished around child education, development, and care.

In Chapter 3, professional growth planning information provides guidelines to increase the reader's chances of goal realization and success. Generalist and specialist training is explained along with career ladders. The chapter urges the development of an individual growth plan tied to an estimated time line. State certification, credentials, in-service training, distance learning, mentors, apprenticing, and financial aid are given attention. Helpful Website information is included. Charts, graphs, and figures clarify textual content when necessary.

Educators currently searching for employment may want to skip ahead to Chapter 4. Career moves involve immediate needs and an analysis of a best career move. Other topics under consideration in Chapter 4 include potential job satisfaction, a job seeker's mental attitude, job options, and the search for work. The legality of wording in classified ads will be of interest. A listing of job titles found on the Web alerts the reader to the diversity of positions available. The chapter recommends fact finding which often clarifies whether a job seeker will continue to pursue a position initially deemed desirable. It also prepares readers for interviews.

Cover letters and resume preparation comes next in Chapter 5. Both are commonly used to uncover available employment, to market oneself, and to impress hiring personnel. The chapter provides guidelines and professional examples. In addition, cover letter and resume templates are available on the accompanying CD.

A naive interviewee fails to prepare for job interviews. Many suggestions for interviewing are found in Chapter 6. The chapter gives readers every chance to interview well. Those being interviewed often wonder if it is proper to ask questions, particularly questions concerning salary, benefits, and chances for advancement. Information and examples are included that provide answers. Interview checklists and possible interview scenarios are available on the accompanying CD.

The workplace skills that keep people employed are covered in Chapter 7. How employees become invaluable to their employers is explained. Chapter 8 is of interest to those heading toward a career as a teacher trainer.

Educators can be uninformed about federal and state laws and the protections these laws afford. Chapter 9 explains rights, liabilities, occupational safety, worker's compensation, and other legal issues.

Chapter 10 describes opportunities for self-employment and features stories of successful educator entrepreneurs.

The final chapter, Chapter 11, deals with how advocacy efforts affect educators. It describes how advocacy groups have obtained increased salary, various benefits, and better working conditions.

The Appendix to this text contains a self-aptitude exercise, a skills checklist, a professional association list, sample forms, and additional examples related to chapter content.

Supplementary Material

This text is accompanied by a back of book CD-ROM that includes additional forms, exercises, cover letters and resume templates with instructions, interview checklists, interview scenarios, and examples of classified ads.

In addition, the personal Datakeeper will become your one-stop resource for resume and job application development. The fill-in-the-blank format allows for simple insertion of your education and employment history with additional space to keep your personalized record up-to-date. Also included are interview preparation questions and interviewing and follow-up tips. Once completed, you will have an easy-to-reference guide available when you need it most.

Acknowledgements

The author and the Thomson Delmar Learning publishing team would like to thank the following reviewers for their thoughtful feedback, which helped to shape the final text.

Julie Bakerlis, M.S.
Quinsigamond Community College
Worcester, MA

Alice D. Beyrent, M.Ed.
Hesser College
Manchester, NH

Kim Brown, Ph.D. (c)
California State University–
Bakersfield
Bakersfield, CA

Marsha Garman, M.S.
Hillsborough Community College
Tampa, FL

Kathleen Hutchison, Ed.D.
Texas A&M–San Antonio
San Antonio, TX

Margaret King, Ed.D.
Ohio University

CHAPTER ONE

Starting Out

The journey of a thousand miles begins with one step.

—Lao Tzu

Guest Speaker

When Zack was 15, his Aunt Meg asked him to be a guest speaker in her summer school class of academically talented third and fourth graders. Meg wanted Zack, who was an avid snow boarder, to describe the sport to her class, bring all his gear, including his board, show photos, talk about how he trained and took lessons, share books on the subject, and identify places he'd been to snow board. She gave Zack a list of possible points to cover in his talk. One was safety.

Arriving at the school, he checked in at the office, and was greeted by the summer school program director, who Meg said would direct him to her classroom. Meg's class was a surprise. There were no students at desks. There were no desks, just tables and chairs. The room looked like a beehive and buzzed with activity. Students were working on individual projects or in small groups. One group was learning how to run the school's audio visual equipment. Another was creating a map of the downtown section of their small town. Zack's impression of the room was—it's cool, not like my fourth grade.

Zack stayed after his presentation to help out. He knew he had been a big hit with the kids. They had been fascinated, asked lots of questions, and laughed at him dressed in his winter snow gear on a warm summer day.

QUESTIONS TO PONDER

1. Was exposing Zack to the field of education at 15 a good idea? If so, why?

2. What possible feelings might Zack have experienced while being a guest speaker? Could some of these encourage him to choose a teaching career in college?

This resource book hopes you already have chosen a career in education and have completed some form of training. It also provides information to those investigating the career field.

The idea of career management may be new to you. Career management requires an awareness of the labor market and opportunities to improve skills, and also knowing what strategies will work best. Instead of feeling that outside factors control your career success, this book places that responsibility on your shoulders as your own **career manager**. It promotes overcoming career obstacles that sometimes arise by becoming flexible and adaptable enough to modify career plans when necessary. As in any other profession, no-control situations, dead end jobs, and unhealthy and unprofessional work environments sometimes exist.

As your own career manager there will be many decisions ahead. Morkes (2003) describes a decision making process as

1) identifying choices.
2) identifying the likely outcomes of choices.
3) considering the pros and cons of choices.
4) identifying alternative outcomes.
5) choosing the option that is not only doable but most likely to succeed.

It is important to weigh multiple factors when making career decisions. These factors include personal job satisfaction, required training, typical compensation, employment opportunities, life balance, and other factors. A good manager takes inventory often. Prudent decisions are based upon self-awareness and self-knowledge. Your personal learning style, identity, values, interests, dispositions, aptitudes, and abilities will influence your individual career plans.

Career development is a process that encompasses identifying what is in your power to control and what is not. It considers work as one factor in your life. Your work life has an entry point, a progression, and a termination. Your work life provides professional identity and value. It involves occupational skills which include self-assessment, ability to apply information, decision-making, and both short- and long-term planning ability.

Goldman's (2004) view of career management suggests thinking about yourself as a creative agent:

> *Being a creative agent is about being able to position yourself as someone who is responsible for your success in your career, as opposed to being someone who is victimized by the economy, globalization or your boss.*
>
> *You have to be able to understand your industry and company with respect to what's happening in the market.*
>
> *You have to sell yourself in ways that are subtle, systematic and reinforce your becoming the person you want to be.*

Your personal life management skills may still be growing and developing as you steer the course of your life and decide what role work will play in it. You will choose a life style, how and where to live, and how to balance work with roles such as student, parent, partner/spouse. Work and its rewards may open life choices. As you interact with others you use interactional skills and other job-keeping or job survival techniques. If you've had success managing your life, managing your career is another adventure where personal skills will likely transfer.

The authors hope to convince you that a confident, competent, informed educator can reach his or her ultimate career goals, find satisfying employment, and discover the best use of training, experience, and talents. A thoughtful, planned approach is recommended.

A first step in a career plan includes an analysis of what brought you this far. Your beliefs about teaching and working with children are usually well established before entering a training program. A beloved educator in your past may have inspired you. Practicing educators frequently mention the intrinsic satisfaction and joy they feel or the fact that their work is meaningful and children in their care are learning. Take a moment to list the factors, people, or experiences that lead you to consider a career in education. A form is available on the CD that accompanies this text.

Occupational Awareness and Labor Market Trends

Census data shows an increase in the number of working parents, and, consequently a demand for child care (Child Care Law Center, 2001). Armas (2002) reports that Census 2000 figures reaffirm that young children are affected and experience some form of child care early in their lives. Figure 1–1 displays the percentage of children, birth through age five, in various types of child care.

Anyone abreast of current events has noted increased awareness and promotion of developmental child care for young children. Increased state spending on developmental programs for pre-kindergarten children is a reality (Greenberg & Springen, 2000).

Employment in the field of education, of which **early childhood** education is a subsection, is expected to increase by 14 percent between 2000 and 2010 according to U.S. Department of Labor predictions (Morkes, 2003). Average employment growth is projected for preschool teachers (Morkes). Faster growth is expected for school counselors, secondary school teachers, special education teachers, teacher assistants, and English as a second language teachers. Teacher job openings will occur both for the replacement of retiring teachers and general employment growth. *The Statistics' Occupational Quarterly 2003–2004* notes that preschool teachers are third on the list of growth occupations that are expected to require an associate degree or vocational certification from 2002 through 2012.

Types of Care

Age of Child	Relative	Nonrelative's Home	Center Based	No Arrangement without Parent
Birth to 1 year	24%	17%	77%	55%
1 year old	24%	19%	11%	50%
2 years old	19%	20%	19%	46%
3 years old	21%	19%	41%	32%
4 years old	18%	15%	65%	22%
5 years old	15%	17%	75%	16%

Figure 1–1   Estimated Percentage of Children Birth through Age Five in Care Situations.

* Note: Estimates based on children younger than six years old who had no prior kindergarten enrollment. Columns will not add up to 100% because some children were in multiple types of care.

Source: U.S. Department of Education. Center for Educational Statistics, 2002.

> **Question:** I learned to speak English at age ten, and I have an accent. Will this affect my chances for a career in education?
>
> **Answer:** Not necessarily. English as a second language teachers are in short supply and actively recruited in many parts of the United States. Numbers of immigrant and non-English speaking children continue to grow. Bilingual programs exist in preschool, elementary school, and for adults. Your spoken classroom English needs to be standard English, but it can be spoken with an accent. Many non-teaching positions exist where speaking a second language will be an advantage.

Krantz (2000) predicts a 26 percent job growth rate for preschool teachers and child care professionals. He notes a large majority of workers in the field are self-employed and points out job turnover is high in the child care industry. He believes most new jobs will occur in heavily populated areas of the country.

Farr (2001) recognizes that turnover in the occupation is high and estimates 1.3 million workers held positions in education in 1998. He states more than 60 percent of all salaried preschool teachers were employed by centers and preschools, and about 14 percent worked for religious institutions. The remainder found employment with community programs, organizations, and with state and local government programs. Additionally about two percent worked in industry-sponsored on-site child centers.

Farr predicts the employment of preschool teachers will increase faster than the average for all occupations through the year 2008. He feels qualified people will have little trouble finding jobs. According to Farr, changes in the public perception of pre-primary education may lead to increased public and private spending on child care. Growth of government-funded programs and increased state subsidization may affect salaries. They should rise as standards are developed mandating advanced training or college degrees for teaching and administrative staff.

Kleiman (2002) discusses the "inside track" for the employment picture for child development professionals in the following excerpt:

> *Good opportunities for qualified people will result from more families seeking alternative child care arrangements, high turnover, and rise in the number of children enrolled in child care and preschool programs. Working environments can vary from private homes and schools to child care centers and religious institutions. Work is never routine, and new challenges will arise each day. Child care can be physically and emotionally demanding, and hours may be long.*

Federal Legislation and State Early Childhood Education Efforts

In July 2001, The White House Summit on Early Childhood Cognitive Development met and focused on the chain of negative educational events that can result when children are unable to master reading in the lower grades of elementary school. There is increased federal emphasis, not only on reading instruction, but also on preparing young children for kindergarten enrollment (Love, 2003).

Guidelines for reading in the federal *No Child Left Behind Act* (U.S. Department of Education, 2002) are designed to improve publicly-funded school children's reading in kindergarten through Grade Three. *Early Reading First*, the portion of the law aimed at improving pre-kindergarten children's skills which influence later reading achievement, specifies that publicly-funded preschool teachers deliver systematic and explicit instruction to increase children's oral language development, print awareness, alphabet knowledge, and phonological awareness (McGee, 2003), Figure 1–2. Pushing formal reading instruction into preschool classrooms was not recommended and was not the legislation's intent. A central concern was that literacy experiences during preschool years are critical for successful learning during elementary school years.

The federal *No Child Left Behind Act* directs states and local school districts to develop academic standards, test all students annually in Grades Three through Eight, and hire "highly qualified" teachers. Many educators feel the emphasis on testing creates undue pressure on teachers and may result in an inordinate amount of time spent on ensuring that children test well. The *No Child Left Behind Act*'s provision that federal grants be contingent on all enrolled primary school children making "adequate yearly progress" in reading created shock waves throughout public educational systems (Hirsch, 2004). As a result, regional areas, states, cities, local communities, school districts, and professional organizations and groups have made attempts to identify age-level literacy characteristics. They also have developed standards and goal statements, pinpointing the literacy skills gained during the early years that may support children's learning to read.

The 2003–2004 school year saw the first widespread public school implementation of the *No Child Left Behind Act*'s accountability measures. Howell and Casserly (2004) point out that these measures were intended to stimulate competition, provide students with better alternatives, and punish under-performing schools. School districts worried about losing federal dollars are designing supplemental services and tutoring programs.

If school districts have not focused yet on the years before kindergarten, especially children's language arts activities, they cannot afford to ignore them much longer. *No Child Left Behind Act*'s "highly qualified" teacher requirement is aimed at ensuring teacher quality in elementary schools (Section 1119). It mandates that teachers have the content knowledge and teaching skills necessary to enable children to succeed. A "highly qualified" teacher of reading must hold a bachelor's degree by the end of the 2005–2006 school year. Subject matter competency tests and/or teacher competency demonstration on a state standard's evaluation may be necessary to hold a teacher's job or gain employment.

President Bush and the U.S. Congress, keen to promote reading success in young primary children, committed $75 million,

Figure 1–2 Legislation Has Focused Attention on Writing and Reading.

part of which helps states develop early intervention programs (Hagel, 2002). State officials in California contend that $1.2 billion was budgeted in 2000 to run both Department of Education and Social Service preschool programs (Hagel).

The California's Children and Families Commission's (known as First 5 California) public opinion survey calculated that more than half of their study's respondents believed it was important for children to attend preschool before kindergarten. Many respondents were dissatisfied with the state's efforts to ensure preschool access to all children (*San Jose Mercury News*, 2004). First 5 plans to provide $1 billion to fund California's early intervention programs. California is also one of six states that requires its programs to meet state academic standards. The Education Commission of the States (ECS) (2001) points out there is ample support for the notion that higher levels of academic qualifications for early childhood teachers yields significant improvements in program effectiveness for all children, especially those from low-income families. Both legislation and subsequent funding have created jobs.

What does all of this interest and funding mean to educators? Hopefully, more jobs for professional educators. As Echaore-McDavid (2001) notes, the education industry is constantly creating new jobs to meet the needs of society.

Women and Work Trends

Winik (2003) believes women are now more likely to become managers and professionals, but they are also putting in longer hours. Since the 1970s increasing numbers of women have gone to work, and by 2010 the estimated percentage of women in the workforce is 48 percent of the labor market. With more women in the workforce, there has been a steady demand for child care (Morkes, 2003).

The Realities of the Early Childhood Field

In the early childhood field, many entry-level jobs exist due to low pay and job turnover. The positive side of this situation is a worker's ability to secure employment while obtaining further education. How high is turnover? Estimates agree there is a turnover rate of more than 30 percent for early childhood teachers who often receive inadequate compensation. This compares to a 14 percent turnover rate for public school teachers whose average annual salary is $39,385.

Elementary, Middle, and Secondary School (High School) Employment

About 168,000 kindergarten teachers, 1.5 million elementary school teachers, 602,000 middle school teachers, and 1.1 million secondary school teachers held jobs in 2002 (U.S. Department of Labor, 2004). Of these, about 10 percent worked for private schools. School districts and private school employers look for educators who have the ability to communicate, inspire trust and confidence, use motivational techniques, and understand each student's emotional and educational needs and uniqueness.

With additional schooling beyond teacher credentialing, certification, and a bachelor's degree, some teachers move into more specialized positions such as literacy specialists, reading specialists, curriculum developers, guidance counselors, and administrators or supervisors such as school principals.

A review by Fine (2000) revealed the following information found in the higher education periodical, *Phi Delta Kappan:*

- The government projects 21 percent growth in demand for teachers, librarians, and counselors from 1996 to 2006.
- The demand for elementary school teachers is projected to increase by 20 percent from 1996 to 2006 compared to 10 percent for preschool or kindergarten teachers.
- Certification and testing standards for new teachers are being toughened, and lower class sizes are being mandated.
- The U.S. Secretary of Education expects demand for additional teachers to reach 200,000 per year for the next 10 years, with first-time teachers accounting for between one-half and two-thirds of them.

Working Conditions: Elementary School

Teachers often work alone in their classrooms, but some teachers have assistants, aides, or volunteer helpers. When school budgets permit, assistants can be full- or part-time staff. Students may be a homogeneous group or extremely diverse. Classes today often consist of a mix of English and English-language learners. School facilities range from new to run down, and class size may vary from overcrowded to small enough for teachers to provide considerable individual attention.

Working Conditions: Middle and Secondary School

Middle and secondary teachers specialize and provide in-depth studies in subjects such as English, history, geography, science, physical education, and art. Some teachers are vocational education specialists and provide career training, technical and/or technology training, and job placement in fields such as auto repair, and health-care.

More audio-visual instruction takes place and, in most cases, more computer use. Assessment, grading papers, preparing report cards, meeting with students and parents, maintaining discipline, conducting study halls, home rooms, extracurricular activities, and field trips are common job tasks. Recently, site-based management policies have increased parent–teacher interaction and teacher workload with parents participating actively in classroom management decisions including budget, personnel, textbook selection, curriculum, and methods.

Other Work Characteristics

Most teachers work 40 hours per week in a traditional 10-month school year and may or may not work at other jobs during the summer. They may obtain **tenure** after a probationary period. Tenure does not absolutely guarantee continued employment (U.S. Department of Labor, 2004). More than half of all elementary, middle school, and secondary teachers belong to unions such as the American Federation of Teachers.

Stress is commonplace in teaching positions; teachers may cope with unmotivated, disrespectful, violent, or out-of-control students. Teachers are expected to produce results such as making sure their students exhibit satisfactory performance on standardized tests in core subjects. Failure to do so may jeopardize their continued employment. Parent–teacher meetings and interactions have also increased stress.

Salary: Kindergarten Through Secondary School

Median annual earnings of kindergarten, elementary, **middle**, and **secondary** school teachers ranged from $39,810 to $44,340 in 2002; the lowest 10 percent earned $24,960 to $29,850; the top 10 percent earned $62,810 to $68,530. The estimated average salary of all public elementary and secondary school teachers in the 2001–2002 school year was $44,367 (U. S. Department of Labor, 2004). Figure 1–3 identifies states paying high and low average salaries. Master's degrees, national certification, or working as a mentor teacher usually raises pay. States such as Idaho are considering merit pay for teacher performance and ability to promote children's academic growth (Roberts, 2004).

Employment Outlook

Job opportunity for the next 10 years varies from good to excellent depending on locality, grade level, and subject taught. Some states are luring teachers with added incentives. Fastest growing regions, and consequently the "hottest" areas in teacher employment are in the South and West—California, Texas, Georgia, Idaho, Hawaii, Alaska, and New Mexico. Currently, many school districts have difficulty hiring qualified teachers of mathematics, science, bilingual education, foreign languages, and vocational teachers. Teachers with ethnic minority background or training are in short supply. Some states have enacted policies to encourage students to become teachers and many have implemented higher teacher standards.

Since the teacher shortages of 1995–2000, school district budgets have dwindled in many localities. Signing bonuses and other job enticements may be things of the past. The National Education Association believes that two million new teachers will be needed to adequately staff the nation's elementary schools in the coming decade (Southworth, 2000).

Compensation and Benefits in Early Childhood Positions

A 2002 survey of 815 National Association for the Education of Young Children (NAEYC) members probed job satisfaction as well as other issues. Answering "If I could change one

High
California
Michigan
Connecticut
New Jersey
District of Columbia

Low
South Dakota
Oklahoma
North Dakota
Mississippi
Montana

Figure 1–3 States Recognized for High and Low Average Teacher Salaries in 2002–2003.

thing about my current position, it would be _____" resulted in the following five most popular responses:

- benefits/pay
- more time (more hours in the day, more time to plan, and so on)
- amount of paperwork
- general respect
- administrative support (McMullen et al 2004)

This survey points out how critical compensation and benefits are to job satisfaction.

When examining the earnings early childhood professionals receive, it is important to understand entry-level, average, and median figures. The median is the figure that best reflects what a worker with some job experience can expect to receive. It is the amount in the middle when earnings of all workers are considered (Morkes, 2003). Those just entering the field may or may not have any form of formal education or training. In some states, early childhood center teachers can work with no pre-service training. Morgan (2003) points out that when researching levels of compensation for the early childhood field in Bureau of Labor Statistics publications, those classified as "child care workers" rather than those classified as "preschool teacher" received roughly $1.75 less in hourly pay.

In part, salary depends on the geographic area and the cost of living where you are employed. In larger cities and metropolitan areas wages are usually higher and benefits more plentiful. The average hourly wage for preschool teachers in Beaumont/Port Arthur, Texas is $5.37 per hour. This compares to $20.27 per hour, a figure that many in the San Francisco area receive (Fisher, 2003). (The Texas figure does not reflect the present minimum wage law.) *The Occupational Outlook Handbook* of the U.S. Department of Labor (2001) calculates the mean hourly wage of preschool teachers at $9.66, the median hourly wage at $8.56, and the average annual wage at $20,100. Krantz (2000) found entry-level annual earnings to be $12,000, mid-level jobs and top jobs at an average of $21,000. Average wages are the **mean** of all the earnings of all workers in the occupation from entry-level to the most experienced.

Farr (2001) suggests the following earnings figures:

Median hourly earnings of child care workers were $6.61 in 1998. The middle fifty percent earned between $6.61 and $8.13. The lowest ten percent earned less than $5.49, and the highest ten percent more than $9.65.

Farr also postulates pay depends on the education of the worker and the type of establishment. Farr's (2001) book, *America's Fastest Growing Jobs in Our Economy,* included preschool teachers. He calculates about 40 percent of preschool teachers and child professionals are self-employed—more than four times the proportion for all workers. Most of these are family child care providers.

Hagel (2002) cites figures from a study of preschool and early childhood teachers funded by the Pew Charitable Trust of Philadelphia:

Teachers reported earning an average of $19,610 a year in 1999, about half the average salary of elementary school teachers.

and

California's preschool teachers annual pay averaged $21,130 in 1999. The national range ran from $15,140 in Alabama to $23,750 in Minnesota.

Many other early childhood occupational experts realize government funding has a tremendous effect on the child care profession. In strong economic times, when child care demand grows, child care businesses thrive. He estimates two-thirds of all child care workers are self-employed, and they are usually better compensated than those working in large child care centers.

The annual publication, *Current Data on Child Care Salaries and Benefits in the United States*, is the most up-to-date and respected source of evolving facts and figures. This can be researched at the Web site of the Center for the Child Care Workforce at http://www.ccw.org.

The 2000 Census Bureaus statistics, reviewed by Armas (2004), paint a dismal picture for women's earnings versus men's earnings in the same field of work:

Indeed, the field with the highest proportion of female workers—kindergarten and preschool teachers, nearly ninety-eight percent women—men had median earnings of $22,000; $5,000 more than for women.

Nationally, the median income for a woman working full-time, year-round was about $28,000, compared with $38,000 for a man. That means a woman earned less than seventy-four cents for every dollar earned by a man.

There are a growing number of male early childhood educators. Why do census statistics find male educators' pay unequal to female educators? To the authors' knowledge, a "double standard" pay schedule does not exist, and males do not receive more pay than female educators. We suspect more males work during the summer months when most all public schools are closed. See Web sites concerning male educator issues at this chapter's end.

Morgan (2003) discusses the public hysteria that took place in the 1980s and 1990s concerning the alleged sexual abuse of children supposedly in centers:

. . . we were having some success in attracting more men to the field. The effort was derailed . . .

Care givers, even women, are not trusted to touch children and give them love. It takes an unusually self-confident man to enjoy the work when surrounded with such distrust.

Question: Men in the education field, including early childhood educators, seem to get positions of responsibility before females, right?

Answer: Very few males enter the field for the express purpose of tapping into a men's network that propels them into administrative positions (Sargent, 2002). Allan (1993) proposes that men can align with male principals and administrators because of their maleness, and seek promotions to administrative positions. Williams (1992) claims that this is what men teachers do. They enjoy a hidden advantage that she terms "the glass escalator," a set of circumstances that ironically causes men to be "tracked" into better paying, more prestigious specialties. Sargent notes there are factors that deter men from selecting a career working with preschool children and the lower grades of elementary school, including suspicion, double standards for behavior, and subtle pressures to move "up and out" and away from teaching young children (Figure 1–4).

Figure 1–4   Teachers Join Children at Play and at Times, Offer Suggestions.

Universal and State Pre-kindergarten Programs

Thirty-seven states have initiated **pre-kindergarten** programs that are focused on helping children enter kindergarten ready to learn (Groginsky, Robinson & Smith, 1999). These programs vary, but commonly target preschoolers from low-income families. State investment in these programs ranges from $1 million annually to more than $20 million. Machado and Botnarescue (2005) believe these state initiatives and newly enacted laws will have a positive impact on early childhood workers:

> *More job opportunities, better compensation (in some cases the same pay as public school teachers), higher standards regarding teacher qualifications and training, a chance for increased benefits, stipends for future training, more specialized job titles, a new public image, and a hope that with all the state and federal interest in quality care, the inequities that exist for early childhood educators will finally disappear.*

Job Benefits for Early Childhood Educators

Some employers offer no job benefits. Others offer paid holidays, sick leave, stock purchase programs, paid leave, retirement plans, insurance including health, liability, disability, and payments to the employee's survivors in the case of death. Some employers provide meals, housing, and travel expenses. Morkes (2003) notes these workers' total compensation including benefits may be greater than at a higher paying job without benefits. The Bureau of Labor Statistics survey, "The Employee Benefits Survey," provides data and information about employee benefits in both private and federal employment sectors. Check http://www.bis.gov/ncs/ebs.

Benefits received by early childhood professionals can be best described as running from nonexistent to "spotty." As was true of wages, larger sponsoring organizations in the publicly-funded sector are the best providers of benefits. Faith-based sponsored or nonprofit employers come next. Profit-generating centers in large metropolitan cities follow. All of these are more generous employers in booming economic and high employment times when they must compete with other sectors for employees.

Bellm and Haack (2001) summed up the realities of the early childhood profession as follows:

> *There is great excitement and pleasure in playing an important role in children's and families lives. With proper pay and a good, supportive working environment, child care can be one of the very best jobs of all. But we also know that for many people in this field, decent pay, benefits and working conditions are a dream that may seem quite far off.*

Gender and Racial Issues in Early Childhood Teaching

The child care workforce is overwhelmingly female with at least one-third women of color (Bellm & Haack, 2001). These authors note the average early childhood educator has achieved a higher level of education than the average worker in the American workforce. Roughly one-third of early childhood teachers are paid minimum wage and even those at the highest end of the pay scale, who are likely to have a baccalaureate degree and several years of experience, rarely earn enough to support a small family (Bellm & Haack). The public elementary school educator workforce is quite different when considering percentage of teachers of color and numbers of females. Twelve percent of elementary school teachers are male (U.S. Department of Education, 1994) and 40 percent of principals (Center for Educational Statistics, 1996). Sargent (2002) notes the percentage of males teaching in the early grades of public elementary schools has not changed significantly in 40 years. In middle and secondary schools the percentage of male teachers has increased.

Question: What about the ethnicity of public school teachers? Are a variety of races adequately represented in light of student population in the United States?

Answer: See Figure 1–5, The Need for Minority Teachers.

The career field pictured so far may seem rather glum if you are considering an early childhood teaching career. However, as you read earlier, both the federal government and a number of state governments have initiated a heavy investment in early childhood programs due to research developments and growing public awareness of the critical learning period called early childhood. The universal pre-K movement has caught on, but it is in its infancy. Another hope is unionization efforts. Though the movement to unionize is still quite small, workers have successfully created unions in some geographic areas, at Head Start, and at a few community-based programs. Military child care administrators have made major improvements to their salary schedules and training. Consequently, they have reduced staff turnover.

Bellm and Haack (2001) describe advancements in the early childhood field:

> *Organizations, such as the National Black Child Development Institute, the Center for the Child Care Workforce, and the "Taking the Lead" project based at*

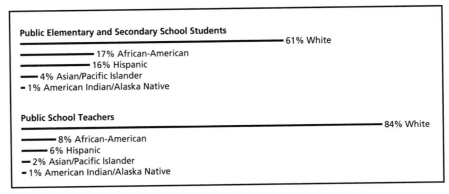

Public Elementary and Secondary School Students

61% White
17% African-American
16% Hispanic
4% Asian/Pacific Islander
1% American Indian/Alaska Native

Public School Teachers

84% White
8% African-American
6% Hispanic
2% Asian/Pacific Islander
1% American Indian/Alaska Native

Figure 1–5 The Need for Minority Teachers.

Source: U.S. Department of Education, Spring 2000.

Wheelock College's Institute for Leadership and Career Initiatives, are actively working to increase leadership and mentoring opportunities for people of color in early childhood education. The TEACH Early Childhood scholarship program, first begun in North Carolina and now operating in many other states, is helping a more diverse population of teachers and providers to pursue their education. The California CARES/Child Development Corps model, which offers stipends to reward and retain the child care workforce, allows for additional stipends to teachers and providers who have bilingual skills.

Prospects for Teachers: Primary, Secondary, and Above

Kleiman (2002) predicts excellent job prospects for teachers based on the large numbers expected to retire over the next 10 years and due to a shortage of qualified applicants. Elementary and secondary school teachers may find the most job openings. Special education teachers and teachers with a background in mathematics, science, foreign languages, and computer science will have opportunities as a result of shortages in some geographic areas. English as a second language (ESL) teachers will have excellent job prospects as the immigrant population rises, as will self-enrichment teachers as more people seek lifelong learning to gain new skills and remain marketable in the workforce. Teachers who are willing to relocate to another city or state and who obtain a license or credential in more than one subject will have a competitive edge.

Although 17 percent of students in K–12 public schools are African American, teachers make up just 8 percent of the teaching force (Dee, 2004). Dee also notes experimental evidence suggests that teachers, in interacting with students, are more favorably disposed toward those who share their racial or ethnic background. Administrators who are aware of this will be eagerly searching for teachers who match their enrolled student profile. An annual American Federation of teachers survey claimed the typical public school teacher's salary in 2002–2003 barely kept up with inflation (*USA Today*, 2004). It also noted teachers' health insurance premiums rose 13 percent while the average salary rose only 3 percent during the same time period.

Do You Have What It Takes?

Passion, dedication, and commitment are necessary for educators at all teaching levels. Educators don't expect to get rich teaching! Helen Harkness, called the Fairy Godmother of career reincarnation, takes her clients on journeys of the soul to find out what will feed their passions.

Harkness has four steps to career renewal.

1. Look inward to define the real you.
2. Look outward at what's going on in the real world.
3. Combine the first two steps to determine what you want and can be.
4. Determine a strategy that immediately begins to fulfill that future (Harkness, 2004).

What Does Having a Passion for Teaching Mean?

It could be defined as a future teacher's natural enthusiasm and desire to create or recreate a classroom that:

- helps or enables children to know they are valued individuals.
- encourages a lifelong joy of learning and children's discovery of the world around them.
- recognizes the value of "student skills" that enable students to take advantage of educational opportunities.
- attending children are eager to enter each school day because their emotional, social, intellectual, and physical needs are met.
- is safe, secure, and fair.
- celebrates **diversity** and reveres innate differences.
- promotes competent, informed future contributors to society.
- offers a daily program of activities to explore and enjoy.
- offers choices, and helps students understand the consequence of their actions in social situations.

This is not a full list but may indicate why people choose and stay in careers in education. Other reasons could be:

- being with students during "aha" or "I get it" experiences as co-explorers, and therefore sharing the joy of discovery or exploration.
- seeing growth, change, and development.
- enjoying the mutual respect of teacher–student relationships.
- helping students overcome behaviors that may block future school success.
- working with parents to magnify their teaching skill and parenting strengths, and their abilities to parent.
- being available to enhance child curiosity, and help them find answers through study, research, and effort.
- witnessing students' cooperation and acceptance of others, Figure 1–6.
- observing and encouraging the many gifts, multiple talents, abilities, and skills students possess.
- recognizing "the child within."

- seeing the world through the eyes of a child.
- receiving visits or letters from former students or parents that reinforce or confirm their efforts to make a positive educational difference in the lives of children.

Edwards and Edwards (2003) describe the dilemma people face when deciding on a career:

Figure 1–6 Finding a Friend Is a Step Forward.

> *For some people, answering the question of what they really want to do comes easily; for others it's more difficult. Some of us have always known what we want from life. Others of us don't have a clue. Some of us knew once upon a time but have forgotten. Others have never even dared to think about what they really want; they just have this inner yearning for something more. If up until now your job, school, or family has pretty much determined the nature and structure of your life, or you're living life the way you saw your parents living theirs, you may not have spent much time thinking about how you'd really like your life to be.*

When you're working in a classroom of students, examine your feelings at the end of the day. You'll know whether helping and guiding children suits you or perhaps providing an indirect service to children and families suits you more. Perhaps there is a magical feeling, a natural high, or sense of a fulfillment when you are with children. You might experience a deep desire to reach out, nurture, share, and give. By doing so, you make the world a better place by touching children's lives. Each day in your education career can be filled with fresh possibilities.

One teacher of our acquaintance described meeting the new group of children each school year. She saw each child as a raw and wondrous gem with hidden characteristics that unfolded during time with her. She spoke of the precious measured time she had to impact their long educational lives. She was excited about her opportunity to touch their lives in a positive way by sharing her "special beloved activities." These activities opened new avenues, promoted new ideas, and built new skills. She envisioned "her children" graduating to the next school year as stronger, better learners who were full of positive self-esteem and heightened awareness because of time spent in her classroom. She saw the challenges ahead when she created and adapted methods and materials to suit her new group's unique educational needs.

Many career counselors, including R. N. Bolles, the author of the bestselling career book *What Color is Your Parachute?* (2003), recommends individuals follow their heart when selecting an occupation. This means focusing on what you really enjoy and have fun doing. Carlson (2004) adds "figure out what you're truly good at and go for it, and discover what makes you happy because that's almost always something that matches your natural skills." He believes hard work ultimately separates the successful from the failed.

> **Question:** As a man who likes being with children, I am also hesitant to choose this career. Should men work with young children?
>
> **Answer:** Definitely. Children need male role models. Parents, especially fathers, relate well to male teachers and often seek their support and parenting tips. Gender is not as important as a nurturing and enthusiastic nature and a desire to positively impact children's lives.

Health and Job Stress

Anyone attempting to be realistic about the physical demands of working directly with children will mention the bending, kneeling, lifting, and the necessary physical stamina. Additional stresses may exist in some job positions. These can include staff conflict, irregular hours, and noise level problems. Stress can arise from awkward, makeshift facilities, staff turnover, and lack of administrative support and can occur at any educational level.

An elementary school teacher performs many roles including communicator, disciplinarian, conveyor of information, evaluator, room manager, counselor, team member, decision maker, role model, and at times, surrogate parent. After school, there are meetings, committees, grading tasks, assignments to check, and communications with parents. There is a need for continual updating of educational skills. You can easily see stress is often considered an occupational hazard.

English Language Usage

Some early childhood education students who enter the field with limited English language facility may experience an employment disadvantage. Ideally, educators at all levels should provide children with an excellent English speaking model. School children who are learning English either as a first or second language need to hear proper English speaking models. Karen Hinds (2003) admonishes "If one is interested in good jobs, one has to know how to speak proper English."

Bilingual teachers often find jobs in centers that enroll the children of immigrant parents where they may be able to translate, communicate, and better understand different cultural groups. Some bilingual early childhood programs provide instruction in the children's native language. Career educators are encouraged to increase the quality of their speaking model as quickly as possible so that their career mobility is enhanced.

Assessing Skills

Now that you are aware of the labor market and the realities of this career, assessing your personal life skills is the next step. As your own career manager you will need to recognize opportunities to improve your competencies to become more marketable. Life skills can help you become the educational professional you want to be. You should know what personal attributes and occupational skills and abilities are present as you develop a career plan with short- and long-range goals. Take a good look at your core values. Your character, personal code of ethics, and personal standards are important considerations. Also assess your communication skills, diplomacy, organizational skills, leadership skills, problem-solving ability, and team work skills. Hopefully, you are open to self-improvement. If so, you will learn from mistakes, acknowledge them, accept criticism, and analyze how different actions yield different results.

We have not yet talked about occupational skills. If you are attending college, the college's counseling offices and/or career guidance center may have commercially developed interest inventories such as the Meyer-Briggs or Strong Interests Inventory available. These and other testing instruments will also help your self-assessment. Of course, employers will want well-trained professionals. They will try to assess a job applicant's personal life skills. Many guidance counselors are well aware that most people unsuccessful at work are not fired because of occupational skills but because they simply can't get along with co-workers. Their interpersonal skills, or lack of them, are the problem. Employers also calculate what a job applicant's image will project to clients. They have in mind a desired image for their particular educational operation. You have acquired skills and abilities through both education and experience. Some of your background experience was assessed in written form or through consultation with others. However, a grade in a class doesn't provide specifics or detailed knowledge about your abilities. College course outlines identify course content and may help in identifying skills you have acquired. Also, college catalogs contain course descriptions that may help you to write a list of your present level of occupational skills.

Student teaching supervisor observations, ratings, and job reviews (if you are employed) offer an analysis and assessment of your skills and abilities. Though not infallible in validity, if a number of observers and/or supervisors make similar comments, you should give these added credibility.

If you completed a college class that required a personal growth portfolio, it identifies the competencies you have attained. Self-rating forms, such as the one in the Appendix, may also help your self-assessment.

Figure 1–7 provides a list of Child Development Association (CDA) competency areas and is probably the best recognized competency list in the early childhood field. Additional competency areas are listed in Figure 1–8.

There are multiple reasons for conducting an analysis of your professional skills. You need to know them well and will want to describe them on job applications, in interviews, and on resumes. When faced with advocacy opportunities, you will want to describe how professional skills promote *quality* services to children and families.

When you create a list of your occupational skills and abilities, remember to include those that you acquired outside of formal educational institutions. You may have become a computer whiz on your own! Your family background might include using sign language. You may have intimate knowledge of another culture. Perhaps you possess sports, cooking, photographic, or musical expertise, or artistic ability. You may have skills from recreational pursuits, club attendance, or hobbies.

Taking the time to pinpoint your present level of skills and abilities, Margaret Sullivan (2004) believes, allows you to better market yourself in a job search. This activity needs to be addressed not once, but over a lifetime. Sullivan states:

Learning how to market yourself is a critical skill for all job seekers because it allows you to apply marketing theory to your most important product—yourself. It's all about a brand *called you, and (it) prepares students not only for their first, but also for their second and third jobs.*

CDA	Competency Goals	Functional Areas	Definitions
I	To establish and maintain a safe, healthy learning environment	1. Safe	Candidate provides a safe environment to prevent and reduce injuries.
		2. Healthy	Candidate promotes good health and nutrition and provides an environment that contributes to the prevention of illness.
		3. Learning Environment	Candidate uses space, relationships, materials, and routines as resources for constructing an interesting, secure, and enjoyable environment that encourages play, exploration, and learning.
II	To advance physical and intellectual competence	4. Physical	Candidate provides a variety of equipment, activities, and opportunities to promote the physical development of children.
		5. Cognitive	Candidate provides activities and opportunities that encourage curiosity, exploration, and problem solving appropriate to the developmental levels and learning styles of children.
		6. Communication	Candidate actively communicates with children and provides opportunities and support for children to understand, acquire, and use verbal and non-verbal means of communicating thoughts and feelings.
		7. Creative	Candidate provides opportunities that stimulate children to play with sound, rhythm, language, materials, space, and ideas in individual ways and to express their creative abilities.

Figure 1–7   Child Development Association (CDA) Competency Goals and Functional Areas.

CDA	Competency Goals	Functional Areas	Definitions
III	To support social and emotional development and provide positive guidance	8. Self	Candidate provides physical and emotional security for each child and helps each child to know, accept, and take pride in himself or herself and to develop a sense of independence.
		9. Social	Candidate helps each child feel accepted in the group, helps children learn to communicate and get along with others, and encourages feelings of empathy and mutual respect among children and adults.
		10. Guidance	Candidate provides a supportive environment in which children can begin to learn and practice appropriate and acceptable behaviors as individuals and as a group.
IV	To establish positive and productive relationships with families	11. Families	Candidate maintains an open, friendly, and cooperative relationship with each child's family, encourages their involvement in the program, and supports the child's relationship with his or her family.
V	To ensure a well-run, purposeful program responsive to participant needs	12. Program Management	Candidate is a manager who uses all available resources to ensure an effective operation. The Candidate is a competent organizer, planner, record keeper, communicator, and a cooperative co-worker.
VI	To maintain a commitment to professionalism	13. Professionalism	Candidate makes decisions based on knowledge of early childhood theories and practices, promotes quality in child care services, and takes advantage of opportunities to improve competence, both for personal and professional growth and for the benefit of children and families.

Figure 1–7　*(Continued)*

From Phillips, C. (Ed.) (April, 1999). *Essentials for child development associates working with young children.* Washington, DC: Council for Early Childhood Professional Recognition. Reprinted by permission.

> preparing the classroom/outside environment
> curriculum activities planning
> interactions with children
> observation, documentation, assessment
> guidance management
> parent relationships/parent supportive assistance
> group instruction
> learning aids
> using community resources
> supervising assistants/aides/volunteers
> cultural awareness
> developing individual learning plans
> staff relationships/teaming
> classroom equipment/materials/media
> awareness of professional techniques/strategies
> translates goals into activities to promote progress
> technical

Figure 1–8   Additional Categories of Competencies.

Think of yourself as an unfinished product, as a growing, learning, and inquisitive educator who always has room to develop more competencies and abilities. Your list is a statement of fact, an accomplishment, and a description of your present state. Be proud of your professional efforts. We recommend that you make a list using forms found on the CD that accompanies this text. The list will also be used for future exercises.

Life factors may dictate where your career path is at the moment. Some of these factors may be out of your control; you may have priorities other than advancing your career at this time. Many people put career dreams on hold while raising families and slowly acquire more training.

Career Goals

Lindgren (2003) outlines the beginning steps that take place in career planning:

- Identify the career.
- Learn more about it.
- Determine which area of the field you want to be part of.
- Develop skills and credentials.
- Begin making contacts.

Each step is put into a time frame such as year one, year two, and so on. You probably feel you have reached a career planning level although you may be open to changing which area of the field you will pursue.

A goal can be defined as a desired end result at a stated time. If you want your dreams and fantasies to become goals, then they need to be clearly stated, described precisely, and have a timeline for achievement. As Carr-Ruffino, (1997) author of *The Promotable Woman*, states, "if you're ready to recognize your self-limiting beliefs and to replace them with self-empowering beliefs" almost any goal is attainable. (Her comments are just as applicable to the promotion of a male!) Now, write about the most fulfilling, satisfying, exciting career future you can imagine. Identify the career job you feel is right for you—the unique you. Remember a career may entail both direct and indirect work with young children and their families. Don't write the steps you'll take to get there, that's another exercise! This career wish isn't set in concrete. Career plans change. Individuals grow. They are presented with unforeseen opportunities. Over time they may understand themselves better. Is there anything positive about wishing about a future job? Many counselors advise that, if you do, dreams can become reality. Read the motivational quotations in Figure 1–9 if you need a nudge.

- Become positive about your goals.
- Realize the tough, real work necessary to get to your goal.
- Know your path, know where you are headed.
- Act as if it will come true.
- Empower yourself to live your dreams and experience your greatness.
- What you believe, you will create.
- Get clear about your end result.
- Don't give energy to negative thoughts.
- Practice positive affirmations every day.
- Accomplishment can be grueling or even boring at times. Put one foot in front of the other. That's what success is all about.
- Many people choose a high goal but won't pay the price to get there.
- Develop a solid foundation.
- Identify and drop baggage that gets in the way of your goal.
- Don't play negative thoughts over and over—forget the junk.
- Believe it and it will happen.
- Believe in yourself.
- Self-talk can be both positive and negative. Analyze which you listen to most.
- Choose your companions wisely.
- Explore your limits. Try to go beyond what you think possible.
- Build on your strengths, and perfect them.
- Concentrate on your accomplishments on dark days, when you need a lift.
- Follow your instincts.
- Seek peace within.
- Be happy with where you are now, but give your goals your best shot.
- Relax and have fun along the way.

Figure 1–9 Career Goal Quotations.

At some point in life an educator decides how career plans and goals fit into the other goals in their lives. Priorities can be examined by looking at choices of activities. Your private life, family life, your leisure time pursuits, spiritual quest, and health goals will vie for your time. Only you can analyze the importance of your career in relation to them.

SkillPath (2003) suggests considering a work/life balance:

> *Having fun at work is an important element in any job, but having the right work/life balance is really what it's all about. Today, more and more successful people maintain that their success revolves around planning their careers around their personal lives.*

Edwards and Edwards (2003) believe that finding and holding down a job that offers a chance to live the way you want has become a puzzling challenge.

Summary

This chapter started with the assumption you have already embarked on a career in education. It urges you to become your own career manager and provides a realistic analysis of the field of education. Your dreams and goals were considered along with your existing occupational skills.

Educators with minimum training may start this career field as an early childhood worker with low wages and few benefits. Those that persevere and continue college credit course work leading to degrees find higher paying jobs and better benefits. Since standards are rising, pay should rise. Those choosing to be early childhood career educators should know that the field is struggling for status, recognition, and wages commensurate with their educational attainment and competency.

As your own career manager, you will plan a path toward professionalism and the career you wish.

The *No Child Left Behind Act* is currently affecting educators at all levels, and the field is experiencing dramatic changes. Many newly funded programs and new job titles are being created.

It is important that you read the entire text to see the number of rewarding job opportunities that are available. Keep in mind statistics tend to slight many job classifications or ignore them altogether.

Helpful Web Sites

America's Career InfoNet
  http://www.acinet.org

American Management Association
  http://www.amanet.org
  offers workshops and training about career management

Center for the Child Care Workforce
  http://www.ccw.org

Education Jobs Page
  http://www.nationjob.com
  job listings

Occupational Outlook Handbook
http://www.bis.gov

Recruiting New Teachers, Inc.
http://www.rnt.org

Teach for America
http://www.teachforamerica.org

Resources

Ayers, W. (1989). *The good preschool teacher: Six teachers*. New York: Teachers College Press.

Ayers, W. (2001). *To teach: The journey of a teacher*. New York: Teachers College Press.

Council for Early Childhood Professional Recognition. (1996). *The Child Development Association assessment system and competency standards: Preschool caregivers in center-based programs*. Washington, DC: Author.

Edelfelt, R. A., & Reiman, A. J. (2004). *Careers in education*. Chicago: VGM Career Books.

Edwards, P., & Edwards, S. (2003). *Finding your perfect work: The new career guide to making a living, creating a life*. New York: Penguin Putnam, Inc.

Gale, L. (1990). *Discover what you're best at: A complete career system that lets you test yourself to discover your own true career abilities*. New York: Fireside Book, Simon & Schuster.

Halton, S. D. (2005). *Teaching by heart: The Foxfire Interviews*. New York: Teachers College Press.

Hendrick, J. (1999). *Why teach?* Washington, DC: National Association for the Education of Young Children.

Katz, L. G. (1995). *Talks with teachers of young children: A collection*. Stamford, CT: Ablex.

Nieto, S. (Ed.). (2005). *Why we teach*. New York: Teachers College Press.

Sunstein, B. S., & Lovell, J. H. (2000). *The portfolio standard: How students can show us what they know and are able to do*. Portsmouth, NH: Heineman.

Wassermann, S. (2005). *This teaching life: How I taught myself to teach*. New York: Teachers College Press.

References

Allan, J. (1993). Male elementary school teachers: Experiences and perspectives. In C. L. Williams (Ed.), *Doing "women's work": Men in nontraditional occupations* (pp. 138–161). Newberry Park, CA: Sage.

Armas, G. C. (2002, May 22). Census: Working parents are finding more child care options. *The Idaho Statesman*, p. B5.

Armas, G. C. (2004, June 4). Jobwise, it's a man's world. *The Idaho Statesman*, p. B2.

Bellm, D., & Haack, P. (2001). *Working for quality child care: Good child care jobs equal good care for children*. Washington, DC: Center for the Child Care Workforce.

Bolles, R. N. (2003). *What color is your parachute?* Berkeley, CA: Ten Speed Press.

Carlson, T. (2004, June). The graduation advice I never got . . . but wish I had. *Reader's Digest*, 153–156.

Carr-Ruffino, N. (1997). *The promotable woman: 10 essential skills for the new millenium*. Franklin Lakes, NJ: Career Press.

Child Care Law Center. (2001, March). *Legal update*. San Francisco: Author.

Dee, T. S. (2004, Spring). The race connection: Are teachers more effective with students who share their ethnicity? *Education Next, 4* (2) 53–59.

Echaore-McDavid, S. (2001). *Career opportunities in education*. New York: Checkmark Books.

Education Commission of the States (2001, June/July). Teacher training. The Progress of Education Reform 1999–2001. *2* (6) 21–26. Denver, CO: Author.

Edwards, P., & Edwards, S. (2003). *Finding your perfect work: The new career guide to making a living, creating a life*. New York: Penguin Putnam, Inc.

Farr, J. M. (2001). *America's fastest growing jobs in our economy*. (6th ed.) Indianapolis, IN: JIST Works.

Fine, J. (2000). *Opportunities in teaching careers*. Lincolnwood, IL: VGM Career Horizons.

Fisher, H. (Ed.) (2003). *American salaries and wages survey* (7th ed.) Farmington Hills, MI: Thomson-Gale.

Goldman, H. Quoted in McAleavy, T. M. (2004, July 4). Author says your employer owes you nothing. *The Idaho Statesman*, p. CB1.

Greenberg, S. H., & Springen, K. (2000, October). Back to day care. *Newsweek*, 61–62.

Groginsky, S., Robinson, S., & Smith, S. (1999). *Making child care better*. Washington, DC: National Conference of State Legislatures.

Hagel, J. (2002, January 8). Study finds preschools short on standards, teacher pay. *San Jose Mercury News*, p. 6A.

Harkness, H. Quoted in Hall, C. (2004, August 1). Find yourself . . . and happiness in a new career that may follow. *The Idaho Statesman*, p. CB1.

Hinds, K. Quoted in Thernstrom, A., & Thernstrom, S. (2003). *No excuses: Closing the racial gap in learning*. New York: Simon and Schuster.

Hirsch, E. D. Jr. (2004, February 25). Many Americans can read but can't comprehend. *USA Today*, 13A.

Howell, W. C., & Casserly, M. (2004, Summer). Where the rubber meets the road. *Education Next, 4* (3), 25.

Kleiman, C. (2002). *Winning the job game: The new rules for finding and keeping the job you want*. Hoboken, NJ: John Wiley and Sons, Inc.

Krantz, L. (2000). *Jobs rated almanac*. (5th ed.) New York: St. Martin's Press.

Love, J. M. (2003). Instrumentation for state readiness assessment: Issues in measuring children's early development and learning. *Assessing the State of State Assessment*. Special Report. Greensboro, NC: The Regional Education Library as SERVE, 43–49.

Lindgren, A. (2003, August 31). Research the key to successful interview, CEO says. *The Idaho Statesman*, p. 2CB.

Machado, J., & Botnarescue, H. (2005). *Student teaching: Early childhood practicum guide*. Clifton Park, NY: Thomson Delmar Learning.

McGee, L. M. (2003, Summer). The influence of early reading first on High/Scope's preschool reading instruction. *High Scope ReSource, 22* (2) 23–25.

McMullen, M. B., Alat, K., Buldu, M., & Lash, M. (2004, March). A snapshot of NAEYC's professionals through the lens of quality. *Young Children*, 59 (2) 87–92.

Morgan, G. (2003). Staff role, education, and compensation. In D. Cryer & R. M. Clifford (Eds.). *Early childhood education and care in the USA* (pp. 87–105). Baltimore, MD: Paul M. Brookes Publishing Co.

Morkes, A. (Ed.) (2003). *Encyclopedia of careers and vocational guidance*. (Vol. 1). Chicago: Ferguson Publishing Co.

Phillips, C. (Ed.) (1999). Essentials for child development associates working with young children. Washington, DC: Council for Professional Recognition.

Roberts, B. (2004, August 17). State Board looks at merit pay for teachers. *The Idaho Statesman*, p. M1, 4.

San Jose Mercury News. (2004, February 11). Californians support universal preschool. In Brief, Sacramento. p. 16A. Author.

Sargent, P. (2002, November). Under the glass: Conversations with men in early childhood education. *Young Children, 57* (6) 22–31.

Skillpath Seminars. (2003, September 8). *Training tips*, 1. Mission, KS: Author.

Southworth, S. A. (2000 January/February). Wanted two million teachers. *Scholastic, 109* (5) 25–26.

Sullivan, M. Quoted in Kleiman, C. (2004, July 18). Marketing skills handy for all job seekers. *The Idaho Statesman*, p. CB1.

USA Today. (2004, July 15). Teacher's group says salaries can't keep up. p. 4D. Author.

U.S. Department of Education. Center for Educational Statistics. (1996). *Teacher follow-up survey: 1991–1992*. Washington, DC: Author.

U.S. Department of Education. Center for Educational Statistics. (1996, October). *Child care and early education program participation of infants, toddlers and preschoolers*. NCES 95–824. Washington, DC: Author.

U.S. Department of Education. (1994). *School and staffing survey: 1990–1991*. Washington, DC: Author.

U.S. Department of Education. (2000). No Child Left Behind Act of 2001: Executive Summary. Retrieved July 15, 2002, http://www.ed.gov/nclb/overview/intro/execsumm.html

U.S. Department of Education. (2000, Spring). *Teacher Profile*. Washington, DC: Author.

U.S. Department of Education. Center for Educational Statistics. (2002, August). *Child Care Situations Summary Report*. NCES 94–71., Washington, DC: Author.

U.S. Department of Labor, Bureau of Labor Statistics (2001). *Occupational Outlook Handbook*. Washington, DC: Author.

U.S. Department of Labor, Bureau of Labor Statistics. (2004, October 19). Teachers—Preschool, Kindergarten, Elementary, Middle, and Secondary. *Occupational outlook handbook, 2004–2005*. Bulletin 2540. http://stats.bls.gov/oco/print/ocos069.htm

Williams, C. L. (1992). The glass escalator: Hidden advantages for men in the female professions. *Social Problems*, 39. 253–267.

Winik, L. W. (2003, October 26). What you may not know about workers in America today. *San Jose Mercury News*, p.4.

Employment Sectors

*The more extensive a man's knowledge
of what has been done, the greater will
be his power of knowing what to do.*

Benjamin Disraeli

Dilemma

Mai works for a child care resource and referral agency. Before this employment, she acquired considerable knowledge of local programs. She accomplished this through employment, serving as a student teacher and a volunteer, and by supervising work experience and work-study students for a community college.

When parents call for information to help them select a child center, Mai provides location, telephone numbers, ages served, licensing particulars, times of operation, staff descriptions, program size and description. She also mentions accreditation and awards and informs parents that the licensing agency may provide additional information. Mai can coach parents concerning how to choose child care, and she can send written material. Mai feels she is providing information about a number of centers she would never recommend to a friend.

QUESTIONS TO PONDER

1. Is Mai concerned needlessly?

2. What might help Mai's dilemma?

3. What could happen if Mai gives strong positive recommendations for some centers and not others?

It is an exciting time to launch or pursue a career in education. Although this book focuses on positions for teaching infants through college level students, it does include most sectors of employment. Many diverse positions exist and new ones are evolving. Changes in public opinion concerning the importance of education have promoted job growth, increased professional training for teachers, higher standards, and training program accreditation. This should result in an increase in the number of better paid positions. Working as your own career manager you will need to know about teacher shortages and employment sectors. A teacher shortage exists in select geographic areas. Southworth (2000) provides teacher shortage information:

- Nearly one half of America's public school system teachers will retire or change careers in the next few years.
- Two million teachers will be hired in the next ten years.
- Many "emergency" or uncertified teachers are currently employed.
- Bilingual and English as a second language (ESL) teachers are being recruited overseas.
- Special education and speech pathology teachers are in short supply.
- In some school districts with higher-than-average salaries or where desirable and pleasant living situations exist, teacher shortages are not as apparent.

Whether or not the employment picture in your area is strong depends on many factors. A knowledgeable educator must know where to look and what possibilities exist. This chapter will identify the best-known sectors. Others will be described in Chapter Four.

Question: A career helping children and families appeals to me, but I'm afraid teaching is not what I want or can do. Are there jobs that don't involve teaching?

Answer: It sounds as if you might be looking for a job in the social or community service area. There are many indirect service positions where a background or degree in education or early childhood education would enhance your understanding of children and their families, and your ability to better serve them. A good number of educators switch from direct to indirect positions as their careers develop.

Sectors of Child Care— Direct and Indirect Service Areas

Looking at the whole field of education you will find two broad categories of services to children and families. These are *direct* and *indirect* services. Direct service involves face-to-face interactions with children or families (Figure 2–1). Indirect services entail supportive and assistive services that indirectly affect classrooms, children, and families. Common indirect services include administrative, technical, training, informational, regulatory, liaison, legislative, supply, and referral functions. See Figure 2–2.

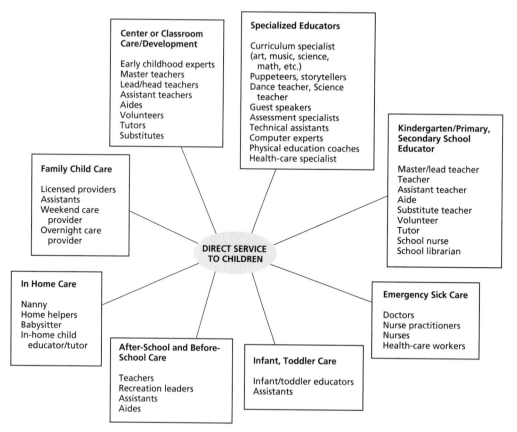

Figure 2–1 (A) Direct Services to Children.

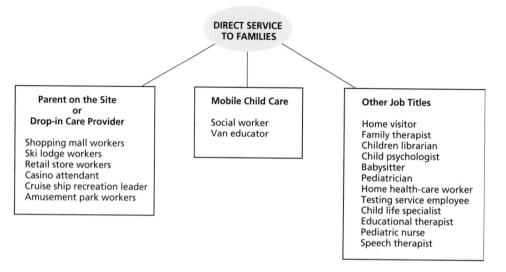

Figure 2–1 (B) Direct Child Care Services with Sample Job Titles.

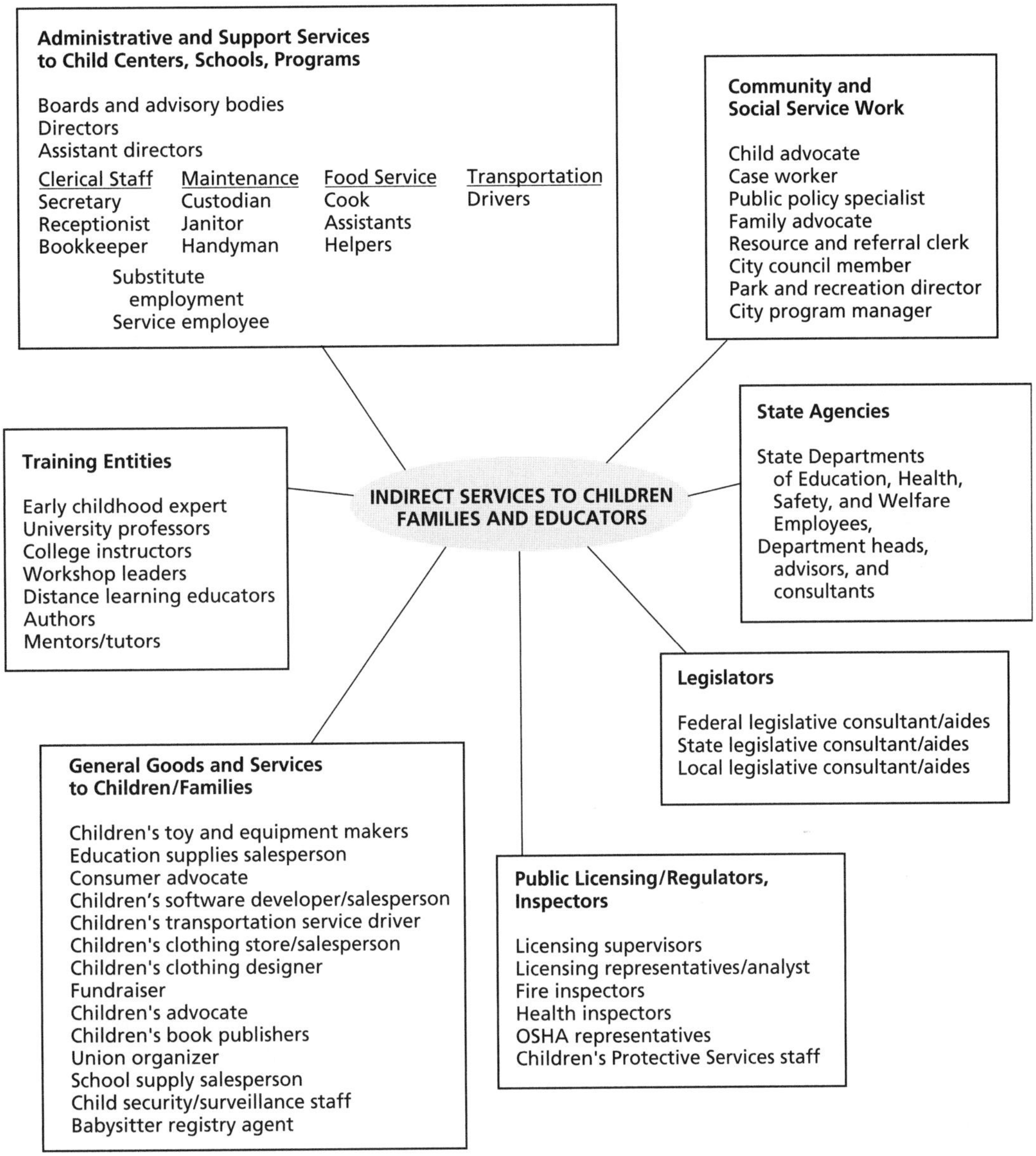

Figure 2–2 Indirect Services to Children, Families, and Educators, with Sample Job Titles.

Public Programs

Educators should be aware of the differences in the ownership of programs and whether they are for profit or nonprofit. Public programs, those funded with federal or state monies, commonly offer employees stability, job benefits, and higher salaries than other job sector programs. In most states, three main types of early childhood programs receive public monies. These are usually administered by different public agencies or departments.

1) *Federal programs* Head Start and other federal child programs enroll eligible children including the children of parents receiving public assistance. Head Start is regulated by a national bureau. Elementary, middle, and secondary schools also have funded child programs. Military programs that serve all military children are also in this category.

2) *State Education Department programs* These are designed to promote school readiness or have some other educational intent. They are usually administered by State Departments of Education.

3) *Welfare Department or Health and Human Service Agency programs* Subsidies (monies) are provided to needy parents for child care services, or fund another education-related purpose.

Families receiving child care in many public programs have qualified for services by proving a low family income, hardship, school district residence, or another eligibility. Parents who are not fully subsidized usually pay fees on a sliding scale based on family income and size. State-funded universal preschools are available for all preschoolers regardless of family income. Staff working in a public support center are usually required to have higher levels of educational preparation and experience than staff in an unfunded center. They must obtain the necessary training and experience to qualify for positions. Job benefits may include health-care insurance, vacations, and retirement plans. Some unionization of workers in public centers has taken place.

Public programs have identifiable policies, goals, and program standards in a published written form. Staff salary schedules and professionally recommended child/adult ratios exist. Facilities usually are located near parent neighborhoods in public buildings. Well-known public programs include Head Start, state preschools, universal pre-K programs and college and university campus laboratory schools. These are public, nonprofit operations. See Figure 2–3 for additional characteristics of public programs.

Public agencies and organizations that administer, regulate, license, or accredit public programs regularly hire individuals with education or social service training.

Sponsor, Owner/Administrator	Characteristics
Public	
Federal, state or county agency such as Office of Economic Opportunity, Department of Health and Human Services, U.S. Military, State Department of Education, Social Services, school districts, college districts	Funds allocated by Congress, state legislatures, or county government or agencies Program developers and supervisors may be quite remote from schools themselves, in off-site offices Programs exceedingly varied May also include schools providing services to special groups such as developmentally delayed or challenged, speech impaired, bilingual, after-school care, etc

Figure 2–3 Features of Private and Public Early Childhood Programs.

Sponsor, Owner/Administrator	Characteristics
Other agencies such as a neighborhood council, community service organization, welfare agency, or community action programs	Often a parent or community board serves an advisory function Program standards and guidelines are available and may be mandatory Program may be accredited Universal pre-kindergarten and some state pre-K programs are open to all interested parents and exist in some states. Nonprofit Enroll greater numbers of English as a second language children Programs may be affected by *No Child Left Behind Act* legislation requiring child testing. Parent fees may be on a sliding scale reflecting parent income Centers may be located in low-income and rural communities Facilities located on public property May be unionized
Private Individual or group business	Profit making Higher parent fees A small or large school operated by a single owner or a large chain with absentee owners, run by a paid director and a staff May be accredited
Religious group (faith based)	May use church personnel for staffing and have secular emphasis or may simply permit use of church facilities May be accredited
Parent cooperative	Parents hire a professional director and serve as assistants on a rotating basis, with regularly scheduled meetings for families, which usually include parenting education
Private nonprofit	An incorporated entity that has been granted nonprofit status through legal application to a federal, state, or local agency A wide variation of programs May be accredited

Figure 2–3 *(Continued)*

Military Child Care

Care for the children of members of the military is funded through public funds. Military child care has its own regulatory system, training, and workforce policies. One of the largest employer-sponsored programs in the world, it serves 200,000 children per day (Morgan, 2003). Morgan believes this program has become a model for success because it is adequately funded, addresses quality, has reasonable personnel policies, and serves all children. She notes 75 percent of military programs are accredited from outside the military at national standards. Wages and wage advancement are tied to staff education and performance. Center care, family child care, school-age care, and resource and referral are all components of the military child care program.

Head Start

Head Start serves more than 900,000 children ages three to four who are from low-income families in the U.S. (U.S. Department of Health and Human Services, 2002). Legislation has extended Head Start benefits with a program called Early Head Start (Katz, 2003). This is a community-based program serving infants and toddlers.

Morgan (2003) notes Congress enacted into law a requirement that 50 percent of Head Start classroom staff have bachelor's degrees by 2003. Many Head Start teachers have Child Development Associate credentials awarded by the Council for Professional Recognition. This credential usually represents about half of a two-year college degree in Early Childhood Education.

Private Sector Programs

Private sector programs, sometimes called purchase-of-service programs, are diverse. About half the children attending preschool in the U.S. attend private centers (Kamerman & Gatenio, 2003). Some are profit making, others are nonprofit. They serve parents who can afford their services. Program philosophies can range from traditional, eclectic, to experimental. Student activities are based on varied philosophical positions and have varied goals of instruction and priorities. Some stress certain activities over others. A number of early childhood centers may be advertised as play centers, while others offer to teach academic subjects. The majority of child centers describe their programs as developmentally appropriate. Current educational theory recognizes that this kind of program promotes child growth and each child's potential.

For-profit centers derive their operating monies from parent fees, and initial set-up monies were invested by owners, others, or corporations expecting a monetary return. Profit centers can be small mom and pop operations or part of a chain of schools (centers) that operate across the United States and overseas. Examine Figure 2–4. Small child care facilities are commonplace because it does not take a tremendous amount of capital to open a small school. As a result, the child care industry is overwhelmingly dominated by small operations. In some states, private schools have contracted with public agencies and may enroll publicly-funded children as well as parent-funded children. Many franchised preschools are part of a chain of centers. Wittenberg (1996) notes:

> *Commercial centers are private profit-making centers, such as KinderCare, Mary Moppet, and The Children's World. The basic model for the center was developed*

Organization	Main Office Location
KinderCare Learning Centers	Portland, OR
Knowledge Learning Corporation	San Rafael, CA
La Petite Academy	Chicago, IL
Bright Horizons Family Solutions	Watertown, MA
Childtime Learning Centers	Novi, MI
Nobel Learning Communities	West Chester, PA
Child Care Network	Columbus, GA
Children's Courtyard	Arlington, TX
The Sunshine House	Greenwood, SC
New Horizon Child Care	Plymouth, MN
Minnieland Private Day School	Woodbridge, VA
Allegheny Child Care Academy	Pittsburgh, PA
Mini-Skool	Scottsdale, AZ
Children's Friend	Warner Robins, GA
Rainbow Child Development Centers	Lathrup Village, MI
Sunrise Preschools	Phoenix, AZ
The Phoenix Schools	Sacramento, CA
Action Day Nurseries / Primary Plus	San Jose, CA
Hildebrandt Learning Centers	Wilkes-Barre, PA
Pinecrest Schools	Sherman Oaks, CA
Stepping Stone School	Austin, TX

Figure 2–4 Private Preschools with More Than Ten Centers.

and then franchised out. The franchised centers are basically built and run the same way as the model.

Morgan (2003) describes the educational background of staff working in privately-funded programs as follows:

In the field of practice, those working in the purchase-of-service system for young children in licensed centers have a wide mix of credentials. A few have master's degrees. More have bachelor's degrees. Still more have associate's degrees or the Child Development Associate (CDA) credential. A large number have no degrees.

Private primary, middle, and secondary schools have as much diversity as early childhood schools.

Private Center Salary

The salaries of staff in some private centers may be slightly above minimum wage. In others, pay is equal to or better than public programs. Job benefits such as health-care insurance are relatively rare unless the center is affiliated with a business with a large number of workers or is situated in an area with a scarcity of workers.

Cooperative Preschools

Cooperative preschools date back to the 1930s, 1940s, and 1950s. These schools operate on a nonprofit basis by a group of parents who hire a qualified director to assist them as they staff their own center (Figure 2–5). Parents teach and maintain the facility. Fees can be low and parents often attend director-led parent education classes that a local school district sponsors. Parents may pay additional fees for this instruction. The majority of cooperative schools are half-day programs.

Community and Church-Sponsored Centers and Schools

Community, charitable, and faith-based programs exist in most communities. Many are nonprofit, but profit-making operations also flourish. Care and/or instruction usually takes place in entity buildings, and enrollment may be based on parental affiliation with the sponsoring group—such as church or club membership, neighborhood residence, or another factor. Elementary, middle, and secondary schools that are faith-based are found in many communities.

Figure 2–5 Parents Work as Assistant Teachers in Cooperative Preschools.

Industry-Sponsored Centers

This is a small but growing sector of child care. Industry-sponsored center existence may depend on the economic factors that influence the sponsoring industry. Probably the best-known centers of this kind were the Kaiser Shipyard Child Centers in the Pacific Northwest. Designed as a necessary fringe benefit for Kaiser workers during World War II, they provided an enviable level of services to families and children. Described as well-equipped, well-designed facilities with qualified, competitively paid staff, they were considered an example of excellent child care provided by a company who "well-conceived" their center's operation, and the needs of their employees. Today, many companies, such as Apple Computer, provide child centers for their employees.

Montessori Schools

The philosophy and curriculum of Montessori schools is based on the work and writings of an Italian physician, Maria Montessori (1870–1952). Children are introduced to materials that present a task. Teachers (facilitators) demonstrate their proper use. Children select and complete activities at will and return materials to assigned places (Epstein, Schweinhart, & McAdoo, 1996). In the early 1900s, Montessori schools opened in the United States. Accredited Montessori teacher training centers prepare many teachers. More than 120,000 teachers have gained Montessori certification worldwide. Not all child centers using a Montessori model have accredited teachers. The Montessori curriculum is found in a variety of school settings including preschools (both profit and nonprofit), family care homes, primary, and middle schools.

Residential Treatment Programs

Residential care facilities serve children with special needs including physical, social, and emotional conditions. Care is provided in group homes, private or state hospitals, other care units, private homes, foster care homes, or special facilities. Some facilities provide custodial care plus educational and recreational activities. Employees can be hired to live in or work shifts. Other professionals on site may be physicians, psychologists, nurses, therapists, and social workers. In some areas, there are both private and publicly supported facilities.

Hospital Care

Child care facilities in hospitals are found in many geographic locations. The needs of children during hospitalization promoted the development of this type of care. An area on the hospital grounds is usually turned into a play or activity center and designed to be a warm and comfortable environment. A child life specialist, an early childhood educator, or another person with a similar title supervises children's welfare and recuperation along with medical staff. Educators frequently work with families providing information, advice, and other supportive assistance both during the child's hospital stay and after the child's release from the hospital. Child life specialist training is offered in some community colleges.

Locations and Permission to Operate

Private schools offer services in locations near or at a distance from parents' homes or work. They are licensed by public agencies that regulate a square footage per child, health and safety features, food service and depending on the state, require an educational and/or developmental program for children. Some choose to adopt the same child/adult ratios as public programs. Others do not. Curriculums are often designed by staff members who meet the staff qualification criteria of the licensing agency. Licensing regulations in any state are available for public review.

Private programs can choose to become nonprofit and to obtain nonprofit status from a state agency. Many churches, private employers, and community service institutions operate this way. Private operators can also contract for their services and operate schools or programs in various community locations.

Neighborhood Play Groups

A group of parents in a particular town or neighborhood may hire an educator to operate a half day or full day program that moves from home to home or from park to park with parents present. Parents usually serve as assistant teachers. Depending on the state, they may need to be licensed.

Figure 2–6 Teachers of Toddlers Monitor Children's Health.

Mall Care and Other Parent On-Site Child Care

Malls, tennis centers, ski centers, cruise ships, casinos, restaurants, and department stores may operate as a pay-by-the-hour or free child care service. A parent who is on-site engaging in another activity can be reached quickly. In many states, these are unlicensed and unregulated by any outside regulatory authority. Wages for staff are often low but may include housing, food, recreational opportunities, or other benefits.

Infant – Toddler Centers

A fast growing segment of child care, infant–toddler care, can be a public, private, profit-making, or a nonprofit operation. This type of child care is believed to require the most interfacing and consulting with parents. Most community colleges offer classes specifically designed to promote occupational skill. A teacher attempts to observe individual infants closely to determine their unique needs, rhythms, and interaction styles in order to aid their growth and development (Figure 2–6). Health and safety is a key concern. Facilities, furnishings, and equipment suit the age level.

Question: What are the working conditions like when working with infants and toddlers?

Answer: Centers differ. Bending, lifting, and tolerating a sometimes high noise level is universally expected. Lots of changing and hand washing is necessary. Professional infant and toddler specialists believe this level of education offers its own special rewards. Child–teacher ratios should be small enough to provide individualized attention.

Before-School and After-School Care

These centers typically handle elementary school-aged children before and after school. They may be operated by a variety of sponsors. They are frequently located on the premises of a public or parochial elementary school. A few club-like operations exist and children are bused from school to other community locations. After-school, weekend, and summer boys' and girls' clubs can be sponsored by charitable organizations for disadvantaged or other special youth groups.

Some private centers are licensed for children up through age 12, and may provide overnight, holiday, vacation, and summer programs in addition to before-and-after-school care.

The popularity of after-school education has increased in recent years as growing evidence indicates that after-school programs can have significant academic and social benefits

(*Harvard Education Letter*, 2002). Programs of quality can reinforce and supplement material students learn in school by offering skills training besides recreational activities. The majority of programs are nonprofit.

Accredited Programs

The most widely established vehicle for early childhood program accreditation is National Association for the Education of Young Children's (NAEYC) accreditation. In 2004, there were over 8,000 NAEYC accredited programs. Both public and private schools and centers have received NAEYC accreditation awards. As a group, these centers continue to demonstrate higher overall quality when compared to non-NAEYC accredited programs (Turner, 2002). Many pay higher than average salaries and attract highly skilled staff members.

The NAEYC accreditation criteria recommends the number of children per group and particular staff–child ratios that, in many states, differ from that state's licensing requirements. Accredited programs provide regular staff training and ongoing staff professional development opportunities. They conduct at least one annual employee evaluation. Staff are informed of evaluation criteria in advance. Consultation is frequent, as is joint staff planning. Staff meetings involve program goals, individual child plans, and working condition issues, as well as other important consultation areas. Since accreditation is a voluntary procedure, a center has demonstrated a commitment to quality and developmentally appropriate practice, if accreditation from a professionally recognized group is received.

Question: Do accredited schools pay higher teacher salaries?

Answer: Not necessarily, but usually. Budget, funding, and school priorities control salaries. Often, accredited programs have better working conditions, and teachers receive administrative support for their efforts.

Bilingual and English as a Second Language (ESL) Programs

If you are fluent in a language other than English, you will most likely have an edge if applying for certain educator positions. Bilingual programs for preschoolers and primary children are often situated in metropolitan areas, but rural areas have classes if a population of English as a second language speakers exists. Secondary schools teach foreign language classes. Adult classes are frequently available at night schools, adult education programs, and at college level.

Most bilingual and ESL programs are funded by public funds, but a considerable number of private schools exist. Parents often believe learning a second language while young is a lifetime advantage. This parental attitude supports schools for preschoolers in the private sector.

When a teacher is licensed or credentialed, overseas positions with schools or businesses increase job prospects. With the number of immigrant, multilingual, and multicultural school children in America today, interviewing committees realize certain teachers may be better able to relate and teach attending children and interact with their families.

Special Education

Edelfelt and Reiman (2004) describe special education teachers as follows:

About 386,000 teachers in the United States work with children who have disabilities. Around 93 percent of them are employed in schools that serve students with disabilities from ages six through twenty-one.

Special education students' conditions can include learning disabilities, speech and language impairments, mental retardation, emotional disturbance, hearing impairments, orthopedic differences, health concerns, visual problems, deafness, blindness, or combinations of disabilities. Federally supported special education programs served 5.7 million children in 1999–2000, and about 386,000 teachers worked with children with disabilities (Edelfelt & Reiman, 2004). Primary, middle, and secondary students have their own facilities.

Job titles in the special education field are diverse with school nurse, educational diagnostician, school psychologist, audiologist, social worker, speech-language pathologist, therapist, and special education teacher being the most common. Administration job titles also are numerous.

License-Exempt Child Care

License-exempt child care is often called "family, friend and neighbor care," "kith and kin care", or "grandma care." It is the most common and largest child care arrangement in the United States. As different and unique as the families concerned, each child care situation is similar in one respect, that is, care is being provided by someone other than the child's parents or guardians. In some cases, such as exercise clubs, mall child care centers, child gyms, and like establishments, parents are on-site, closely available, or reachable by telephone or electronic devices.

Fees may or may not be involved. In number, family relatives provide the bulk of licensed-exempt care, followed by providers who care for children in their own or the child's home. Infants and toddlers are the largest age group served, then preschoolers.

Federal, state, and local programs have been developed to provide license-exempt caretakers, especially low-income and immigrant group providers, with supportive assistance that recognizes and bolsters their existing nurturing and developmental care skills. To qualify for services in many of these supportive programs, the child in care must never have participated in a licensed child care program.

These assistance programs employ administrators, home visitors, parent partners, care coaches, and other professionals who monitor children's health and growth in addition to providing child care tips and suggestions. Parents prefer this license-exempt care for a multitude of reasons including safety, convenience, cost, cultural similarity, and linguistic features.

Public Elementary School

The U.S. Department of Labor (2001) calculates teachers held over 3 million jobs in the year 2000. Of these, about 1.5 million were elementary school teacher positions, 175,000 were kindergarten teachers, and 423,000 were preschool teachers.

Figure 2–7 Working in an Elementary School is a Possibility.

Most states require applicants for teacher licensing be tested for competency in basic skills. All states require general education teachers to have a bachelor's degree and to have completed an approved teacher training program. Some states require a minimal grade point average.

Many states are implementing policies that encourage more students to become teachers. Some school districts without tight budgets are offering large signing bonuses that are distributed over the teacher's first few years of teaching. States having a difficult time finding teachers have offered incentives including state scholarships and loans for moving expenses. Loan-forgiveness programs allow education majors with at least a B average to receive state-paid tuition as long as they agree to teach in that state for four years.

Qualifications in private elementary and secondary schools varies. Out-of-state or overseas degrees may be acceptable. Each school decides what level of teacher training is required (Figure 2–7).

The *No Child Left Behind Act* and the Teaching Profession

Will the *No Child Left Behind Act* affect the careers of elementary school educators? Yes, in diverse ways. There is no doubt teachers will need to demonstrate their ability to help all children show "adequate yearly progress." Many school districts are considering increasing teacher pay to teachers who do so. Some are awarding bonuses. The National Council of Teachers of English (2004) reports that one teacher boosted her yearly pay with an extra $7,000. Federal grants, which totaled over two billion in 2003, were designated to improve teacher quality and teacher skill in reading and mathematics instruction (Peyser & Costrell, 2004). In many cases, teachers will have to accumulate advanced degrees and participate in lifelong learning. The need for assessment professionals and literacy specialists has increased dramatically, as has the need for tutors and classroom assistant teachers. Because the *No Child Left Behind Act*'s target date extends to 2014, these jobs are not likely to disappear. The federal administration in Washington will have to be responsive to the public, particularly parents, who view the legislation as a positive change in American education.

No Child Left Behind Act grants for "innovative programs" have totaled close to $380 million. This will create additional job opportunities. It is actually a very turbulent time in the field of education, but an exciting time. Job titles in elementary, middle, and secondary schools are featured in Figure 2–8.

Superintendent	Occupational therapist
Principal	Physical therapist
Elementary teacher	Speech-language pathologist
Private school teacher	Speech-language audiologist
Central Office administrator	Educational diagnostician
Central Office supervisor	Art therapist
Central Office manager	Mentor teacher
Central Office director	Substitute teacher
Central Office coordinator	Reading specialist
Art, music, physical education teacher	Department head
School library media specialist	Career guidance specialist
Computer specialist	**School Support Staff**
School counselor	Instructional aide
School psychologist	Career guidance technician
School social worker	Bus driver
English as a second language teacher	Cafeteria manager
Special education teacher	Campus monitor
	School nurse

Figure 2–8   Sample Job Titles in Elementary, Middle, and Secondary Schools.

Note: This is not a complete list of job titles.

Middle and High Schools (Secondary Schools)

Sometimes called junior high, middle schools can be described as being similar to both elementary and high school. Students between eleven and fourteen years old, still require the use of teacher guidance techniques and social direction. Teachers instruct in their area of specialty. Students change classes and learn from teachers specializing in academic, artistic, physical development, and other subjects. Secondary school teaching involves the instruction of teenagers and their extracurricular activities. Increased use of instructional technology has taken place. Paperwork at the secondary level is considerable due to examinations and general record keeping, and student counseling and advisement are included in teacher's duties. A field of specialization is required for credentialing and many teachers hold master's or doctoral degrees. Continual updating in their chosen subject field is undertaken so that teachers retain the instructional depth needed to plan, prepare, and present advanced knowledge and sophisticated skills.

College and university teaching is covered later in Chapter Nine. Chapter Eleven is devoted to self-employment.

Summary

There are many ways to categorize educational programs. This chapter covered well-known education and care programs, from infancy through high school. It divided schools into two broad sectors—publicly-funded and private programs. Employment positions were separated into direct or administrative and other support services. Infant–toddler centers, preschools, kindergartens, elementary, middle, and secondary schools were described along with their employment characteristics. Other educational or care-related group programs that are licensed or unlicensed were mentioned. As your own career manager, this chapter presents a view of possible employment sites, and affords a glimpse of job qualifications, tasks, and duties. You may have been able to clarify which sectors in the field of education appeal to you.

Helpful Web Sites

Center for the Future of Teaching and Learning
  http://www.cftl.org
  search for "The status of the teaching profession 2003 (California)."

Council for Exceptional Children
  http://www.sped.org

Early Childhood and Parenting (ECAP)
  http:ecap.crc.uiuc.edu/
  use key words such as "employment in education" *on search for publications.*

Ecumenical Child Care Network
  http://www.eccn.org
  church-affiliated child care

State Child Care Regulatory Offices
  http://www.nccic.org/

National Afterschool Association (NAA)
  http://www.naaweb.org
  an association of public, private, and community-based programs

Teachers of English to Speakers of Other Languages
  http://www.tesol.org
  information on teaching

Resources

Bloom, P. J. (1995). The quality of work life in early childhood programs. In S. Bredekamp & B. Willer (Eds.), *NAEYC accreditation: A decade of learning and the years ahead* (pp. 13–24) Washington, DC: National Association for the Education of Young Children.

Center for the Child Care Workforce. (1998). *Current data on child care salaries and benefits in the United States*. Washington, DC: Author.

Cryer, D., & Clifford, R. M. (Eds.) (2003). *Early childhood education and care*. Baltimore, MD: Paul H. Brookes Publishing Co.

National Association for the Education of Young Children. (1998). *Accreditation criteria and procedures of the National Academy of Early Childhood Programs (rev. ed)*. Washington, DC: Author.

References

Edelfelt, R. A., & Reiman, A. J. (2004). Careers in education. Chicago: VGM Career Books.

Epstein, A. S., Sweinhart, L. F., & McAdoo, L. (1996). *Models of early childhood education.* Ypsilanti, MI: High/Scope Press.

Harvard Education Letter. Reviewed in *ASCD SmartBrief* (2002, November 11). Schools supplement curricula with afterschool programs. Author: 1.

Kamerman, S. B., & Gatenio, S. (2003). Overview of the current policy context. In D. Cryer, & R. M. Clifford (Eds.), *Early childhood education and care in the USA,* pp. 1–30. Baltimore, MD: Paul H. Brookes Publishing, Co.

Katz, L. G. (2003). Program content and implementation. In D. Cryer & R. M. Clifford (Eds.). *Early childhood education and care in the USA,* pp. 107–117. Baltimore, MD: Paul H. Brookes Publishing Co.

Morgan, G. (2003). Staff roles, education, and compensation. In D. Cryer & R. M. Clifford (Eds.). *Early childhood education and care in the USA,* pp. 87–106. Baltimore, MD: Paul H. Brookes Publishing Co.

National Council of Teachers of English. (2004, August 17). . . . news, views, and ideas you can use! *The NCTE Inbox. 3* (48) 2. Retrieved September 18, 2004. http//www.ncte.org/about/

Peyser, J., & Costrell, R. (2004, Spring). Claims that the *No Child Left Behind Act* represents an "unfunded mandate" wilt under close scrutiny. *Education Next, 4* (2) 23–29.

Southworth, S. A. (2000, January/February). Wanted two million teachers. *Scholastic Instructor, 109* (5) 25–26.

Turner, P. (Ed.) (2002). *La ristra: New Mexico's comprehensive professional development system in early care, education and family support.* Santa Fe, NM: Office of Child Development, Youth and Family Department.

U.S. Department of Health and Human Services, Administration on Children and Families. (2002). 2002 Head Start fact sheet. Retrieved November 5, 2003. http:112.acf.dhhs.gov/programs/

U.S. Department of Labor. (2001). *Occupational outlook handbook,* Washington, DC. Author.

Wittenberg, R. (1996). *Opportunities in child care careers.* Lincolnwood, IL: VGM Career Horizons.

CHAPTER THREE

Professional Growth Planning

Education is learning what you didn't
even know you didn't know.

Daniel Boorstin

Struggling Family

Rance and Barbara, a struggling young, married couple, plan to consult their financial advisor about a decision that would affect them financially. With two children under the age of six, another on the way, and a new condo, their budget is tight. Their six-year-old daughter, Reba, was bored in kindergarten. They conferred with her teacher who confirmed Reba was performing two to three years ahead of her peers. Rance and Barbara identified a private school with a long waiting list for their daughter's next school year, and it was expensive. They felt she needed more specialized attention than the public school was able to provide. They were contemplating refinancing their home to afford school fees.

QUESTIONS TO PONDER

1. What would you like to know about this family before you judge whether this is a wise or unwise plan?
2. Is this family unusual, or do many parents value their child's early education to this degree?
3. Are you aware of the course credits, degrees, certification, or licensing requirements you need to be eligible for the employment position you desire? or Do you know where to get the education or training that qualifies you?

Chapter One ended with your development of a career goal. You were not asked to put this goal into successive steps or to develop a timeline because you will need additional information first.

Professional Growth Plans

Continuous learning is the mark of a professional in any occupational field. Mary Ann Davies (2001) notes "what is required of teachers in today's world."

> *The emerging complexities of today's world require teachers to be adaptable to change, be reform oriented, and conscious of their roles in addressing the evolving needs of children. These teacher demands necessitate a disposition focusing on continuous professional growth and a willingness to use reflective practice to drive this growth. They must be willing to peer through the looking glass. Like Alice in Wonderland, life becomes the wonderment of self-discovery.*

According to Morkes (2003), rapid developments in technology have resulted in changes in the skills required for many occupations. Skill growth is necessary for the occupational survival of career professionals. Occupations with the most job growth are the ones that require the most skills, the most lifelong learning (Kleiman, 2002).

The *Elementary and Secondary Education Act*, as re-authorized by the *No Child Left Behind Act*, has set high standards to ensure the quality of teachers in the United States. It requires teachers to be highly qualified and have content knowledge and the teaching skills that enable their students to succeed. In order to be considered highly qualified, a teacher in elementary, middle, and secondary schools must hold a bachelor's degree. They also must demonstrate required subject matter competency and teaching skills either by passing a rigorous subject-matter competency test in each core academic subject they will teach, or by demonstrating competency through a state evaluation procedure (U.S. Department of Education, 2003). Core academic subjects include English, reading, language arts, mathematics, science, foreign languages, civics (or government), economics, arts, history, and geography.

Most states require that their elementary school teachers enroll in college as a major or minor in education, while their middle and high school counterparts need a college major in the subject they plan to teach.

Early childhood teacher requirements in publicly funded programs have increased. Many states have mandated, as has Head Start, that teachers hold or are working toward a four-year degree.

Teale (2003) observes:

> *Early childhood development and early childhood education are hot items these days. Brain research, Head Start, early education opportunities, early intervention, and many other issues related to funding, policies, facilities, and curriculum for young children seem omnipresent in both professional and public media.*

Early childhood professionals working in publicly funded programs and public schools may find their states or their program administrators have developed and adopted a state professional growth planning guide for them. Planning guides specify years of experience and cite specific degrees, certificates, licenses, permits or training courses that must be completed for upward job mobility and continued employment. If your state, like New Mexico and New Jersey, has a written plan, obtain it. Such written plans continue to be developed as states move to ensure their early childhood educators have a good handle on what constitutes quality and developmental early education and care.

New Jersey's Professional Development Center for Early Care and Education (NJPD-CECE) has implemented a five-year plan to develop a statewide system of coordinated and accessible professional development opportunities for early care and education professionals. The plan attempts to ensure that early childhood programs in New Jersey offer appropriate and developmental learning experiences. Their planners believe that this curriculum consistently promotes the highest levels of physical, emotional, social, and intellectual well-being in children. This state plan identifies occupational core knowledge and competency areas (NJPDCECE, 2002). These guides are used in the following ways:

- to plan entry to the field
- to establish a career path and plan for advancement
- to enhance professional growth within a level
- to explore options for professional growth across levels
- to self-evaluate using core knowledge and competency levels

Copies of core knowledge and competency areas can be downloaded from the NJPDCECE Web site, http://www.njpdc.org.

State professional growth plans to guide educators may be flexible and allow a choice in professional growth activities. Often, stipends covering employee costs are available, and completion of coursework is tied to upward movement on a salary scale. Research has repeatedly substantiated the idea that teachers' educational training is closely related to staff turnover and the quality of program services. A California program, The Child Development Corps, also provides a professional stipend ($500–600 per year) to early childhood teachers, directors, and family care providers who meet educational and training qualifications and who commit to continuing their professional development (Whitebook & Eichberg, 2002).

NAEYC's definitions of early childhood professional categories have been used as a framework in many states. They have also been used by educators who plan their own professional growth. Figure 3–1 displays levels of accomplishment. Obtain a copy of your state's required qualifications for early childhood workers. Some cities, such as Boise, Idaho, have also adopted city requirements.

County Offices of Education and licensing agencies are sources of written requirements.

In Chapter One you identified your dream job. If your dream job is in early education, examine the six levels of responsibility in Figure 3–1. What professional level of attainment might be necessary for that dream position?

Definitions of Professionalism

VanderVen (1988) defines professionalism as the ability to plan knowledgeably and competently, to make a sustained difference, to diagnose and analyze situations, to select the most appropriate interventions, to apply them skillfully, and to describe why they were selected.

This is designed to reflect a continuum of professional development. The levels identify levels of preparation programs for which standards have been established nationally.

Early Childhood Professional Level VI

Successful completion of a Ph.D. or Ed.D in a program conforming to NAEYC guidelines; OR

Successful demonstration of the knowledge, performance, and dispositions expected as outcomes of a doctorate degree program conforming to NAEYC guidelines.

Early Childhood Professional Level V

Successful completion of a master's degree in a program conforming to NAEYC guidelines; OR

Successful demonstration of the knowledge, performance, and dispositions expected as outcomes of a master's degree program conforming to NAEYC guidelines.

Early Childhood Professional Level IV

Successful completion of a baccalaureate degree from a program conforming to NAEYC guidelines; OR

State certification meeting NAEYC/ATE certification guidelines; OR

Successful completion of a baccalaureate degree in another field with more than thirty professional units in early childhood development/education including 300 hours of supervised teaching experience, including 150 hours each for two of the following three age groups: infants and toddlers, three- to five-year-olds, or the primary grades; OR

Successful demonstration of the knowledge, performance, and dispositions expected as outcomes of a baccalaureate degree program conforming to NAEYC guidelines.

Early Childhood Professional Level III

Successful completion of an associate degree from a program conforming to NAEYC guidelines; OR

Successful completion of an associate degree in a related field, plus thirty units of professional studies in early childhood development/education including 300 hours of supervised teaching experience in an early childhood program; OR

Successful demonstration of the knowledge, performance, and dispositions expected as outcomes of an associate degree program conforming to NAEYC guidelines.

Early Childhood Professional Level II

II. A. Successful completion of the CDA Professional Preparation Program OR completion of a systematic, comprehensive training program that prepares an individual to successfully acquire the CDA Credential through direct assessment.

II. B. Successful completion of a one-year early childhood certification program.

Early Childhood Professional Level I

Individuals who are employed in an early childhood professional role working under supervision or with support (e.g., linkages with provider association or network or enrollment in supervised practicum) and participating in training designed to lead to the assessment of individual competencies or acquisition of a degree.

Figure 3–1   Definitions of Early Childhood Professional Categories.

Source: From Professional development. (1994, March). *Young Children, 49*(3). Reprinted with permission from the National Association for the Education of Young Children, NAEYC, © 1994.

Another definition states that a professional is one engaged in a limited number of occupations or vocations involving special learning and a certain social prestige.

An educator needs to be a generalist—it is the nature of the work. A multitude of teaching skills and competencies are necessary to promote students' development and to ensure effective interaction with parents, other staff, and community. To reach a training program's graduating competency level you need to acquire a number of general skills. As an educator, you may be aware of your limitations and also proud of your strengths. Specializing involves magnifying strengths. In job hunting, specialization is an important consideration. By working to improve limitations and build strength in one or more areas, you can improve your career opportunities.

Ladder and Lateral Mobility

Job mobility can progress in two directions—upward (moving to higher levels of responsibility), or laterally (becoming increasingly adept and skillful at the same level). Aiming for an administrative position while being a teacher entails reaching for a higher rung on a career ladder. Becoming an expert teacher puppeteer, while working in the same position, typifies lateral development, Figure 3–2.

Individual goals may involve both ladder and lateral features. The revision of goals and action plans is a lifelong process. Will there be elements of lateral development necessary in your career plan? Your answer is probably yes.

Individual Growth Plans and Learning Cycles

Just as you have observed children's learning cycles in classrooms, you can expect your own professional growth to vary from times when you take leaps and bounds to times when you pause to reflect, and periods that are as slow as a snail's pace. Harrison (1978) suggests a risk and retreat cycle exists in self-directed learning:

> *The learning cycle is our name for the natural process of advance and retreat in learning. We observed early in our experiments with self-directed learning that individuals would move out and take personal risks and then would move back to reflect and integrate the experience.*

Caruso and Fawcett (1999) point out that life stages influence growth plans:

> *Staff members working in early childhood programs represent all adult age groups. Women beginning or returning to work as their children grow up, and senior citizens working part-time to earn extra income or to have something to do. These adults are at varying points in their life cycles. As they develop and change, so do their personal and professional needs and priorities.*

You may envision your career growth plan as a path, a journey, a ladder, or a mountain to conquer. Whichever plan you envision, time and financial resources will need to be considered if your plan involves further education or self-employment. Figure 3–3 reports the frequency with which the 815 participants in a nationwide study of employed preschool professionals reported they engaged in professional development activities (McMullen et al., 2004).

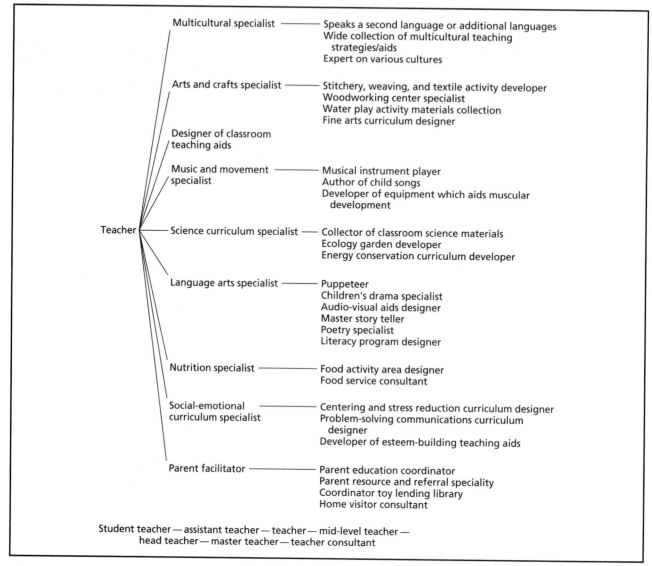

Figure 3–2 Examples of Lateral Development.

The following Web sites are recommended for more information on selecting a college or training program:

http://www.allaboutcollege.com/

This site contains links to the home pages of colleges and universities in the United States and overseas. Internet addresses for admissions offices are available.

http://www.mcli.dist.maricopa.edu/

This site offers 1,242 community college Web sites. Home pages give specific information concerning college offerings, financial help, and counseling. Search geographically, alphabetically, or by key word.

http://www.rwm.org/

Profile of Participants' Ongoing Professional Development

	Never/Not applicable to me	Rarely	Sometimes	Often
I attend regular staff/faculty meetings.	4.0%	1.2%	6.2%	88.6%
I attend inservice trainings/workshops.	1.4%	1.2%	22.9%	74.5%
I read newsletters, magazines, and/or journals written for professionals.	0.1%	1.3%	27.0%	71.6%
I consult with colleagues about my work.	0.7%	3.1%	31.4%	64.8%
I read books that are related to my profession.	0.5%	4.2%	42.8%	52.5%
I attend conferences run by professional organizations locally.	2.7%	8.5%	42.6%	46.2%
I get advice/feedback from my supervisors(s).	14.7%	7.8%	33.0%	44.5%
I attend conferences run by professional organizations in my state.	4.0%	14.2%	47.4%	34.4%
I consult with a mentor about my practice.	32.3%	16.3%	31.7%	19.7%
I consult with fellow professionals electronically through e-mail or Web.	37.0%	18.8%	25.7%	18.5%
I attend conferences run by professional organizations nationally or internationally.	27.9%	24.2%	35.1%	12.8%
I write in a personal journal about my practice.	56.4%	25.0%	13.8%	4.8%

Figure 3–3 Profile of Participants' Ongoing Professional Development.

Source: McMullen, M. B., Alat, K. Buldu, M. & Lash, M. (2004, March). A snapshot of NAEYC's preschool professionals through the less of quality. *Young Children, 59* (2) 87–92.

This site contains a vocational school database. Select a state and research early childhood (preschool teaching) training programs.

http://www.graduateguide.com/
A directory of U.S. schools offering doctorate, masters, and professional degree programs.

Trade or Technical Schools and Colleges

Referred to as private career schools, vocational schools, or trade and technical schools, these schools typically offer programs of study for specific occupations including early childhood teaching. Not all trade and technical schools are accredited to award associate's degrees. Private school and college fees are often higher than fees at public colleges.

Community Colleges and Two-Year Degrees

Once called junior colleges, public community colleges are found in every state. Along with other colleges and universities, they award two-year degrees. A two-year training program in

Early Childhood Education typically consists of instruction and a practical experience leading to an Associate of Arts (AA) degree, an Associate of Sciences (AS) degree, or an Associate of Applied Science (AAS) degree. Some community colleges offer training necessary for a Child Development Associate (CDA) credential.

Coursework leading to a degree includes general education requirements. These units (credits) often transfer easily into a baccalaureate degree program at a four-year college. This is not so for all early childhood coursework. Although efforts to promote a smooth transfer of early childhood coursework credits have increased dramatically, articulation agreements do not exist in some states. It is important to seek department or instructor counseling concerning credit transferability at both the two-year college level and the bachelor's degree institution you plan to attend. There can be a difference in coursework transferability. Sometimes credits are accepted as elective units in a major at an institution offering baccalaureate degrees. In other cases, they are accepted as fulfilling required coursework.

> **Question:** I have a good job working with preschool children, and I have a few college units. Will an Associate of Arts (AA) degree help me get a better-paying job?
>
> **Answer:** Yes, usually. You are probably working at a private sector program where wages may be low compared with most public early childhood programs. Publicly funded employers also tend to provide benefits such as health insurance. Since standards for teachers are rising and affecting staff qualifications, getting more education is a prudent move.

College catalogs may use diverse terms—such as preschool teaching, family and child studies, child development, or assistant or aide training to describe their early childhood education major. Speciality training programs may be offered, such as infant/toddler teacher, special education aide, preschool director, bilingual aide, or school-aged practitioner, or another speciality related to the care and education of young children. The college departments where early childhood training takes place are also diverse. The most common departments are early childhood education, human or child development, home economics, psychology, or family and child studies. Community colleges usually provide counseling staff, a financial aid officer, an employment office, and a tutoring center. College catalogs outline and describe training programs and both major and general education classes. A prescribed course pattern is required for the completion of a two-year degree and/or a certificate program.

Community College Certificate Programs in Early Childhood Education

Community colleges may offer a certificate of completion issued by a college department for completion of a training program's major coursework. Usually, no general education classes are required, and specific coursework often reflects the number and type of college credits necessary to satisfy the required credits for an entry-level early childhood teacher, aide, or director in the licensing requirements of that state.

> **Question :** Should I start with an Associate of Arts (AA) degree from a community college in early childhood education if I eventually want an elementary school teaching or administrative position?
>
> **Answer:** That depends on your individual circumstances. Many individuals choose to get an AA degree for reasons including the convenience and cost of community colleges, the ability to get a job and work while completing an elementary teaching credential program, campus child care facilities, and the experience of student teaching early in their career.

According to Lutton (2004), community colleges are playing an increasingly critical role in the development of the pre-K through grade 12 teacher workforce, and she notes that 20 percent of America's current teachers started their education at a community college. The alternate route to a teaching credential is to enroll in a four-year college or university and become an education major.

Bachelor's Degree Programs

Bachelor's degrees are awarded at four-year colleges and universities. Universities are often bigger than colleges, and many offer undergraduate, baccalaureate, master's, doctorate, and professional degrees. Tuition is often less at public institutions. Some higher education schools and training programs in every profession are recognized for their excellence and considered prestigious. Many Ivy League universities and colleges fit this description.

The National Council for Accreditation of Teacher Education (NCATE) has accredited over 550 teacher education programs nationwide. Many students enter these programs in their sophomore year. These college programs instruct majors in subject matter and professional education courses covering educational theory and practice. Students aiming for secondary level teaching will major in the subject they wish to teach, while also taking teacher preparation courses. Some states offer professional development schools that merge theory and practice and provide a year of teaching under professional guidance.

In early childhood college training, Pacific Oaks in California, Wheelock College in Boston, Bank Street College in New York, Lesley University in Massachusetts, and Erikson Institute in Chicago are well-known for their training programs. Getting a degree from a NAEYC accredited training program at a college or university may provide an advantage in the job market. Many career counselors recommend selecting a "top flight" institution. Others point out good training programs that are available nationwide. Morkes (2003) states that although it is possible to enter many occupations with a liberal arts degree, the people who are the most competitive for positions seek specific courses and experiences to prepare for occupational entry. Educators desiring employment at the middle school or secondary school level should select a major in a "core academic subject."

Individuals Entering Education with a Degree in Another Discipline or from Another Institution

If you already have a college degree, seek information and counseling from the Education Department at the college or university you wish to attend. Usually a year and a half of full-time college work is needed to attain a teaching credential. It may be wise to shop around.

Some colleges offer more services to returning students than others. Some may accept former coursework more readily. If possible, consult an instructor or professor personally and bring copies of your transcripts. Instructors occasionally have the power to decide which courses may be waived in light of past experience or coursework. They can also alert you about how to negotiate for credit for a class you feel you have already completed. This advice applies to students transferring to another higher education institution with coursework completed or to students with a degree from an overseas university.

Individuals with Degrees from Other Countries

A teacher who received a degree in another country that is at least equivalent to a bachelor's degree offered by an American institution of higher education can be employed by an American school district. Foreign teacher qualifications must be consistent with the statutory requirements found in the *No Child Left Behind Act* that define a "highly qualified teacher" (U.S. Department of Education, 2003).

Graduate Study

Graduate study usually requires two to six years after the undergraduate degree. Master's, doctorate, specialist, and professional degrees are awarded by accredited institutions. In a graduate program, the student concentrates on one particular field or occupation.

A Master of Arts in Education (M.Ed.) usually requires 36 to 64 graduate semester credit hours within a limited time period. Specialist degrees, such as Education Specialist in Education Administration, Early Childhood Leadership, School Psychology, and many other similar degrees, may go beyond the master's level. For elementary school teachers, a master's degree is required for permanent certification in some states, and 56 percent of public school teachers hold master's degrees. This is an increase from 27 percent in 1971 (Grant & Murray, 1999). A doctorate degree in education (Ed.D.) usually requires 90 graduate semester credit hours beyond an undergraduate degree. A Doctor of Philosophy in Education (Ph.D.) can require additional coursework that includes research. Most institutions require both academic coursework and experiential learning in addition to a comprehensive examination and a research project that includes writing a doctoral dissertation.

The San Jose State University Career Center (2003) offers information for students contemplating graduate school and describes what is usually required for admission.

> *Is grad school right for you? Some factors you may wish to honestly appraise when deciding whether graduate school is for you include:*
>
> ***Interest.*** *Do you have an interest in a particular field? Graduate work is intense and arduous. Do you like to learn?*
>
> ***Ability.*** *Are you an above-average student who has good study skills and can work independently? Do you have strong research techniques and writing abilities?*
>
> ***Financial Consideration.*** *If you need financial assistance, will the graduate school of your choice be able to provide you with financial support? Are teaching or graduate assistantships readily available?*

Although admission requirements vary, the following are basic to most programs:

- admission test scores
- university application/personal statement

- official transcripts
- undergraduate degree and/or course requirements
- interviews
- letters of recommendation from faculty
- language/residency requirements
- unique major requirements

Keep in mind that university admission requirements and deadlines are often different from individual department (or program) requirements.

State Teacher Certification

Teacher qualifications are regulated by two separate processes—state child care licensing and state teacher certification requirements. Each state develops unique stipulations. A description of state teacher certification follows:

> *Teacher certification is a process by which a state's department of education qualifies* individuals *for teaching positions in the public school system. Although states certify roles such as teachers, principals, and superintendents, the focus for early care and education is on the single role of the teacher.* Certification requirements *specify the amount of training and education a prospective teacher must complete before employment, although the way these are measured varies from state to state. Requirements for certification include degrees in early childhood education, credit hours or demonstrated competencies in early care and education subject areas, and degrees from accredited institutions' teacher-training programs. When individuals meet these requirements, they receive a* certificate, *a document granted by a state for teachers, administrators, and related professional staff to indicate that an individual met specific state standards.*
>
> *In some states, the certificate is not specific to early childhood. Instead, individuals receive both a certificate and an* endorsement, *which is the information added to a certificate indicating the services the endorsed individual can perform because of special training (Morgan et al., 1993).*

Teacher Licensing/Credentialing—Public Elementary, Middle, and Secondary School

The U.S. Labor Department's *Occupational Outlook Handbook* (2003) notes:

> *With additional preparation, teachers may move into positions as school librarians, reading specialists, curriculum specialists, or guidance counselors. Teachers in kindergarten through Grade 12 may become administrators or supervisors, although the number of these positions is limited, and competition can be intense. In some systems, highly qualified, experienced teachers can become senior or mentor teachers, with higher pay and additional responsibilities. They guide and assist less experienced teachers while keeping most of their own teaching responsibilities.*

All states and the District of Columbia require public school teachers to be licensed or credentialed. The State Board of Education or a licensing advisory committee can grant a license/credential to teach preschool through Grade 3, the elementary grades, the middle grades, a secondary education subject area, or a special subject such as reading or music.

These licenses/credentials vary by grade and title from state to state. Figure 3–4 displays typical licenses and/or credentials needed for different teaching levels. However, all states require general education teachers to have a bachelor's degree and to have completed an approved training program with a prescribed number of subject and education credits, as well as student teaching (supervised practice teaching), Figure 3–5. Master's degree completion is required in some states during a specific time frame after individuals are hired. Most states test licensing or credentialing candidates' competency in basic skills, and they require a level of proficiency in subject matter. Performance-based testing is gaining acceptance along with an examination of candidate's subject matter knowledge.

Teacher Titles and Credentials

Teacher Title	Type of School	Typical License/Credential and Education Requirements
Early Childhood Educator/Teacher	Pre-kindergarten, Preschool, Infant/Toddler Program, After-school Program	Usually a specified number of credits/units in early childhood education in private schools; an A.A. or B.A. degree in public programs
Elementary School Teacher, Kindergarten Teacher	Kindergarten	An early childhood, kindergarten, or elementary license/credential; a B.A. degree and in some states eventually a M.A. degree
Elementary School Teacher	Grades 1–6	A K–6 license/credential; a B.A. degree and in some states eventually a M.A. degree.
Middle School Teacher	Grades 4–8, 5–7, 6–9	K–6, K–8, or secondary school license/credential; depends on grades encompassed; a B.A. degree; M.A. degree in some states; degrees in a subject area
Junior/Senior High School Core Subjects Teacher	Grades 6–8, 7–9, 7–12, 9–12, or 10–12	K–8 or secondary school license/credential endorsed in field of specialization or core subject; a B.A. degree and M.A. degree in some states
Special Area Teacher (music, art, physical education, special education, home economics, industrial arts, science, foreign language, geography, social studies, etc.)	K–6, K–8, K–12, Grades 7–12, 9–12, 10–12	License/credential B.A., M.A., doctorate degree in a subject area

Figure 3–4   Teacher Titles and Credentials.

Figure 3–5 Different States Require Different Qualifications for Their Teachers.

Source: U.S. Department of Education. Spring 2000.

Alternate routes to licenses/credentials usually exist. Emergency and provisional licenses/credentials may be issued but require meeting full requirements in a stated period of time.

Voluntary Certification

The National Board for Professional Teaching Standards, composed of representatives from two dozen organizations, issues a certificate that signifies the holder has met the highest standards established for the teaching profession (Wiebke, 2000). To qualify, applicants pay fees, undergo a year-long process to assess their own effectiveness, develop a professional portfolio, and pass a series of exams. This is a voluntary procedure and 17 different certificates of national merit are available including Early Childhood/Generalist. More information is available at http://www.nbpts.org or 1-800-22-TEACH.

Guiding and Hyson (2002) believe successful applicants join a distinguished group of 3,800 educators. The professional advantages of this credential, in addition to advanced teaching skill, may be upward mobility and recognition as a leader in the field.

Early Childhood CDA (Child Development Associate) Credential

Developed in the 1970s, CDA training is found in some community colleges and other training institutions. It is a nationally recognized system that provides a validated statement of early childhood education competence for early childhood workers. The nonprofit Council for Early Childhood Recognition in Washington, DC, administers the program. Caruso and Fawcett (1999) describe the system as follows:

> *This system allows people with varying amounts of formal or informal education, with or without degrees, to focus on the same goals (career development goals) and reach them at their own pace, and in a way most appropriate for them. The requirements are flexible, both in time and in the type of training needed. CDA competencies are based on sound child development principles and the credential is awarded on the basis of a caregiver's actual work with children. The CDA credential is awarded in three child care settings.*

- Center-based, for which candidates receive endorsements to work with infants, toddlers, and preschool children
- Family child care
- Home visitors

Coursework or training taken for college credit is more advantageous, flexible, and desirable for upward career mobility. Not all CDA training programs award college credit for training classes. (See Figure 3–6 for the number of credentialed CDAs.)

Distance Learning

Distance learning offers many options including the opportunity to study at home during the day, night, and weekend. It is frequently connected to college course credits that lead to a degree or credits that are transferable to another institution. When in doubt concerning transferability, ask specific questions about course credits. Ask whether credits are accepted as elective or required units (credits) in a college major. Each college has their own policy regarding which credits are accepted at their institutions. Colleges offering distance learning may have articulation agreements with only certain other colleges. The cost of distance learning courses usually exceeds on-campus fees.

The availability of distance learning has grown, and there are many delivery methods. Courses can be offered via video conferencing, the Internet, e-mail, or a combination of these. There is a wide variety of institutional sponsors including government agencies, professional associations, and colleges and universities. Accredited educational institutions are listed in the Resources section at http://www.usdla.org. College and coursework information is also available.

College correspondence courses, though considered by some to be old fashioned, are still offered. Academic coursework is transmitted by mail to sponsoring institutions. There is usually a set fee per course, and often a certificate is awarded for completion of a course of study.

Mentors

Mentoring is most common in elementary school teaching settings. School districts have used mentoring programs to help retain first-year teachers. Feiman-Nemser and associates (1999) point out that formal mentoring programs to assist beginning teachers are not new, but they have gained considerable momentum since the mid-1980s. The cost of mentors is a fiscal expenditure. However, studies show the approach is financially effective in retaining new teachers.

A mentor is a more experienced person with a higher level of expertise who seems to possess a parental or personal interest or paid interest in promoting a protégé's professional growth. It is possible to have multiple mentor relationships.

The responsibilities of a mentor are described in Figure 3–7. After reading this list of responsibilities, most practicing teachers agree that mentors can provide professional growth. Mentors are available for some

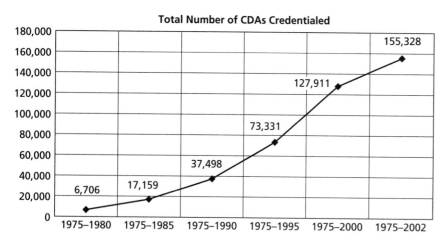

Figure 3–6   Total Number of CDAs Credentialed.

Source: Improving child care through programs of the Council for Professional Recognition. Brochure. Council for Professional Recognition. Washington, DC.

Responsibilities of a Mentor

- Get involved in solving specific problems about curriculum, instruction, and relationships.

- Provide opportunities for classroom visits with feedback (beginning teacher's classroom, mentor's classroom, colleague's classrooms). Encourage visits to other classrooms by offering to cover the beginning teacher's classroom.

- Express positive feelings about teaching and help the beginning teacher attain those same feelings. Address the new teacher's thoughts about being a teacher.

- Help the new teacher cope with practical details of being a teacher.

- Assist with the new teacher's understanding and management of school authority.

- Listen to daily concerns, progress, and questions.

- Serve as a source of ideas.

- Be easily accessible, trustworthy, and understanding.

- Offer assistance on classroom management.

- Demonstrate professional competence.

- Help expand the beginning teacher's repertoire of teaching strategies.

- Show awareness of, commitment to, and familiarity with the new teacher's classroom.

- Schedule time willingly with the beginning teacher.

- Provide a task-oriented focus established through a two-way interchange about goals and procedures.

Figure 3–7   Responsibilities of a Mentor.

Source: Brooks, M. (1999). Mentors matter. In M. Scherer (Ed.). *A better beginning: Supporting and mentoring new teachers.* Reprinted by permission of the Association for Supervision and Curriculum Development. The Association for Supervision and Curriculum Development is a worldwide community of educators advocating sound policies and sharing best practices to achieve the success of each learner. To learn more, visit ASCD at http://www.ascd.org.

early childhood educators, and they are paid by the educator's employer or by public funding. Mentors can be private contractors who charge fees or fellow teachers who voluntarily become mentors to new colleagues.

Carol Schlank (2004), a new teacher, describes an experienced teacher (also named Carol) who became her mentor:

> On that first day, Carol took time away from her own work to help me find furniture and supplies for my classroom and to lend me pictures to brighten its walls. She invited me to lunch with some of the staff and offered to answer questions and help me in any way she could. We taught in neighboring classrooms for many years. Carol would bring me narcissus bulbs from her greenhouse, pollywog eggs when they appeared in her pond, or books of special interest to my students. When she borrowed farm animals from a nearby animal shelter, she shared them with my class. She listened when I needed help with a child's behavior, and she offered support and suggestions.

Schlank believes:

> . . . most inexperienced teachers would do well to seek out mentors with the following characteristics: expertise and dedication, warmth and caring, energy and enthusiasm, creativity and imagination.

Epperheimer (2004) points out that having a sounding board (coach, mentor, colleague) accelerates professional growth and provides insight. Training programs for mentors include the newly developed Mentoring North Carolina Novice Teachers Training Program. Mentors vary in style; some co-teach while others observe and consult. The Center for the Early Childhood Workforce maintains a state listing of early childhood mentor programs with program director names and numbers. See the Helpful Web Sites at the end of the chapter.

Internships

Morkes (2003) observes that students who intend to enter an occupation requiring a bachelor's degree or who want a competitive advantage on the job market after graduation should seek out opportunities such as internships. Internships are an opportunity to perform the job duties expected of an employee in an actual workplace for a short period of time. Some colleges and university-sponsored learning programs offer internships with or without academic credit. Internships are considered exploratory in nature. They provide a taste of work in a chosen field.

Apprenticeships

Apprenticeships help students learn occupational skills by working under the tutelage of a skilled professional worker. An apprentice is taught skills in exchange for working at lower wages. Apprentices sometimes agree to working under contract and may also enroll in academic coursework. If so, they pay for their own tuition, books, and associated costs.

Fellowships

Fellowships are sponsored by a growing number of professional associations, foundations, private donors, and government agencies. They are created to promote leadership in individuals showing promise and/or a desire to contribute substantially to their career field. Fellowships are granted based on the applicant's accomplishments and future potential. Fellowships are usually designed to recruit talent from diverse groups of people. They provide unique learning opportunities such as working as a special legislative assistant or a staff person for a member of Congress or a congressional committee, or working with an investigative federal agency concerned with children's welfare. Some fellowship programs involve working with a foundation, such as the Annie E. Casey Foundation, and assuming a significant leadership position to improve children's lives (Hyson, 2003). In the Columbia University summer fellowship program, fellowship interns are placed in New York City agencies while participating in seminars to deepen their understanding of the links between their academic learning and child and family policy. Fellowship programs are sponsored by Head Start; The American Psychological Association; The National Center for Infants, Toddlers, and Families; The Society of Research in Child Development; and The State Early Childhood Policy Leadership Forum (Hyson, 2003).

Question: Are there scholarships especially for early childhood educators?

Answer: Yes. These may be local or state programs, or those of other sponsoring organizations. Scholarships have qualification criteria such as need, years of experience, grade point average, or other factors. The Teacher Education and Compensation Helps (T.E.A.C.H.) Early Childhood scholarship programs supported more than 16,000 students attending over 400 community colleges in 2004 (Russell, 2004). A number of career education students have joined the military to earn granted years of college education for years of military service. A good number of clubs, associations, lodges, churches, and other community entities offer scholarships. Check with family members and secondary school counselors who are aware of financial aid options. It pays to look around and do the research to obtain the means to reach your dreams.

Financial Aid

College financial aid officers and counselors assist in finding money or supportive assistance. Options include Pell Grants, federal loans, private scholarships, Hope Scholarships, and family loans. Ask for information about loan forgiveness programs, tax credits, and student employment opportunities.

The federal government, states, and colleges assist students who would not otherwise be able to attend college. Financial aid is intended to close the gap between educational expenses and a student's ability to pay for them. Unfortunately, in difficult economic times (recession), the trend has been for colleges to increase tuition and decrease financial aid, making it even more difficult for students to pay for college expenses (Walton, 2004). Financial aid usually consists of low-interest loans that need to be paid back after graduation, need-based grants that do not have to be repaid, scholarships for academic performance that are not repaid, and work-study awards. Work-study awards require a student to perform work for an hourly wage while they attend college. Loans from private or public sources can be subsidized and have a low interest rate or are unsubsidized. Students must apply for federal loans and grants. Successful recipients become eligible based upon the need for financial aid, the cost of tuition, and on their full- or part-time student status. Federal Pell Grants are only awarded to low-income, undergraduate students. Twenty percent of students attending community colleges in the 1990–2000 school year received some financial aid (*The Chronicle of Higher Education*, 2004).

Students can expect to pay back college loans over a period of years. Walton (2004) notes that in the 2003–2004 school year, the average college tuition and fees rose 47 percent at public four-year colleges and universities.

Many states have shifted grant aid funds from college need-based financial aid to merit-based financial aid. In merit-based grant programs, scholarships usually are awarded to students who excel academically and maintain a B average in a required number or type of college courses. Florida, Georgia, Kentucky, Louisiana, and Michigan and nine other states have some type of merit-based scholarship program. Eligibility may be based upon student class rank, grade point average, or SAT or ACT scores. In 2003 only six states committed a substantial amount of their financial aid budgets to need-based aid—New York, California, Illinois, Pennsylvania, Texas, and New Jersey.

When Congress passed the *Taxpayer Relief Act of 1997*, it included two programs to help taxpaying families pay for college: the Hope Scholarship and the Lifetime Learning Tax Credit. These programs are not financial aid but tax relief in the form of tax credits.

College and university education is becoming more expensive. Students and their families are taking on more debt to fund higher education expenses. A person who obtains a college degree averages an 80 percent higher income than does a high school graduate, and the college graduate can expect to find a decent job. College students face more financial obstacles when the national economy is in a slump.

What are the current college tuition costs and fees per year? In the 2003–2004 school year, two-year public colleges fees averaged $1,905, at four- year public colleges $4,694,

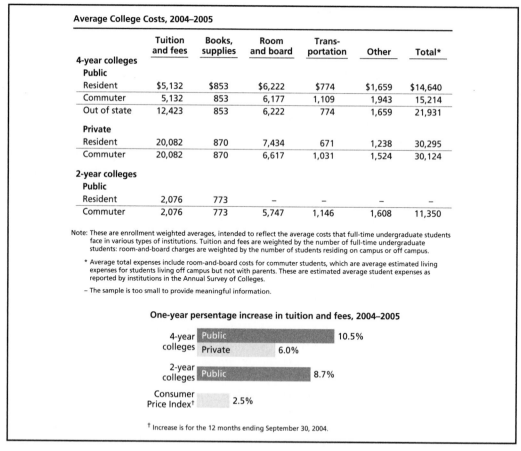

Average College Costs, 2004–2005

	Tuition and fees	Books, supplies	Room and board	Trans- portation	Other	Total*
4-year colleges						
Public						
Resident	$5,132	$853	$6,222	$774	$1,659	$14,640
Commuter	5,132	853	6,177	1,109	1,943	15,214
Out of state	12,423	853	6,222	774	1,659	21,931
Private						
Resident	20,082	870	7,434	671	1,238	30,295
Commuter	20,082	870	6,617	1,031	1,524	30,124
2-year colleges						
Public						
Resident	2,076	773	–	–	–	–
Commuter	2,076	773	5,747	1,146	1,608	11,350

Note: These are enrollment weighted averages, intended to reflect the average costs that full-time undergraduate students face in various types of institutions. Tuition and fees are weighted by the number of full-time undergraduate students: room-and-board charges are weighted by the number of students residing on campus or off campus.

* Average total expenses include room-and-board costs for commuter students, which are average estimated living expenses for students living off campus but not with parents. These are estimated average student expenses as reported by institutions in the Annual Survey of Colleges.

– The sample is too small to provide meaningful information.

One-year persentage increase in tuition and fees, 2004–2005

4-year colleges	Public 10.5%
	Private 6.0%
2-year colleges	Public 8.7%
Consumer Price Index[†]	2.5%

† Increase is for the 12 months ending September 30, 2004.

Figure 3–8 Average College Costs, 2004–2005.

and at four-year private colleges, $19,710 (The College Board, 2004). Additional costs include books and supplies, room and board, transportation, and miscellaneous expenses. Figure 3–8 provides additional information.

In-Service Training

Teachers' institutes, in-service training sessions, and workshops take place on a regular basis for elementary school teachers and also for some early childhood teachers. Children get the day off, or teachers are replaced by substitutes. Weekend or summer in-service training is commonplace also.

Training topics include updating teachers on current techniques and educational trends. School districts try to obtain innovative, dynamic, and motivational speakers who explain and demonstrate new ideas. Teaching aids such as computers, technical or electronic equipment, and prepackaged commercial educational programs may be a subject of study. Early childhood educators are more likely to receive their updating through unpaid conferences or workshops, independent reading, or college classes.

Professional Association Conferences

Professional association conferences are held throughout the United States and overseas. They are prime opportunities to increase occupational skills and practices. Conference attendees are exposed to national leaders, experts, researchers, seminars, institutes, and other learning opportunities. They choose sessions based on their own lines of interest and inquiry. The National Association for the Education of Young Children (NAEYC) and the Association for Childhood Education International (ACEI) promote high-quality early learning for all children. NAEYC is the world's largest early education association, with more than 100,000 members and a network of nearly 450 local, state, and regional affiliates. See the Appendix for a list of additional professional associations. More than 25,000 people attend NAEYC's annual conferences. Conference exhibit halls contain information, displays, commercially developed teaching materials, aids, books, and other items of interst to those who work with children.

In Idaho a number of different programs administered by the Idaho Association for the Education of Young Children, a chapter of NAEYC, promote early childhood worker's professional growth through the following activities:

- Teacher Education and Compensation Helps (TEACH) is a program with college scholarships for some individuals working in an early childhood setting who are thinking about taking college classes.
- Mentors for Early Care and Education (MECE) is a program supplying a guide or mentor for an early childhood worker. Mentoring can include business planning or other training issues.
- Idaho STARS is a new training and registration system for child care professionals that offers professional development opportunities, and possibly monetary incentives as level of training, experience, and education increase (Boazman, 2004).

Check chapters of associations in your area for professional growth opportunities.

Campus Education: Major Student Groups

Student organizations (clubs, groups) meet on college campuses and actively support the professional growth of members. It is a great way to start networking early in your career. Meetings may be social, informal, and educational with speakers such as alumni, local employers, and guidance counselors. Club attendance at local, regional, or national conferences with follow-up discussions enrich everyone present.

Visitation and Travel

There is a lot to be learned through visiting classrooms and facilities and observing, discussing, and analyzing child activities, outcomes, and/or program operations. Professional courtesy to teachers and educators is extended worldwide. All programs expect visitors to obtain administrative permission before arriving.

Self-Directed Learning

Most teachers have nightstands piled with books. They read for pleasure, and they read to know. They may read to understand a specific behavior or to understand other ways to help children. They read because they have intellectual curiosity. Carlson (2004) urges college graduates to read and believes that simple act separates the leaders from the followers, the real achievers from the rest of the crowd. He states that the habit of reading is the path to knowledge. Take a moment to fill out the professional growth probe form in Figure 3–9.

Making a Step-by-Step Plan

Look at the list of the occupational skills that you made in Chapter One. Decide which skills are absent or need enhancing. Only you, as your own career manager, can decide your goals and professional growth path. If a state or employer plan is tied to your employment mobility, hopefully it will be flexible enough to allow training choices. Remember, all plans are tentative, and ignoring planning is unwise. When you know your long-range goal, select coursework and training activities to reach that goal.

Edwards and Edwards (2004) believe that goals help us to clarify what we want in life and provide us with a focus for how to use our time, money, and energy to create a rewarding life. They make the following observations:

> *Some of the most successful people we've met achieved their success not only because they set goals, but also because they didn't let their goals limit their ability to see other possibilities.*

Figure 3–10 is a sample of one educator's plan. It includes a time line for accomplishment. Each step can be considered a short-range goal. Selected coursework, even college electives, can relate to a long-range plan. See Figure 3–11 for college minor choices that might be influenced by a long-range goal.

Each step is important, and, there are going to be obstacles. This is when you, as your own career manager, can analyze what is causing problems, decide the best courses of action, and take actions that will produce the outcomes that aid your professional progress. Carr-Ruffino (1997) believes target dates will keep you on target.

	Yes	No
1. Is your chosen career education?	____	____
A specialty career field?	____	____
2. Were you enrolled in college credit courses this year or last year?	____	____
3. Are you working toward an advanced degree ? Or advanced expertise?	____	____
4. Do you belong to a student club, professional group, or association?	____	____
Specify those in which you are an active member.		

_____

_____

5. Do you do professional reading other than assigned reading?

Journals? _____

Magazines? _____

Books? Number read in last six months? _____

6. In which advocacy activities have you participated? Check all that apply.

written letters	____	elected official contacts	____
phone calls	____	association activities	____
e-mails	____	letters to newspapers	____
local or state rallies	____	Week of the Young Child	____

7. Conferences or workshops with an emphasis on careers in education.

    Number attended in the last two-year period. ____

	Yes	No
8. Will you be working with children three years from now?	____	____

If no, why? _____

	Yes	No
9. Do you have a long-range career goal?	____	____

10. What do you feel is the best professional growth activity? _____

Figure 3–9   Sample Professional Growth Probe Form.

Edwards & Edwards (2003) advise:

> *You'll want to find a path that assures you the highest possible degree of success because research shows that most people need to be successful in their efforts about 75 percent of the time in order to sustain their motivation.*

You might think of your career journey as a step-by-step adventure, but in reality a career path has many unknowns that may cause your path to turn corners and twist upward or downward, climb mountains, or cross deserts.

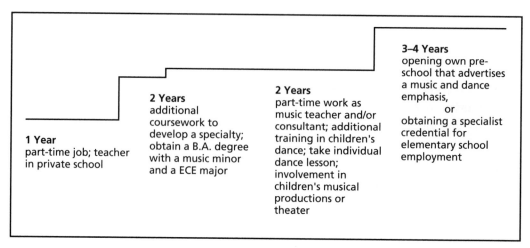

1 Year
part-time job; teacher in private school

2 Years
additional coursework to develop a specialty; obtain a B.A. degree with a music minor and a ECE major

2 Years
part-time work as music teacher and/or consultant; additional training in children's dance; take individual dance lesson; involvement in children's musical productions or theater

3–4 Years
opening own pre-school that advertises a music and dance emphasis,
or
obtaining a specialist credential for elementary school employment

Figure 3–10   Example of a Step-by-Step Planning Graph.

Many people say they have not discovered a natural talent. Edwards and Edwards (2003) suggest that even if you are unaware of any one outstanding talent, do not neglect the gifts you do have. They believe we each have natural abilities that are an expression of our personalities, and sometimes by nurturing, polishing, and using these abilities we can develop them and shine. Some of us shine at interpersonal skills such as listening, understanding, consoling, teaching, healing, helping, or team building. Others have outstanding communication skills for persuading, motivating, debating, negotiating, mediating, explaining ideas and concepts, writing and speaking. According to Edwards, recognizing special gifts, talents, and skills becomes a route to a satisfying livelihood. Do not overlook them because someone has not yet called them to your attention or encouraged you to use them.

College Minor	Possible Long-Range Goal
Journalism	children's literature consultant
Accounting	support service business
Music	curriculum specialist
Social Service	public agency employee
Economics	fundraiser
Psychology	child psychologist
Public Relations	human resource specialist
Business	self-employment
Criminal Justice	juvenile counselor
Foreign Language	bilingual educator
Political Science	advocacy coordinator
Science	researcher
Computer Science	support service business

Figure 3–11   College Minor Choices.

Self-Awareness and Professional Growth Planning

Analyzing what may limit your professional growth plans involves an inward look at what is holding you back. This might be your beliefs connected to the view others have of you. Are you giving yourself messages that hold you back? The Appendix has a useful form to help you investigate ways you may be limiting your potential. Stereotypical thinking may be involved. Preconceived notions of female and male traits, abilities, strengths, and weaknesses can also get in the way of professional growth.

Summary

Continuous growth in occupational skills is the hallmark of professionals in the field of education. Many educators develop their own growth plan based upon their career goals. Others follow plans outlined by their employers and include additional professional growth activities that help them achieve their long-range career goals.

There are many routes to professional development. They all involve further education and/or training. As your own career manager, you will make your own decisions, identify choices and likely outcomes, consider the pros and cons of professional growth activities, identify alternative outcomes, and choose which activities are possible and most likely to help you succeed on your career path.

Helpful Web Sites

Association for Career and Technical Education
http://acteonline.org

Careers in Child and Family Policy
http://cfp.igpa.uiuc.edu
fellowship and internship information

Center for the Early Childhood Workforce
http://www.ccw.org
mentoring information

College Invest
http://www.CollegeInvest.org
information concerning loans and repayment programs

Columbia University
http://www.tc.columbia.edu
fellowship and research opportunities

Council for Early Childhood Professional Recognition
http://www.cdacouncil.org
resource for CDA information and standards

Degree Net
http://www.degree.net
distance education

National Association of Child Care Resource and Referral Agencies
http://www.childcareer.org
training information

National Council for Accreditation of Teacher Education
http://www.ncate.org

National Directory of Teacher Preparation Programs for Cultural and Linguistic Diversity
http://www.crede.ucsc.edu

National Latino Children's Institute
http://www.nlci.org
search training opportunities

Teach for America
http://www.teachforamerica.org

Think College
http://www.ed.gov/thinkcollege

U.S. Department of Education
http://www.ed.gov
No Child Left Behind Act *description*

Resources

Bellm, D., Whitebook, M. & Hnatiuk, P. (1997). *The early childhood mentoring curriculum: A handbook for mentors.* Washington, DC: Center for the Early Childhood Workforce.

California Commission on Teacher Credentials and the California Department of Education. (1997). *California standards for the teaching profession.* Sacramento, CA: Author.

Duff, E. R., Brown, M. H. & Van Scoy, J. (1995). Refection and self-evaluation: Keys to professional development. *Young Children. 50* (4), 81–86.

Ingersoll, R., & Alsalam, N. (1997). *Teacher professionalism and teacher commitment: A multilevel analysis.* NCES 97–069. Washington, DC: Department of Education.

Katz, L. G. (1972). Developmental stages of preschool teachers. *Elementary School Journal, 73* (1), 50–54.

King, J. E. (2002). *How student's financial decisions affect their academic success.* Washington, DC: American Council on Education.

National Commission on Teaching and America's Future. (1996). *What matters most: Teaching for America's future.* New York: Author.

National Conference of State Legislatures. (2004). *College affordability.* Author.

Reeher, G., & Mariani, M. (Eds.) (2002). *The insider's guide to political internships: What to do once you're in the door.* Denver, CO: National Conference of State Legislatures.

The Chronicle of Higher Education. (2004, October 29). Community colleges by the numbers. B46.

References

Boazman, H. (2004, Spring). President's message. *Idaho Association for the Education of Young Children.* Boise, ID: Idaho Association for the Education of Young Children. 1.

Brooks, M., (1999). Mentors matter. In M. Scherer (Ed.). *A better beginning: Supporting and mentoring new teachers.* Alexandria, VA: Association for Supervision and Curriculum Development.

Bureau of Labor Statistics. (2005). Summary report on U.S. college costs, 2003–2005. LPN 5740-1-634. Washington, DC: Author.

Carlson, T. (2004, June). The graduation advice I never got . . . but wished I had. *Reader's Digest.* 153–156.

Carr-Ruffino, N. (1997). *The promotable woman: 10 essential skills for the new millennium.* Franklin Lakes, NJ: Career Press.

Caruso, J. J., & Fawcett, M. T. (1999). *Supervision in early education: A developmental perspective*. New York: Teachers College Press.

Council for Professional Recognition (2002). Improving child care through programs of the Council for Professional Recognition. Washington, DC: Brochure.

Davies, M. A. (2001, Summer). Through the looking glass . . . preservice professional portfolios. *The Teacher Educator. 37* (1) 27–36.

Edwards, P., & Edwards, S. (2003). *Finding your perfect work: The new career guide to making a living, creating a life*. New York: Penguin Putnam, Inc.

Edwards, P., & Edwards, S. (2004). Set your goals but not in concrete. *Costco Connection. 19* (11) 9.

Epperheimer, J. (2004, November 18). Align your goals with your boss's. *San Jose Mercury News*. 3C.

Feiman-Nemser, S., Carver, C., Schwille, S., & Yusko, B. (1999). Beyond support. Taking new teachers seriously as learners. In M. Scherer (Ed.) *A better beginning: Supporting and mentoring new teachers*. Alexandria, VA: Association for Supervision and Curriculum Development. 3–12.

Grant, C., & Murray, C. (1999). *Teaching in America: The slow revolution*. Cambridge, MA: Harvard University Press.

Guiding, R., & Hyson, M. (2002, September). National board certification: The next professional step? *Young Children. 57* (5) 60–61.

Harrison, R. (1978). Self-directed learning. *Human growth games*. Beverly Hills, CA: Sage Publications.

Hyson, M. (2003, November). New directions for emerging leaders: National fellowships. *Young Children. 58* (6) 70–71.

Kleiman, C. (2002). *Winning the job game: The new rules for finding and keeping the job you want*. Hoboken, NJ: John Wiley and Sons, Inc.

Lutton, A. Quoted in Hyson, M., & Duru, M. (2004, July). Accrediting associate degree programs: N.A.E.Y.C. launches a new system to recognize excellence. *Young Children. 59* (4) 92–95.

McMullen, M. B. Alat, K., Buldu, M., & Lash, M. (2004, March). A snapshot of N.A.E.Y.C.'s preschool professionals through the lens of quality. *Young Children. 59* (2) 87–92.

Morgan, G., Azer, S. L., Costley, J. B., Genser, A., Goodman, I. F., Lombardi, J., & McGimsey, B. (1993). *Making a career of it: The state of the states report on career development in early care and education*. Boston: Wheelock College, Center for Career Development and Education.

Morkes, A. (Ed.) (2003). *Encyclopedia of careers and vocational guidance*. Vol. 1, Chicago, IL: Ferguson Publishing Co.

National Association for the Education of Young Children. (1994, March). Professional development. *Young Children. 49* (3) 66–77.

New Jersey Professional Development Center for Early Care and Education. (2002). *Using the core knowledge and competency areas*. Union, NY: Author, Brochure.

Russell, S. Quoted in Hyson, M., & Duru, M. (2004, July). Accrediting associate degree programs: NAEYC launches a new system to recognize excellence. *Young Children. 59* (4) 92–95.

San Jose State University Career Center. (2003). *Job and internship guide: Your link to the employment community*. Chicago, IL: Career Recruitment Media, Inc.

Schlank, C. H. (2004, March). To teach until we die: The importance of mentoring. *Young Children. 59* (2) 67.

Teale, W. H. (2003). In D. M. Barone & L. M. Morrow (Eds.), *Literacy and young children: Research-based practices*. (23–44) New York: The Guilford Press.

The Chronicle of Higher Education (2004, October 29). Community colleges by the numbers. LI (10) B46.

The College Board (2004). *Trends in college pricing: 2004*. Report on the College Board's Annual Survey of Colleges. Washington, DC: Author.

U.S. Department of Education (2003, March 24). Key policy letters signed by the Education Secretary or Deputy Secretary. http://www.ED.gov.

U.S. Department of Labor (2003). *Occupational Outlook Handbook.* Washington, DC: United States Department of Labor Statistics.

VanderVen, K. (1988). Pathways to professionalism. In B. Spodedk, O. Saracho, & D. Peters (Eds.), *Professionalism and the early childhood educator.* New York: Columbia University Press. 137–160.

Walton, C. (2004). *College affordability.* Denver, CO: National Conference of State Legislatures.

Whitebook, M., & Eichberg, A. (2002, May). Defining polices to improve child care workforce compensation. *Young Children, 57* (3) 66–72.

Wiebke, K. (2000, November/December). My journey through national board certification. *Scholastic Instructor. 110* (4) 26–27.

CHAPTER FOUR

The Search

*Luck is a matter of preparation
meeting opportunity.*
Oprah Winfrey

The Good News is . . .

Ernesto had taken a lot of good-natured teasing about finding a job from his brothers. Because he was the first to obtain a college degree in his family, they were all interested. He knew in the spring before his credential was completed that teaching positions were difficult to obtain. School district budgets weren't allowing much hiring in his city. Other graduates in his class were offered jobs upstate. His job search strategy was to substitute teach until he found a kinder-garten opening. He was pleased when he was called for an interview and was hired. He'd kept it a secret, and wanted to spring his good news at a family dinner. Substitute teaching during the past few months had given him a good idea about where he wanted to work. The staff rooms in schools were very different and eye opening. Sometimes friendly, sometimes downright unprofessional, they had provided a picture of staff dynamics and morale. He'd also observed that schools differed noticeably in furnishings, supplies, rules, and student population. He was hired at the most notori-ous school in the district, in the most depressed section of the city. There were frequent stories in the newspapers about drive-by shootings and violence in the area.

QUESTIONS TO PONDER

1. What reactions should Ernesto expect from his family? What reaction can he expect from one of his brothers who works in law enforcement?

2. Would you hold out longer and refuse the position?

3. Are you willing to work at a school where you might need to be a change agent?

There are many ways to approach a search for employment. We recommend a calculated search. Webster (1988) defines *calculate* as "to figure out in one's head, to intend, to plan, to arrange for a particular purpose, and to scheme for one's own ends."

In your role as your own career manager, you will need to identify what employment characteristics will provide the opportunities necessary to move you toward your goal. Think best-case scenario. What kind of position? What type of child facility? What geographic location? What salary or benefits? What hours of the day? What career step or short-range goal in your plan will be involved? And what must be present to insure that life balance and immediate needs are met? Write these down. Immediate needs may include the following:

- immediate income at a certain level of pay
- part-time work
- a location close to a bus line
- a center that enrolls it's staff's own children

Then look at desired school features. These are individual choices and may include the following:

- accredited or professional practices
- a philosophy of education that you believe is close or compatible with your own
- health care benefits
- a particular ethnic or religious affiliation
- children whose second language is English
- administrative support
- opportunities to participate in training workshops, conferences, etc.
- regularly held staff meetings

A Head Start Bureau's research study identified these early childhood school elements promoting teacher job satisfaction:

- school (center) policies that are clear
- administrative support
- administrator–teacher communication
- well-qualified teachers and aides
- lower staff turnover
- staff feelings that a center is collegial, innovative, and one's supervisor is supportive (Head Start Bulletin, 2001)

Some job seekers can afford to be choosy and hold out for positions that allow job satisfaction, professional growth, and opportunity. Your mental attitude is of prime importance. Positive thoughts, affirmations, and visualization may aid your search. Written affirmations can bolster your spirits and motivation to select a job that best suits talents and career plans. Affirmations can describe the job you want, why you deserve it, and how you will obtain it. In order for something to occur, it helps to really believe it will occur. Is this hocus-pocus? Couple positive thinking with a sense of humor, an ability to roll with the punches, persistence, and an awareness of life's options, and you have every chance of succeeding. These are the characteristics of individuals who achieve their goals and obtain their desired employment.

Consider your caring, nurturing nature, and your desire to make a real difference in children's lives and learning. The education field needs your enthusiasm, dedication, and commitment to quality and excellence. At times, you will need to be your own cheerleader—job hunting may be one of those times. In a way, a job search is like stepping into the unknown!

You'll want to approach a job search with self-esteem and confidence in your worth and value. This comes from within and knowing who you are. This involves self-talk, so monitor what you are telling yourself.

Moving from One Job to Another

If you are planning a switch from one job to another, Treasurer (2003), a workplace consultant, suggests "make sure you feel passionate about what you plan to do next." Kleiman (2003) discusses changing jobs in a tough job market when employers are scaling back:

> . . . *it makes sense that this may be the time for employees simply to lie low.*

and

> *Keep your head down and fly below the radar—especially if you like to eat three meals a day or have health insurance.*

Treasurer (2003) goes on to recommend even if it is a difficult time to find another job, it still may be wise to risk and move on if you are feeling that the work you perform is meaningless. He suggests asking yourself not what a job move will get you, but where will it take you—and to question whether it meets your personal values. It also makes sense not to give up one job before you have another.

Networking

Networking can be thought of as making friends so that you can use them to further your career. Not a pretty picture is it? This view overlooks the social/emotional comforts of friendships and what friends add to the fullness of our lives. Friends educate us, if we listen. Carlson (2004) promotes establishing friendships with diverse individuals as a way to be in touch with the world of work:

> *Start by getting to know people whose skin is a different color from yours. Surround yourself with friends of every political stripe, and listen to them respectfully. And get to know others in very different professions (Carlson, 2004).*

Abrams (2004) believes in initiating new friendships to receive "fresh input," and suggests staying open to new friendships and developing new interests. In group situations, she suggests taking the first step and starting conversations. Be sure to listen and follow up on a first contact. Abrams notes that friendship opportunities are there for everyone—so why not take advantage of them? (The opportunities, that is.)

Is it possible to make mistakes when networking? Definitely. Nierenberg (2003) lists the five most common errors:

- asking instead of giving
- hit-and-run networking, which is defined as quickly moving from person to person
- blatant selling by probing for job information

- ignoring people you feel don't count, instead of viewing everyone you meet as an important contact
- not following up with a thank-you for any and all efforts people make on your behalf

No one likes to feel "used." There is a fine line between getting someone's respectful attention and turning someone off (Nierenberg).

Solomons (2003) describes visualizing networking as a diamond in three segments:

> *You have a triangle at the bottom where people should start—your friends and family. They're the kind of people you can bounce any idea off of. So you start there and then you broaden out and get to know more people. The next section of the diamond is the middle section, the bridging contacts. These people may not be able to get you a job, but you can do an informational interview with them. If that goes well, they can get you to the last part of the diamond—the decision makers. Those are the people who can actually hire you. To get to the decision makers, you have to go through the bridging contacts, and your friends and family are the key people to get you to the bridging contacts.*

Networking is an ongoing activity. It is a social behavior that impacts your knowledge base and social connectedness. Many believe that it affects your overall health. Having a wide circle of friends certainly involves energy, opportunity, and inclination, but it is well worth the effort. Friends enrich your life, and they simply give you many more contacts who will likely know where employment openings exist.

Many educators find job openings through the contacts they made in professional organizations, or with former staff members. Bolles (2003) recommends networking and rates it as a very successful technique. Raymond (2002) also reports networking as the best search method. He states it accounts for 40 percent of all successful job searches.

In a tight job market, *The San Jose Mercury News* (2002) suggests making a list of friends, relatives, and acquaintances and asking for guidance and advice. The newspaper cautions "It's important that people don't think you're calling them for a job." A job seeker gets more results asking for input on search strategies or options.

Professional Networking

Establishing professional relationships and a support network with people working in the education field takes time. Networking involves valuing professional friendships. It requires a sincere interest in what is important to others and recognizing their wants and needs. Effective networkers are friendly, available to chat, and supportive. They also offer constructive opinions and sincere praise, keep confidences, listen closely, and recognize others' accomplishments.

Morkes (2003) describes "the hidden job market," the job openings that are not advertised but are filled by personal contact with other professionals. Network contacts, he believes, can help by providing emotional support through difficult career transitions and job searches. These contacts can also share resources and ideas about personal marketing strategies. Ask your contacts for letters of recommendation or references. They can help you meet others who might provide information and let you know when openings occur. As your own career manager, part of your job is developing a professional network.

Phillips (2003) urges men and women to use professional support groups to reach out to others, and to have a regular "reality check" with those who can identify with their situation. Professional association membership often fulfills this function. A professional association list is found in the Appendix.

Searching the World Wide Web

The World Wide Web is user-friendly and has a vast number of sites related to job searching and career management. Most career counselors, educational institutions, employers and government organizations have Web addresses. Web sites may disappear, change, or newly appear. Morkes (2003) cautions that it's easy to get "bogged down" looking at sites that do not tell you what you want to know, and many sites will want to sell you something. It is wise to identify where job listings are usually found for your sector of the education field. Most employers use fairly traditional media such as newspaper advertisements with Web addresses. Institutions such as hospitals, colleges, foundations, and government-sponsored programs post listings on the Web. Some of the job titles found on the Web are displayed in Figure 4–1.

Salem State College (2003) in New England attempted to identify their early childhood majors' employment search success; see Figure 4–2. Internet search success accounted for only 15 percent of respondents, compared to 30 percent for newspaper and journal use or 40 percent for those who found work through friends and relatives. Although this was a small survey group, this survey can be an accurate picture of graduate

Academic director	Director of development	English as a new language teacher
Administrative office assistant	Demonstration teacher	Exceptional children's aide
After school associate teacher	Deputy director	Exceptional needs specialist
Assistant cottage supervisor	Developmental instructional aide	Family advocate
Assistant director	Early childhood care and education instructional paraprofessional	Family counselor
Assistant teacher		Family program advisor
Associate professor in ECE		Family support specialist
Associate teacher	Early childhood education professor	Family support worker
Campus demonstration project director	Early childhood educator	Funding specialist
Career and technical educator	Early childhood educator assistant	Grant specialist
Case worker	Early childhood instructor	Guest teacher
Certified childbirth educator	Early childhood museum director	Human studies professor
Child caregiver	Early childhood parent involvement coordinator	Infant advisor
Child care practitioner		Infant developer
Child care worker	Early childhood program director	Infant/toddler educator
Child center teacher		Infant/toddler specialist
Child development assistant	Early childhood program staff	In service program coordinator
Child development specialist	Early childhood project leader	Instructional aide
Child development teacher	Early childhood recreation supervisor	In-home provider
Childhood generalist		Intergenerational aide
Child life specialist	Early childhood special education assistant	Lab teacher
Client eligibility specialist		Lead retail sales and birthday program associate
Coordinator	Early childhood teacher	
Director	Educational researcher	Lead teacher
Dance and music specialist	Educational services specialist	Lecturer early years
Day-care helper		Library media assistant
Day-care supervisor		Literacy specialist
Day-care worker		Master teacher
Day-care worker's assistant		Materials procurement agent

Figure 4–1 Job Titles Found on the World Wide Web.

Montessori teacher	Professional governess	Site developer
Nanny service director	Program aide	Site director
Nursery school teacher	Program manager	Speech and language
Outreach recruitment worker	Residential counselor	pathologist
Permit teacher	Senior lecturer	Substitute teacher
Preschool helper	Services coordinator	Summer camp teacher
Preschool recreation supervisor	School age assistant	Support teacher
Preschool teacher	School age clinical supervisor	Training specialist
Prekindergarten aide	School age community worker	Team leader coordinator
Prekindergarten teacher	School age recreation leader	Therapeutic behavior coach
Pre-primary school teacher	School age teacher	Therapeutic recreation assistant
Primary intervention aide	School-community coordinator	Wraparound community worker
Playground assistant	Site coordinator	

Figure 4–1   *(Continued)*

Early Childhood Employment Search Scope	Responses	% of Respondents
25 Miles	19	95.0%
50 Miles	0	0.0%
Home State	0	0.0%
New England	0	0.0%
Outside New England	0	0.0%
Outside U.S.	1	5.0%
Total	20	100.0%
Early Childhood Employment Search Source	**Responses**	**% of Respondents**
SSC Career Services	0	0.0%
Faculty	0	0.0%
Employment Agency	0	0.0%
Direct Application	2	10.0%
Internship/Field Placement/ Student Teaching/Clinicians	3	15.0%
Newspaper/Journal Advertisement	6	30.0%
Friend/Relative	8	40.0%
Prior Employment w/ Organization	1	5.0%
Other	0	0.0%
Total	20	100.0%

Figure 4–2   Selected Sections of a Survey of Salem State College Early Childhood Majors.
Reprinted by permission of Salem State College, Career Services Office.

- Information on college and other training programs.
- Free career assessment.
- Free audio tapes (including 21 ways to get a job you want).
- Free personality tests.
- Free resume posting and distribution.
- "Find a Job" publications.
- For fee resume distribution to recruiters.
- For fee recruiter contacts.
- For fee professionally written resumes.
- For fee resume writing software.
- Professional chat rooms.
- Question and answer services.
- Discussion groups.
- Sign-up for newsletters.
- Sign-up for job postings.
- Job applications.
- Job descriptions.
- A review of college training programs.
- Information on current employment picture in different U.S. and overseas locations.
- Job requirements.
- Free publications.
- Scholarship information.
- Employment outlook in specific locations.
- Government study reports.
- Salary schedules.
- Fax addresses for resumes.
- Self assessment.

Figure 4–3   What Some Web Sites Offer, a Partial Listing.

search success in their geographic area. Your search success may depend on your use of other search techniques.

To narrow Web searches, use these search terms: *early childhood employment* or *early childhood education, elementary school education, middle school education,* and *secondary school.* Web sites offer much more than position postings. Figure 4–3 lists other items or services available on Web sites.

Steen (2003) believes e-mail and the Web have made it easier to find job openings and apply for them. But she notes that some companies are flooded with resumes from applicants who haven't read the job description for the position they are seeking. Personal referrals by employees play an important role when a stack of e-mail applications are received. These referred job hunters are the biggest source of new hires in many companies.

Online Job Boards and Services

According to Raymond (2002), online job boards and services have grown in number, and Monster.com serves more than 93,000 companies. Hotjobs.com has 7,000 members, including

40 of the country's 50 largest employers. It is estimated that from 2003 through 2005 online recruitment service revenues will top $4 billion (Forrester Research, 2002). Online boards are generally free to job seekers and are a quick way for employers to find talented workers.

The success rate of workers obtaining interviews after using an online job board in the $30,000–$40,000 job earning bracket is 56 percent (Harrison 2002). Raymond (2002) estimates Career Builder.com had about 4 million resumes online in 2002. Bolles (2003) states that only 10 percent of those using job boards and employer Web sites get hired.

Online Newspaper Classified Ads

Newspapers nationwide post their classified employment advertising online. For professionals willing to relocate, this is an invaluable free service. Employer's Web addresses are included in the majority of ads, and other ads suggest sending a fax to gain additional application information.

College and University Web Sites

Some colleges and universities operate Web sites that help job seekers use Internet information, search strategies, and search engines. Links to other helpful sites can also be found.

Chapter Eight has much more interesting information concerning positions in higher education.

Job Service Offices

Workforce or job service agencies exist in most states. Job hunters have access to employment help, training services, and information. Your state's Department of Labor can provide their locations. To find your state offices on the Web, use your favorite search engine and enter "state workforce agency offices."

College and University Career Centers

Career centers on college campuses offer varied services. They provide customized career consultation, job listings, information on internship opportunities, and they usually have a helpful network of alumni. Many career centers require registration and issue membership cards. Following is a list of other common services and features provided by career centers:

- an online profile on the center's Web site
- positions posted online that are exclusively offered to the college's students or graduates
- timely e-mails about job trends, job opportunities, employer events
- drop-in advice on resume preparation and free resume critiques plus sample resumes
- news and information concerning job fairs and participating employers
- periodic sessions and informational meetings dealing with interviewing, resumes, cover letters, networking, and internships that often highlight specific professions such as teaching
- networking opportunities with the community and alumni in specific fields of study
- access to a career library with assessment software, books, videos, computers, and a variety of publications

- hosting job fairs on campus
- special services for students with disabilities

Your online profile can be updated with your further accomplishments and become available at a later time when you again seek employment.

San Jose State University's Career Center has developed a "Principles of Professional Conduct" statement that it expects all student job hunters to follow. This appears in Figure 4–4.

Principles of Professional Conduct

Employers expect professional behavior as you search for employment. In accordance with the professional standards of Western Association of Colleges and Employers (WACE); National Association of Colleges and Employers (NACE); American Association for Employment in Education; and the California Association for Employment in Education (CAEE), the **Career Center expects all candidates conducting job searches to adhere to the following university recruitment principles:**

1. Candidates should interview only with employers in whom they have a genuine interest. They should consult available sources of information (employer lists, Career Resource Lab, etc.) about the employer and position so they can organize their thoughts to ask and answer questions intelligently. Attendance at Career Center or employer workshops is encouraged.

2. If it is necessary to cancel an interview, notify the employer as soon as possible. Under no circumstances should candidates fail to keep an interview appointment without previously canceling that interview.

3. Candidates should honestly and accurately present themselves orally and in written materials.

4. Candidates should recognize that they are representing SISU as well as themselves. Businesslike conduct, dress, and punctuality for all interviews is expected.

5. Prompt acknowledgement of invitations for on-site visitations is expected. These invitations should be accepted only if the candidate has a sincere interest in considering an employment opportunity.

6. Candidates invited for second interviews at the employer's expense should include only those costs that legitimately pertain to the trip on expense reports. If several employers are visited on the same trip, costs should be prorated among them.

7. The employer's deadline for acceptance of employment offers should be met unless an extension has been obtained from the employer. If candidates have legitimate reasons for the extended consideration of more than one offer, they should notify employers whose offers they are refusing, as well as communicate with employers under consideration, to establish mutually satisfactory decision dates. The final choice should be made at the earliest possible date.

8. Acceptance of employment offers should be made in good faith with the sincere intention of honoring these employment commitments.

9. After an offer has been accepted, all other employers with whom a candidate has pending offers should be informed that the candidate is no longer available for employment.

10. Candidates are expected to inform the Career Center of their plans once they become finalized.

11. Career Center assistance is provided as a service to students and alumni and may be denied for the following reasons:

    →Unethical behavior

    →Discourtesy to office staff or visiting representatives

    →Failure to adhere to these recruiting principles ■

Figure 4–4 Principles of Professional Conduct.

From San Jose State University Career Center. (2003). *Job and internship guide: Your link to the employment community.* Chicago, IL. Career Recruitment Media, Inc.

Job Postings: America's Monthly Student Job Magazine is usually available at campus career centers. For subscription information check http://www.jobposting.net.

Newspaper Classified Ads

Kleiman (2002) advises "Don't confine yourself to classified ads for one job title. Look at everything that may pertain to your field." Classified ads are carefully written. If an employment advertisement or announcement indicates a preference or limitation based on the following areas, it breaks federal law:

- age (An ad can pinpoint a minimum age as long as this age is under age 40 and relates to some job task such as driving.)
- race
- gender (An ad can specify male or female under certain conditions such as boys' school live-in housing supervisor.)
- color
- religion
- national origin or ancestry
- physical or mental disability

Additional suspect wording and phrases which could be judged discriminatory include *young, married, single, male, female, college student*, and *recent graduate*. Employer penalties for discriminating and therefore breaking federal Equal Employment Opportunity (EEO) laws can include fines, stopping the ad, paying lost wages to a prospective job seeker (whether hired or not), hiring a particular applicant, and giving compensation to former job applicants who were victims of discrimination. Equal opportunity employers are defined as employers functioning under laws enforced and interpreted by The Equal Employment Opportunity Commission.

These laws include the following:

- *Equal Payment Act*
- *American with Disabilities Act*
- gender, religious, and national origin discrimination
- Affirmative Action
- *Rehabilitation Act*
- employers with government contracts
- organizations receiving federal financial assistance

Ads can specify applicant requirements such as a license, credential, permit, clearance, years of experience, and a driver's license. Job seekers offered employment may then need to satisfy additional requirements which may include fingerprinting, first aid training, drug testing, CPR certificates, or TB skin tests. These may be paid by the employer or the new employee. Qualifying exams, though relatively rare, sometimes exist. Education is considered "safety-sensitive" employment, and law enforcement agencies conduct background checks or criminal offense reports in a growing number of states.

Answering an Ad or Conducting a Telephone Search

If you contemplate answering an ad or doing a telephone search, telephone skills are necessary. Garza (2003) reports that many colleges are preparing their graduating students in telephone etiquette and the art of "elevator pitch," which is how to use interesting tricks to share personal information that allow conversations to flow more easily. Training also focuses on effective speaking, preparation, attitude, and thoroughly thinking about what you want to say before lifting the receiver. Practicing a few times is recommended. Mentioning someone who referred you to the school early on is prudent, and knowing something about the education center or school gives you a conversational edge just as it does in interviews. (Fact finding is covered later in the chapter.)

The person answering the telephone at a job site, after a job has been announced or advertised, gives an applicant an initial image of the center or school. Information about the school or center's unique features, the type of person they are seeking, and why the school is a good place to work may be offered. Take notes. These comments can be useful in interviews. Usually the job seeker is urged to obtain and/or submit an application form or schedule an interview.

Telephoning all schools in an area's phone book, what salesmen call "cold calling," can work. The caller queries present openings and also future ones. If you try this approach, ask if job announcements or job applications are available. Also ask who is the proper person to contact, and if the school accepts resumes and keeps them on file. Again practicing beforehand is recommended. Tape record your telephone "pitch," and critique it yourself, or have a friend do so. A. Hemming (2003), the author of *Work It*, offers the following tips for job hunting by telephone:

> *Leave voice mail messages at night so they are the first thing a potential employer hears in the morning. Schedule a specific time per day for your calls. Keep your sense of humor—making a potential employer smile is a big plus. Tape and listen to a sample of your calls from time to time to decide how to improve the way you sound.*

It's a good idea to follow up your telephone conversations with a letter. A letter of thanks is a great personal touch and usually is not forgotten. Be sure to proofread your letter.

To find school or center telephone numbers, check the local library for a reference book called the *Child Care Service Directory*. Annual editions contain thousands of telephone company listings and regional editions are available.

Job Announcements

Position announcements may be posted in career centers, personnel or human resource offices, at work sites, or at various other locations. Position announcements usually include the position title, responsibilities, details such as duties, length of employment, education and experience requirements, certificates, degrees, permits, salary, benefits, application procedures, and time lines.

Professional Association Job Listings

Early childhood professional associations were mentioned in Chapter Three as a resource for professional growth. They are an excellent source of information for job openings. Local chapters often have an employment officer, and local association newsletters may list openings. Association Web sites may also maintain an employment page or list. Conferences usually have job boards where help wanted ads are posted. Association magazines and journals also frequently include job announcements.

Job Fairs

College and community job fairs are a great place to gather information about employers looking for applicants. Job fairs are also a good way to make contact and interact with employer representatives. Obtaining a list of participating employers or school districts beforehand is suggested, and many times these are publicized. Following are some preparation tips when attending job fairs:

- Research participating employers on their Web sites.
- Review your resume.
- Prepare a short one-minute chat about your career interests, degrees or training, work experience, and the type of work you are seeking. Include how your background and career goal would benefit the employer. (See Tips for a One-Minute Opener).
- Prepare questions such as: Does your school (organization, agency, district, etc.) have a need for a staff member (teacher, etc.) with a degree? What do you look for in applicants? What skills/experiences are highly desirable?

TIPS FOR A ONE-MINUTE OPENER

- Try to condense important points about yourself down to 60 seconds.
- Practice and have a friend critique you.
- Smile and don't seem rushed.
- Base your comments on what you think the employer may be seeking.
- Example. Hello, I'm _____. I just graduated from _____, and I'm looking for employment in a school that _____. I have special interest in _____, and I have worked with children who _____ and families that _____. I have developed skills in _____ and created a system that _____. I have team-working experience _____. Also, I developed activities for (or to) _____. I am available on _____.
- Have a resume copy or personal card available.

For further tips, information, or additional job fair strategies, visit the following Web sites.

Career Mart
  http://www.careerfairs.com
  lists job fairs by month, occupation, and state

Quintessential Careers
  http:www.quintcareers.com
  tips on dress and preparations

College Grad Job Hunter
  http://www.collegegrad.com
  tips on making lasting impressions

Bring copies of your resume and/or personal business cards. Scan any employer hand-outs that may be available on tables. Try to approach a representative when he/she is less busy. Introduce yourself and give a copy of your resume. Ask about application procedure, not salary or benefits. Present your one-minute opening chat if you feel it is appropriate. Ask if the representative can be contacted later. A pocket calender should be quickly available if an interview is scheduled. Above all, listen and appear interested. Follow up your job fair contacts with a letter thanking representatives for their time and help.

Public Elementary School District Employment

If your ultimate or short-term goal is public kindergarten and elementary school teaching, each county office, school district office, and some state Department Office of Education offices post position announcements. A large percentage of early childhood majors eventually work for public or private elementary schools. Most early childhood AA degree graduates immediately qualify for teacher assistant or paraprofessional positions.

If you are just finishing an academic training program leading to a kindergarten/elementary credential, open a profile at your college or university career or placement center. Center staff will advise you on what to include in your profile. Often a profile includes a resume, a personal philosophy statement, and letters of recommendation. Update your profile as you gain experience.

If you apply directly to a school district, do some fact finding. Your application form should emphasize skills that match the needs you've discovered through fact finding. Find out the time of year a district hires, and whether applications are kept on file for a specific time period. In a tight job market, substitute teaching can acquaint administrators with your talents.

Independent and Private Elementary School Employment

Private independent primary schools are diverse, both profit-making and nonprofit. They flourish because some parents are looking for a particular educational program, and parents have the resources to pay fees. California has over 500 independent and private schools. Many of these use an educator's placement service to recruit both preschool and primary staff members. In western states, check out the website of CAL/WEST Educators at http://www.calwesteducators.com. Further information can be obtained by contacting The National Association of Independent Schools, and researching how recruitment for staff positions is handled in your state.

Mailings

Many graduating students send out resumes with a cover letter a few months before their training ends. An early childhood education student teacher composed a cover (inquiry) letter and went to a "quick print" store. Using shades of pastel paper, she made multiple copies. She had definite ideas about the rate of pay she wanted, so she included a salary range. It was slightly above what could be expected in the area. Most of her classmates, with whom she shared her letter, felt including a salary range was pushy. The student had a job offer before she graduated, and it was within the range she mentioned. Resumes and cover letters are discussed in Chapter Five.

Field Work Experience

Substitutes, interns, volunteers, and **practicum** students have opportunities to gain inside information about position openings. When students and substitute teachers demonstrate desirable employee skills and fit in with the regular staff, they are natural candidates for employment. Many substitutes and students secure positions in this manner. Field experiences afford chances to network with other professionals and to make decisions about possible employment at the school or center.

Ordinary and Not-So-Ordinary Job Titles

Educators are sure to find varying job titles in their job search. Some job titles may seem to demean early childhood work, while others recognize the professional status of educators. Return to the job titles in Figure 4–2 for examples.

Newly Evolving Jobs

There are always new jobs due to legislation. *The Washington Post* (2002) reports the federal *No Child Left Behind Act* mandates that elementary school classroom aides hold an associate degree or pass a state test by the year 2006. This will open training ground opportunities and interest early childhood two-year degree graduates whose ultimate career goal is elementary school or kindergarten teaching. Congressional re-authorization of Head Start in the coming years is likely to increase teachers' education expectations, and states are increasing education requirements (Hyson & Duru, 2004).

A strategy known as "following the legislation and/or money (funding) technique" requires keeping abreast of news in the field of education and knowing where public money is following public interest and legislation. *A Directory of Federal Programs: Helping Child Care* is available from ERIC Document Reproduction Service, 7420 Fullerton Rd., Suite 110, Springfield, VA 22153–2852. Each entry in the directory contains a name, address, telephone number, contact person, a description of a program, and financial data.

Places Others May Not Look

There are times when an educator may have to look outside the box, plus outside the triangle and circle for employment. The field is growing so fast that it is increasingly difficult to be aware of all sectors of possible employment opportunity. One of the authors was surprised to find on the Island of Terceira in the middle of the Atlantic, an American company called Computertots. This computer learning center for children offers instruction in English and Portuguese. We are also amazed at the number of child life professionals working in hospitals who attend national conferences. Finding new areas of employment may take effort, but this can be well worth your while.

Seeking Secondary School District Employment with an Early Childhood Degree

Some secondary schools offer child development instruction and establish child and infant care facilities to both train high school students and to provide child care for the community and student parents. These schools may enroll any high school students or be continuing schools enrolling only students who are parents.

A school district or personnel office can give you information concerning available positions. Job duties in secondary schools involve both infant and preschool child care and teenage student supervision. Check secondary school Web sites for information.

Corporate Child Care and Office Park Centers

Though economic times and unemployment rates have affected the growth of employer-sponsored child care, it is expected to rebound. Wittenberg (1996) notes that in 1990 only 11 percent of all employers offered direct child care benefits to their workers. In 1991, about 250 companies, 900 hospitals, and 250 government agencies either provided financial support for child care or sponsored child care centers on or near the workplace (Wittenberg, 1996).

It will take some investigation to discover a complex of businesses or an office park in your area that includes a child center. Bright Horizons Family Solutions, the leading supplier of child care for employers, boosted the number of child spaces it provided in 2003 by nearly 7 percent, and a significant part of this growth resulted from current employer clients opening additional centers (Neugebauer, 2003). Employment can be available from both the company sponsoring a child center or from a supplier (contractor) like Bright Horizons. City planning departments may know of new child care developments.

Resource and Referral Agencies

Resource and referral agencies, often supported by local, city, county, and/or state funds, offer an array of services to families, family child care home providers, early childhood workers, infant and toddler staff, and school-aged programs. In addition, these agencies provide parents with referrals to existing child care programs. Agencies often furnish training and information such as enrollment in low-cost health coverage programs. They commonly maintain an educational library, publish newsletters, work with food service companies, and child nutrition programs. Staff positions may vary greatly from executive director, program manager, consultant, provider assistant, trainer, or coordinator, depending on the services the agency provides.

To find locations check the local telephone book, or contact the National Association of Child Care Resource and Referral Agencies (NACCRRA) (http://www.naccrra.net). Then, call local agencies to see if they post staff openings.

Child and Family Service Agencies

Nonprofit and other children's and family service agencies are sometimes called "wraparound" service agencies. They serve children who have emotional disturbances or other conditions. Supportive assistance is provided to their families. This entails working cooperatively with other agencies. Mentor positions in this type of agency are advertised. Jobs often require an AA degree and/or some work experience with families and children. Accepted experience can be work in any education-related job, such as an early childhood center, a children's camp, or a recreation facility. Community groups and churches may run similar programs and are another place to look. A college minor with an emphasis in criminal justice, social service, special education, or social welfare can make a positive difference to these employers.

Job titles found at such agencies (besides mentor) include child counselor, case manager, social worker, family specialist, wraparound care facilitator, clinician, psychiatrist, administrative assistant, family partner, and therapist.

Summer and Vacation Jobs

For these positions, you must research early, select early, and apply early. Many summer jobs are filled by February. Children's camps, family camps, tourist and hotel jobs are available. Housing and food is often part of the compensation. Individuals with special skills in sports, crafts, music, art, recreational planning, dance, science, and nature study are highly valued. Jobs run the gamut from host, counselor, instructor, coach, performer, to positions that have no natural connection to an education or family studies background, such as porter, waitress, maid, and cook.

Library reference books are invaluable. They list pay and duration of employment, plus worker recreational and educational benefits and other perks. Two reference books follow:

Summer Jobs in the U.S.A. 2004–2005. (2003). Lawrenceville, NJ: Thomson/Peterson.

Woodworth, D., & Pybus, V. (2004): *Summer Jobs Abroad 2004.* Guilford, CT: The Globe Pequot Press.

If you want to learn a foreign language, or absorb a foreign culture, or to earn and save while learning new skills, then consider overseas teaching and summer employment.

Foundations and Charities

The best way to find this type of employment is to do library research. A directory of nonprofits or a book describing nonprofits will help. Locate the following helpful reference books.

Directory of Federal Programs: Helping Child Care. (Try ERIC Document and Reproduction Service.) This directory includes name, address, telephone number, contact person, description of program, and financial information.

Krannich, R., & Krannich, C. (1999). *Jobs and careers with nonprofit organizations: Profitable opportunities with nonprofits.* Manassas, Park, VA: Impact Publications.

National Directory of Nonprofit Organizations. (1999). Washington, DC: The Taft Group.

Jobs in this sector can involve humanitarian causes. There are many that involve children and families. Nonprofit organizations provide numerous entry-level opportunities for individuals without work experience. Volunteers often move on to full-time staff positions (Krannich & Krannich, 1999). See Figure 4–5 for samples of nonprofit operations.

Military Child Care

Civilian jobs with the United States Army are located in the U.S. and overseas. Submit a resume online after selecting a classification code at http://www.mwrjobs.army.mil. A job kit, program information, and job vacancy announcements are available at the same Web site.

EDUCATORS FOR SOCIAL RESPONSIBILITY

Offices: Cambridge, MA; New York, NY; Madison, WI; Concord, NH; Carrboro, NC

Web site: http://www.esrnational.org

Cause: to help young people develop a commitment to the well being of others and to make a positive difference in the world

Employees: 14

EDUCATION DEVELOPMENT CENTER

Office: Newton, MA

Web site: http://www.edu.org

Cause: promote the comprehensive improvement of education through work with teachers, administrators, curriculum specialists, researchers, media specialists, academicians, scientists, technicians, and concerned citizens

Employees: 350

EDUCATION LAW CENTER

Offices: Philadelphia, PA; Pittsburgh, PA

Web site: http://www.afj.org

Cause: to provide free legal representation to parents and students relating to preschool, primary, and secondary public education issues in Pennsylvania, and to provide quality public education for Pennsylvania students

Employees: 9

LOS NINOS

Offices: Chula Vista, CA; Calexico, CA

Cause: to improve the quality of life for Mexican children and their families, and to simultaneously provide education on the benefits of self-help community development through cultural interaction

Employees: 9

NATIONAL ASSOCIATION OF PARTNERS IN EDUCATION

Office: Alexandria, VA

Web site: http://www.napehg.org

Cause: to provide leadership in the formation and growth of effective partnerships in education that ensure success for all students

Employees: 16

NATIONAL COMMUNITY EDUCATION ASSOCIATION

Office: Fairfax, VA

Web site: http://www.ncea.com

Cause: to provide the tools and knowledge for lifelong learning; parent and community involvement in education; community use of schools; leadership training for community members and to improve the quality of community life through education and learning.

Employees: 6

Figure 4–5 Nonprofit Employment Samples.

Child and youth services jobs include positions at child development centers, family child care homes, school-age service facilities, and other youth service operations.

The Army Child Development Centers (CDC) and school-age services are required to achieve and maintain accreditation. Family Child Care (FCC) homes may also be accredited. Accreditation is achieved through NAEYC, the National School Age Care Alliance, and the Military Family Child Care Home Accreditation Agency. For more information check http://www.cysjobs.com. or http://www.mwr-europe.com.

Jobs with the U.S. Army in Europe for directors, teachers, and training specialists may offer the following perks and benefits:

- a tax-free housing allowance
- vacation and sick leave
- shopping at military facilities
- paid moving expenses
- ten paid holidays a year
- accredited American colleges
- medical and life insurance and 401K retirement cost-sharing benefits
- travel, culture, and recreation opportunities

For more information on teaching, child care, or other jobs in other branches of the military contact the following:

United States Air Force
      Child Development Programs
      Community Activities
      1111 Jefferson Davis Highway
      Crystal Gateway North, Tower E, Ste. 401
      Arlington, VA 22203
      http://www.usajobs.opm.gov

United States Navy
      Head, Naval Child Development Progams
      BUPERS–653
      MWR Division
      Washington, DC 20370

United States Marine Corps.
      Child Care Program Director
      CMC HQ USMC (MHF) Code 40
      #2 Navy Annex
      Washington, DC 20308–1775

Military Child Development Programs
      http://military-childrenandyouth.calib.com

School-Age Care

If you are searching for part-time employment while you take college courses, consider working before and/or after elementary school hours. School district programs usually offer higher rates of pay than private schools. Those educators whose long term goal is becoming

Figure 4–6   School-age Programs Provide Recreational Activities.

an elementary school teacher should consider school-age work as an opportunity to acquire skills. Or, use this part-time employment experience to analyze whether a long- range goal will provide satisfying employment, Figure 4–6. School district, district offices, and county offices of education usually post and advertise these positions. Volunteering can get your foot in the door.

Teacher Assistants—Primary and Secondary Schools

A job as a teaching assistant with a public or private elementary or secondary school can be a well-paid position. Often, assistants provide clerical support and perform individual tutoring chores. Good record-keeping skills, and computer and audiovisual equipment skills are valuable for these positions. Kleiman (2003) describes prospects and advantages:

> *Excellent job prospects are expected due to a shortage of teachers, thus spurring the need for assistants to provide clerical assistance and classroom monitoring. The best opportunities will be in special education and English as a second language (ESL) classes. An increasing number of after-school and summer programs also will create opportunities. Assistants who speak a second language, particularly Spanish, are in great demand to communicate with the increasing number of students and parents whose first language is not English. Many assistants work toward a teaching degree while gaining experience. About 4 out of 10 teacher assistants belonged to unions in 2000, mainly the American Federation of Teachers and the National Education Association.*

Tutoring

The *No Child Left Behind Act* requires public school districts to offer tutorial services under certain circumstances. To obtain these services, parents usually select a public or private tutoring provider from a list of state-approved providers (Casserly, 2004). Providers of tutoring services vary from city to city and state to state but often include private providers such as Huntington Learning Centers, Kaplan K12 Learning Services, and Sylvan Learning.

Consider researching private tutoring services in your area for possible employment, in addition to researching school districts. Public school district offices are found in local telephone books.

Educational and Technology- Influenced Toy Companies

A University of California study in 1997 implied a positive impact occurred when babies were exposed to classical music (della Cava, 2002). This set the stage for a new industry. Positions exist for educators as consultants, innovators, developers, experimenters, researchers, sales representatives, marketers, etc. Educators can emphasize the creative aspects of toys, and young children's need for "first-hand" manipulatives.

Hospital Child Care

An increasing number of hospitals are hiring employees to provide therapeutic child and family services for hospitalized and pre-hospitalized children. Some workers do family outreach, visitation, and parent training. This becomes necessary because of the child's medical condition. Specialized training is offered at a few colleges such as Pacific Oaks College in California, and at some community colleges. To locate job opportunities use the search term *child life specialists.*

Sick Care

Many communities have developed facilities that serve the children of working parents while the children recuperate from illness. Local resource and referral agencies can provide names and locations.

Child and Parent Magazines

Many metropolitan areas have free publications like the San Francisco Bay Area's *Baby* and *Bay Area Parent* magazines. These publications are full of local child care business advertisements. They also include articles of parent interest, lists of child and family-related events, a child care and preschool directory, and information on sales, coupons, and discounts for local merchants. These magazines are good sources of information concerning businesses that might offer local employment. The Appendix has a list of sample job possibilities from one metropolitan area's free publications. The length of the list will surprise you!

Substituting and Substitute Agencies

Agencies that supply schools, early childhood centers, private elementary schools, and other child programs with qualified substitute teachers are found in most large cities. The agency pays for its services by taking a portion of a substitute's pay. Substitutes need up-to-date clearances to perform substitute duties. Individuals can also make direct contact with programs. Many schools will place names on a substitute list. Although substitute teachers do not have the security of regular employment, there are definite advantages to substituting. When a job arises, and the program already knows a substitute's skills and abilities, it is likely that a well-regarded substitute will eventually be offered a regular position. Substituting provides networking opportunity, and an inside knowledge of working conditions. For public school work, inquire at district offices or a county office of education. Take along copies of credentials for the district or country office to keep on file. Clerks will tell you about necessary clearances.

Nanny and Au Pair Positions

Many early childhood educators have accepted positions as nannies, au pairs, or family helpers. Although specific nanny training programs exist, most parents also value educators with degrees. Many nannies work as family employees, but others are self-employed. Consult library publications such as *The Au Pair and Nanny's Guide to Working Abroad* (Vacation Week Publications) for descriptions of overseas work. Web sites are included at the end of this chapter. Woodworth and Pybus (2004) describe this overseas work:

> *Young women and (increasingly) young men can arrange to live with a family, helping to look after the children in exchange for pocket money. The terms* au pair, mother's helper *and* nanny *are often applied rather loosely, since all are primarily live-in jobs concerned with looking after children. Nannies may have some formal training and take full charge of the children. Mother's helpers (a European term) work full-time and undertake general housework and/or cooking as well as child care. Au pairs are supposed to work fewer hours and are expected to learn a foreign language (except in the United States) while living with a family. The Council of Europe Guidelines stipulate that au pairs should be aged 18–27 (though these limits are flexible), should be expected to work about five hours a day, five days per week plus a couple of evenings of babysitting, must be given a private room and full board, health insurance, opportunities to learn the language and weekly pocket money of 40 to 50 pounds in most cases plus board and lodging.*

Nanny agencies and newspaper advertisements are used extensively for finding nanny positions in the United States, and salaries vary greatly. Education, experience, and references are all factors parents consider, and many nannies are well rewarded for their services.

Overseas Teaching

Teachers may qualify for positions worldwide, and scholarships, grants, and exchange programs can be available. Usually a bachelor's degree with a credential/license is expected, and preference is given to those who speak a country's native language. English majors with a credential are particularly employable. Apply at least six months or a year ahead. Best known categories of overseas teaching jobs are:

- the Peace Corps and Teacher Exchange programs; both are government sponsored
- Department of Defense schools for dependents of military personnel
- private schools and faith-sponsored schools
- American schools
- international schools

The following resources will be of help:

Peace Corps
   http://www.peacecorps.gov
One Small Planet
   http://www.onesmallplanet.com
American-Sponsored Overseas Schools
   http://www.state.gov
Bureau of Educational and Cultural Affairs
   http://exchanges.state.gov

It usually takes considerable investigation before an individual accepts overseas employment. Usually this involves contacting the American Embassy in the foreign city and securing a passport. Knowing about housing is crucial.

Children's Museums, Discovery Centers, Adventure Playgrounds, and Community Art Centers

This sector of employment offers young children hands-on experiences and discovery opportunities. Program funding usually comes from a public entity or foundation. Educators, once employed, often become city, county, or state employees. A work site can be part of, or attached to zoos, natural history areas, botanical gardens, outdoor play parks, art collections, exhibits, nature displays, train parks, unique playgrounds, aquariums, virtual voyages, science projects, simulators, physical exploring activities, or other attractions. Director or coordinator positions typically require public relations and fundraising skills.

Companies that Offer Goods and Services to Schools and/or Staff Members

One walk through the exhibit hall of a major national early childhood professional association conference or a teacher's supply store will open your eyes to the large number of businesses that sell products and/or services to schools and teachers. You will find:

- book publishers and booksellers
- toy makers
- teaching aid manufacturers
- art supply companies
- computer programs
- home surveillance companies (evaluating babysitters)
- school equipment and furnishings manufacturers
- puppet and flannel board makers
- food service vendors
- audio-visual companies
- magazine publishers
- insurance companies
- music companies
- teacher personal item and jewelry makers

The list goes on and on. Employment in this sector may appeal to the educator who might enjoy consulting, innovating, designing, marketing, and of course, sales work.

Consider these other places to look for employment:

- child food service programs
- educational testing services
- children's clothing designers and manufacturers
- teacher supply stores
- child-related American businesses with overseas branches
- recreation centers and city or county recreation departments
- theme parks and entertainment centers

General Job Search Advice

Krannich and Krannich (1999) provide advice about obtaining a job with a nonprofit organization, but their advice also applies to other job searches. Their advice follows:

- Work hard at finding a job with a nonprofit organization. Make this a daily endeavor and involve your family.
- Do not be discouraged with setbacks: You are playing the odds, so expect disappointments and handle them in stride.
- Get organized. Translate your plans into activities, targets, names, addresses, telephone numbers, and materials. Develop an efficient and effective filing system. Use a large calendar to set time targets, record appointments, and compile useful information.
- Be polite, courteous, and thoughtful. Treat gatekeepers, especially receptionists and secretaries, like important people.
- Evaluate your progress and make the necessary adjustments.

Fact Finding

It is a wise move to do an analysis of your values, needs, and personal preferences concerning employment. If you are currently employed, you may have a specific idea concerning the type of employment you will be seeking based on your past job experience and knowledge of the opportunities your current employment provides.

There are three steps involved as you move toward realization of your short- and long-term career goals.

1) Decide what is right for you.
2) Conduct your own investigation and personal survey of available positions.
3) Investigate programs you choose to see if they fit into your career plan.

There probably will be times in your career when fact finding, during a job search or after an interview offer, isn't practical. Through past experience such as student teaching and internships, you may already intimately know the employer, working conditions, and how an offered position will fit into your career plans. You also may not have the time, energy, or resources to be selective about your employment. The job market may be so tight that you can't afford to be choosy.

Your Philosophy of Education

Will you know what kind of job, center, school you are looking for when you see it? Since centers differ greatly concerning their philosophical base, we urge you to find a center that meshes with your own philosophy of learning.

As Albrecht (2002) points out, this may not be an easy task:

Every program has an educational philosophy. In some programs, philosophies are written down, understood, and embraced by all. When this is the case, we say there is strong goal consensus—people agree on what they hope to achieve in their work with young children. In other programs, philosophies are less definitive, less clearly understood.

You already have an idea about how children best learn, the type of curriculum that best suits children's age and developmental level, the room arrangement and materials you prefer, and the guidance techniques you believe are professional. There are centers whose staff members and administrative staff have differences of opinion, and differences are resolved through discussion and compromise which allows professional growth for all parties. When selecting employment, keep your philosophic position in mind. Interviewers will probe your beliefs. If you haven't yet developed a written philosophy of education or early childhood learning, do so. Try to pinpoint the source of your statements if they come up in interviews. Examples follow:

- Children develop cognitive thinking by acting on the environment through spontaneous active play (Piaget, 1952).
- Children learn in enriched environments (Gesell et al, 1974).
- Children learn to function through interactions with peers and in reflective solutions to problems that occur through teacher supportive assistance that leads to resolutions that are socially appropriate (Erikson, 1963–1993).
- Children learn when teachers are enthusiastic about learning and wanting to find out (personal experience).
- Children learn best when rules in a classroom are understood and children know the reason for the rule (cooperating teacher/mentor).
- Children learn best when their ideas are respected, accepted, and given status (personal experience).

Most teachers will tell you that they have learned about learning from observing and interacting with children. Students in training and practicing professionals are reflective, questioning, and open to new ideas. Consequently, their philosophy, though established and guiding their classroom decisions, is still in revision. There is nothing more miserable than working in a program that you feel is unethical or being supervised by someone you don't respect. Fact finding can take place before one has applied, before one has a job interview scheduled, or as you conduct a job search or answer an ad. It involves investigating before telephoning, visiting, observing, or interviewing.

Characteristics to Consider

Caruso and Fawcett (1999) identified characteristics of schools, centers, and child care operations. These include economic, political, physical, organizational, cultural, psychological, and sociological factors.

Economic factors include salary, benefits, job security, and the upward mobility of staff. Political factors encompass staff participation in decision making. This is a factor that often leads to staff dissatisfaction, if absent. Whether a physical plant is adequate or "above" adequate for both children and adults will affect working conditions. A school's organizational structure reflects the school's values. Each school or center you investigate has cultural, psychological, and sociological aspects. A feeling or tone can exist that may range from supportive to destructive, warm to icy, tense to relaxed, stale to invigorating, and so on. The philosophy of education upon which programing is based is an important characteristic. Some programs describe themselves as eclectic, experimental, or perhaps based upon the tenets of an identified educational theorist.

Albrecht (2002) identified several ways that centers and schools differ; see Figure 4–7. As you look at this figure, notice there are many items listed that are only understood when one has worked onsite. But how many other characteristics can be surmised by an outside observer? You can learn more about a center by taking a tour of a school or center, or by reading their operational and employee handbooks and promotional brochures, or by interviewing a school staff and parents.

Some of the Ways Centers Differ

- educational philosophy as it relates to appropriate curriculum, the role of teachers, and expectations for children
- history and traditions
- shared values and beliefs; organizational ethics
- norms about everyday demeanor and how things should be done (for example, degree of formality in how children address teachers, expectations for noise level, appropriate dress for staff)
- legal governing structure, size, and program options for children and families
- division of labor, workload expectations, accountability systems, and opportunities for advancement
- leadership and management practices including decision-making and problem-solving processes, goal setting, supervision, performance appraisal practices, and emphasis on equity and fairness
- parent relations—frequency of, type of involvement in, and expectations about parents' role in program operations and governance
- instructional practices, including daily routines and child assessment procedures
- co-worker relations and expectations for collaboration
- communication processes, including formal and informal patterns of verbal and written communication and approaches to conflict resolution
- physical environment—the arrangement of space and the availability of instructional resources
- collective expertise, talents, and skills of the staff
- innovativeness and technology—the extent to which the center adapts to change and encourages staff to find creative ways to solve problems
- accounting and fiscal management system, including level of pay and benefits
- task orientation—emphasis placed on getting things done
- professional orientation—emphasis placed on improving teaching and professional competence

Figure 4–7 Some of the Ways Centers Differ.
From Albrecht, K. (2002) *The right fit: Recruiting, selecting, and orienting staff.* Lake Forest, IL: New Horizons: Reprinted with permission.

What Written Sources Say about Center Quality

The National Child Care Staffing Study gives clues to job hunters trying to judge both a school's quality and whether satisfactory working conditions exist. These elements are listed here so education applicants on a fact finding quest can investigate them:

- level of staff training (Better care is offered when staff has completed more years of formal education.)
- wages and benefits (High wages can mean higher quality.)
- percentage of the operating budget devoted to teaching personnel (A higher percentage was a predictor of quality.)
- nonprofit status (more likely to be quality)
- staff turnover percentage (low wages, higher turnover)
- income level of families (low income and high income families more likely to attend a center providing higher quality care) (Whitebook, Phillips, Howes, 1993.)

If you are looking for a school that has a work atmosphere that re-invigorates, motivates, and empowers employees to reach new heights of creativity, productivity, and personal fulfillment, consider the working conditions and job aspects that seem to allow it. Kituku (2003) identified elements that may do so:

- clear expectations, visions, and goals
- continuous opportunities for employee growth
- identification of ways to reduce work-related stresses
- eradication of small talk and gossip
- adequate training and refresher courses
- no continuous unexplained changes
- recognition of small and large staff accomplishments
- zero demeaning behavior or talk by superiors
- involvement in team projects
- family friendly workplace environment
- healthy communication within and between staff working in different areas

Cryer (1999) identified widely recognized core elements in the professional definition of quality in early childhood programs. The elements in Figure 4–8 were included and can be kept in mind if you are an early childhood educator beginning fact finding efforts.

Starting Your Investigation

Your first contact with a school may be a telephone call. Previously, you were urged to keep notes and politely probe with prepared questions. Hopefully the person answering your call will want to tell you about the school and its program. Besides asking if a position announcement, job description, and application forms are available, ask if a school brochure is obtainable, or if a school tour is possible. Does the school have a Web site? Home pages can provide considerable information. If salary schedules are attached to application forms, these will be useful during negotiations that follow a job offer.

Consider driving by the school to see the size and exterior of the school, its upkeep, and perhaps the children's neighborhood. A school that has parents dropping off children from a row of "Hummers" or classy SUVs will probably ask you different interview questions than an inner city school where parents walk to the school from their neighborhoods.

- **Safe care**—with sufficient diligent adult supervision that is appropriate for children's ages and abilities, safe toys, equipment, and furnishings.

- **Healthful care**—in a clean environment where sanitary measures to prevent the spread of illness are taken and where children have opportunities for activity, rest, developing, self-help skills in cleanliness, and having their nutritional needs met.

- **Developmentally appropriate stimulation**—where children have wide choices of opportunities for learning through play in a variety of areas such as language, creativity through art, music, dramatic play, fine and gross motor, [numeracy], and nature/science.

- **Positive interactions with adults**—where children can trust, learn from, and enjoy the adults [who] care for and educate them.

- **Encouragement of individual, emotional growth**—allowing children to operate independently, cooperatively, securely, and competently.

- **Promotion of positive relationships**—with other children allowing children to interact with their peers with the environmental supports and adult guidance required to help interactions go smoothly (Cryer, 1999, p. 42).

Figure 4–8   Elements of Quality.

From Cryer, D. (1999, May). Defining and assessing early childhood program quality. *The Annals of the American Academy of Political and Social Science*, 563, 39–55. Copyright 1999 by the American Academy of Political and Social Science. Reprinted by permission.

Fact finding involves making inferences concerning why parents selected the school, or finding out what parents who qualified for publicly funded centers are seeking for their children. Fact finding helps you prepare, so look closely at what you see. Think reflectively about what a particular school might value in their teachers.

The Reputation of Early Childhood Centers

Most centers and schools have a neighborhood reputation. Baby Center (2003) provides parents with the following advice when looking for a good child care center:

> *A good preschool should have a welcoming, friendly atmosphere and be known for its nurturing environment and stimulating curriculum. Ask the school for names and numbers of other parents and call them, or stop by during afternoon pickup time and approach other parents then. Of course, take anything you hear about a school with a grain of salt and wait to judge it until you see it for yourself—disgruntled parents may simply have had a personality conflict with the preschool director. Also, your own first impressions definitely matter here. Be sure to observe the children when you visit. If they don't seem happy to be there, that's probably a signal to look elsewhere.*
>
> ***Bottom line:*** *If you don't hear too many good opinions about a certain school, and if it doesn't feel right, look elsewhere.*

As a job seeker, seek out conversations with people who live in the community or neighborhood. But don't quiz parents entering or exiting a center or school.

Public Licensing Agencies

Public licensing agencies have public records that can be reviewed. However, information may not be available by telephone. Inspection records will give you the most information. The American Federation of State, County, and Municipal Employees (AFSCME) urges parents looking for child care to do the following:

Ask your local agency (licensing) to send you the state's licensing and registration requirements for caregivers. This information can be used to determine if the provider meets minimum state requirements. You may also be able to get information about recent inspections, licensing violations, and complaints about the center. Some resource and referral agencies also will know which providers are accredited. The agency may charge a small fee for providing information (AFSCME, 2000).

Better Business Bureaus and the Chamber of Commerce may have additional information you can research.

National Association for the Education of Young Children (NAEYC) Accreditation

Should you look for a center that is NAEYC accredited? If you read the findings of a study of accreditation conducted by Whitebook, Sakai, and Howes (1997), we think you will. Higher quality centers were found to have less turnover of staff, and highly skilled staff were believed more likely to remain at their job. Wages in higher quality centers were higher than average. Remember these programs have voluntarily chosen to meet higher standards.

Library Research

Library research is a necessary component of fact finding activities. The nitty-gritty of a job hunt is doing your homework, finding out everything you can about the community and industry you're interested in, and researching the companies that are hiring, (including which jobs are open, what salaries they pay) (Kleiman, 2002.) Kleiman also urges you not to feel embarrassed about asking for help because that is what librarians and search engines are there for.

If you are looking for a kindergarten, elementary, middle, or secondary school position, knowing a lot about the community, town, area, and its industries, economy, and population will equip you to understand particular questions that an interview panel might deem important. You'll also be much better able to ask relevant questions.

Checking with Other Professionals

Checking with professional friends about a school or center is a good idea. It is surprising how much information might be forthcoming from a center's or school's present or past employees. You may get information you can't get from any other source.

Thinking about Moving for Employment

You can investigate the employment picture in other geographic areas by researching micro economies region by region. Some regions may still be in recession while others can offer brighter prospects. Economists divide the United States into the following regions—New England, mid-Atlantic, southeast, Midwest, Pacific northwest, northern California, and southwest/southern California. You can gather information concerning whether employment is strong and also which job sector areas are experiencing growth. Cochrane (2004), an economist, noticed the greater Boston area's technology sector was gaining jobs and the employment picture was moderate. On the other hand, housing in New England was less affordable and recent home prices had experienced a steep climb. Cochrane believed the Midwest region, which includes Illinois, Indiana, Michigan, Ohio, and Wisconsin, was about to pull out of a recession. The housing prices there were stable, with bargains to be found. He suggests checking Web sites such as http://www.economy.com.

Garber (2004) notes:

> *Labor market statistics can be found at college career offices. There are also online resources that compile this sort of data, like* Jobstart.org *and* salaryexpert.com. *Salary-Expert uses the Bureau of Labor Statistics to obtain the information that is personalized for new entrants into the work force.*

Sources, such as those mentioned by Garber, can provide pay ranges for jobs, average salaries for a particular location, the national average salary for job titles, and the cost of rent in select cities.

Does the location you are investigating offer the type of living environment you prefer? It's a good idea to identify essential services, housing costs and availability, educational, recreational, and cultural offerings. Every community has a unique profile that includes its demographics, geography, weather, industry, history, amenities, cost of living, and other factors. Visiting a local planning department and a city's Chamber of Commerce can provide abundant information. Ask questions and pick up written handouts. It is surprising how much of this background material will come up during a job interview.

In the final analysis, you are the best judge of whether a particular school or location is the right fit for you. As your own career manager, having participated in fact finding, you will be a more competitive contender for any job opening. Think carefully about what you feel a particular school may be looking for in the person they expect to hire, and also what need or problems the center may have. Interviewers will try to find a new hire who will address those problems, solve them, or contribute to solutions.

Summary   Before searching for employment, you should clarify what you are searching for and how this fits into your long-range career plan. Networking is important and starts when you decide to train for an eventual position in education. A job search can be conducted many ways including through your networking efforts or by using Web searches, online job boards, classified ads, college career centers, family contacts, professional association services, and attending job fares. Other strategies were also discussed: job titles, telephone techniques, and follow-up activities. Fact finding and its relationship to job satisfaction and future interviews should convince you that fact finding is well worth the time and effort.

Helpful Web Sites

America's Job Bank
http://www.ajb.org
maintained by the U.S. Department of Labor, geographic locations

Association for Childhood Education International
http://www.acei.org
information on education careers and issues that affect early childhood educators

Child Care Licensing Study, The Children's Foundation
http://www.childrensfoundation.net
publications of interest

Children's Defense Fund
http://www.childrensdefense.org
information on state pre-kindergarten initiatives

Directory of State Child Care Regulatory Offices
http://necic.org

College Career Centers
http:www.careerresource.net

Employment Services
http://www.careerbuilder.com
http://www.monster.com
http://www.starttodayjobs.com
http://www.flipdog.com

Families and Work Institute
http://www.familiesandwork.org
information on pre-kindergarten programs funded by states

Federal Child Care Provider Loan Forgiveness Program
http://www.aesuccess.org
research this federal demonstration program

Head Start
http://www2.acf.dhhs.gov

Job Bank U.S.A.
http://www.jobbankusa.com
provides job hunting services

Jobs in Higher Education
http://chronicle.com

Job Profiles
http://www.jobprofiles.org
profiles of individuals working in various occupations

Manpower
http://www.manpower.com
international staffing agency

My Job Search
http://www.myjobsearch.com

NAEYC (National Association for the Education of Young Children)
   http://www.naeyc.org
   search for NAEYC's Early Childhood Career Forum

National Resource Center for Health and Safety in Child Care
   http://nrc.uchsc.edu
   http://www.careerjournal.com
   a job search guide and career management information

National School-Age Care Alliance
   http://www.nsaca.org
   publications, standards, accreditation, and an online national directory

Online Job Service
   http://www.nonprofitjobs.org

Society for Nonprofit Organizations
   http://www.danenet.wicip.org

Sterling Medical Group
   http://www.sterlingmedcorp.com
   a company offering overseas employment to educators

The Center for the Child Care Workforce
   http://www.ccw.org
   information and studies of child care quality

The National Association of Child Care Resource and Referral Agencies
   http://www.naccra.org
   lists recent job openings

The National Community Education Association (NCEA)
   http://www.ncea.com
   available career opportunities at community education organizations

U.S. Department of Labor—Office of Occupational Statistics
   http://www.bls.gov
   search preschool teachers, kindergarten, elementary, middle and secondary, provides significant information on teaching professions

Wall Street Journal
   http://www.bestjobsusa.com
   http://www.edsearch.com
   lists positions
   http://www.interbiznet.com
   links to job searching sites
   http://www.anyworkanywhere.com
   http://www.summerjobseeker.com

Resources

Eikleberry, C. (1995). *The career guide for creative and unconventional people*. Berkeley, CA: Ten Speed Press.

Fujawa, J. (1998). (*Almost*) *Everything you need to know about early childhood education*. Beltsville, MD: Gryphon House.

Griffin, S. (1999). *Teaching English abroad. Talk yourself around the world.* Princeton, NJ: Vacation-Work.

International jobs: Where they are, how to get them. Menlo Park, CA: Addison Wesley.

Study and teaching opportunities abroad: Sources of information about overseas study, teaching, work, and travel. Washington, DC: U.S. Government Printing Office.

References

Abrams, M. (2004, June 1). Making friends: Not just for kids. Editor's note. *Bottom Line*, p. 2.

AFSCME (The American Federation of State, County, and Municipal Employees). (2000). *Choosing quality child care.* Brochure. Washington, DC: Author.

Albrecht, K. (2002). *The right fit: Recruiting and orienting staff.* Lake Forest, IL: New Horizons.

Baby Center. (2003, October 20). Signs of a good preschool. http://www.babycenter.com

Bolles, R. N. (2003). *What color is your parachute?* Berkeley, CA: Ten Speed Press.

Carlson, T. (2004, June). The graduation advice I never got. . . . but wish I had. *Reader's Digest*, 153–156.

Caruso, J. J., & Fawcett, M. T. (1999). *Supervision in early childhood education: A developmental perspective.* New York: Teacher's College Press.

Casserly, M. (2004, Summer). Driving change. *Education Next. 4* (3) 32–37.

Cochrane, S. (2004, October 15). If the economy is recovering—why don't we feel any richer? *Bottom Line 25* (20) 1–3.

Cryer, D.(1999, May). Defining and assessing early childhood program quality. *The Annals of the American Academy of Political and Social Science*, 563, 39–55.

della Cava, M. R. (2002, July 23). Building a brainier baby: Parents clamor for educational toys—to the tune of $1 billion. *The Idaho Statesman*, p. 1 Life.

Erikson, E. (1963–1993). *Childhood and society.* New York: Norton.

Forrester Research. Quoted in Raymond, J. (2002, March 18). The jaws of victory. *Newsweek*, p. 38P.

Garber, R. (2004, August 15). How to negotiate your first salary: Play it smart. *The Idaho Statesman*, p. CB1.

Garza, M. M. (2003, June 1). Is your job search getting a busy signal? *The Idaho Statesman*, p. 2CB.

Gesell, A., Ilg, F. L., & Ames, L. B. (1974). *The child from five to ten.* New York: Harper & Row.

Harrison, L. H. Quoted in Raymond, J. (2002, March 18). The jaws of victory. *Newsweek*, p. 38P.

Head Start Bulletin. (2001, April). Improving quality in the classroom: Observations and recommendations from the Head Start Quality Research Centers 70, 35–36.

Hemming, A. (2003, October). Your job search. *Bottom Line Personal. 24* (20) 15.

Hyson, M., & Duru, M. (2004, July). Accrediting Associate Degree programs: NAEYC launches a new system to recognize excellence. *Young Children. 59* (4) 75.

Kituku, V. (2003, September 7). Strategies to invigorate, motivate, and empower employees. *The Idaho Statesman*, p. 1BC.

Kleiman, C. (2002). *Winning the job game: The new rules for finding and keeping the job you want.* Hoboken, NJ: John Wiley and Sons, Inc.

Kleiman, C. (2003, September 28). Don't play it safe in tough times. *The Idaho Statesman*, p. 1CB.

Krannich, R., & Krannich, C. (1999). *Jobs and careers with non-profit organizations: Profitable opportunities with nonprofits.* Manassas Park, VA: Impact Publications.

Morkes, A. (Ed.) (2003). *Encyclopedia of careers and vocational guidance.* (Vol. 1). Chicago, IL: Ferguson Publishing Co.

Neugebauer, R. (2003, September/October). Employer child care languishes—awaiting economic upturn. *Child Care Information Exchange.* 153, 22.

Nierenberg, A. R. (2003, November 1). The five most common networking mistakes. *Bottom Line Personal.* *24* (21) 8.

Phillips, B. E. (2003, October). Feeling stressed? What women of color should know about depression. *Women of Color Conference. 3* (1) 39.

Piaget, J. (1952). *The language and thought of the child.* London: Routledge and Kegan Paul.

Raymond, J. (2002, March 18). The jaws of victory. *Newsweek*, p. 38P.

Salem State College. (2003). Early childhood majors survey. Retrieved August 3, 2004 from http://www.salemstate.edu/careersvs/O2ECH.pdf.

San Jose State University Career Center (2003). *Job and internship guide 2003–2004.* Chicago, IL: Career Recruitment Media, Inc.

The San Jose Mercury News. (2002, December 29). Backed into a corner. p. 1PC. Author.

Solomons, J. Quoted in *Chicago Tribune* (2003, October 5). Personal contacts can bridge the gap to new career. Career Builder. 1. Author.

Steen, M. (2003, March 9). The new resume reality. *San Jose Mercury News.* 1F.

The New Lexicon Webster's Dictionary of the English Language. (1988). New York: Lexicon Press.

Treasurer, B. Quoted in Kleiman, C. (2003, September 28). Don't play it safe in tough times. *The Idaho Statesman*, p. 1 CB.

The Washington Post. (2002, November 12). Teacher aides and the *No Child Left Behind Act*, p. 4C.

Whitaker, L. (2004, September 12). Friends help land jobs, get raises. *The Idaho Statesman,* p. CB1

Whitebook, M, Sakai, L., & Howes, C. (1997). *NAEYC accreditation as a strategy for improving child care quality: An assessment.* Washington, DC: Center for the Child Care Workforce.

Whitebook, M., Phillips, D., & Howes, C. (1993). *The National Child Care Staffing Study revisited.* Oakland, CA: Child Care Employee Project.

Wittenberg, R. (1996). *Opportunities in child care careers.* Lincolnwood, IL: VGM Career Horizons.

Woodworth, D., & Pybus, V. (2004). *Summer jobs abroad 2004.* Guilfort, CT: Globe Pequot Press.

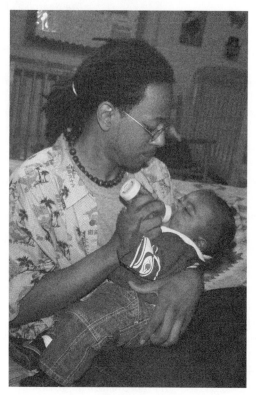

CHAPTER FIVE

Cover Letters and Resumes

If you tell the truth you don't have to remember anything.

Mark Twain

Really Not a Surprise

Christine's grandmother, a tireless and well-known figure in her community, was active in local charities. Christine thought it unlikely that Granny knew anyone that could help her land a job in education, but Christine took her to lunch anyway. Granny said she'd work on it, think about it, and wanted a copy of her resume. They both agreed Christine was going about her job search efficiently, and both felt the great numbers of resumes she was sending out would work eventually even in the current high unemployment job market. She had not received one response yet, and it had been three months.

About a month later, a letter arrived from a company requesting an interview. It turned out to be an American company with a branch in Spain. They were looking for a Spanish-speaking educator to teach English. Since the offer was a good one, and because overseas work appealed to her, and she was fluent in Spanish, she took the position. It wasn't until almost a year later that she found out that Granny had an old school chum with the company.

QUESTIONS TO PONDER

1. If Christine realized her cover letter and resume were not getting her an interview, what she should have done?

2. Christine's grandmother has remained silent concerning her role in Christine's new position. Should Christine say anything? Why?

3. Might there still be some problems with Christine's cover letter and/or resume? Why?

Cover Letters

A brief, well written cover (inquiry) letter displays your first efforts to lure and woo an employer to review your resume and to obtain an interview. The letter's primary function is to grab attention. Think of a cover letter as the wrapping on a present—the present is your qualified services. Assume your cover letter and resume are sitting in a stack of others. You will want them to stand out and be memorable. Decisions regarding the quality and color of the paper you use may contribute to its being noticed.

Knowdell (2002) believes a cover letter's secondary purpose is "to communicate more specific things about yourself that you cannot address in a resume." You can mention something that sets you apart. Figure 5–1 provides characteristics of good and bad cover letters. Figures 5–2 and 5–3 are cover letter examples that have slightly different formats.

Morkes (2003) suggests cover letters are a way to market oneself and specify what you can do for the employer. Your fact-finding efforts, covered in Chapter 4, will be helpful. He also advises you to emphasize experiences and skills matching those found in the ad or job announcement.

Good	Bad
■ simple gray, white, or beige paper	■ vague references
■ states why you are interested	■ poor English usage
■ states why you are a best job fit	■ misspellings
■ specifies subject of letter (re: infant-toddler educator in subject line)	■ run-on sentences
■ addressed to an individual or uses neutral yet formal greeting such as Dear Hiring Manager or Dear Personnel Manager	■ offensive language
	■ repetition
	■ omits the date on a published advertisement
■ a typed signature	■ omission of a position title
■ contact information complete with message telephone or an e-mail address	■ unnecessarily creative
	■ gimmicks
■ straightforward	■ uncalled for humor
■ brief	■ odd stationery
■ is well written	■ long-winded
■ grabs attention	■ longer than one or two pages
■ is one page	■ a gender-specific opening such as Dear Sir
■ refers to date on the employer's ad or to position announcement	■ includes a personal signature only
■ mentions a personal referral (who suggested you apply and how that person is connected to the employer)	■ lack of up-to-date contact information.
	■ not proofread
	■ unnecessary attachments (photo, references)
■ applies for one position opening only	■ seeking more than one job title if the employer has numerous openings
■ uses standard ending such as Sincerely, or Yours Very Truly	

Figure 5–1   Characteristics of Good and Bad Cover Letters.

> 1635 Carter Lane
> Campbell, CA 95017
> March 30, 2004
>
> Mrs. Thelma Harvey
> Director
> First Avenue Early Learning Center
> 125 First Avenue
> Eastridge, CA 94121
>
> Dear Mrs. Harvey:
>
> In June of this year, I will graduate from Central College with an Associate of Arts degree in Early Childhood Education. I would like to talk with you about the possibility of becoming a teacher with your program.
>
> As you can see from my enclosed resume, I concentrated on music and dance curricula for young children both in my studies and spare time. I can offer children special depth in this area, as well as a well-rounded learning program.
>
> Would it be possible to arrange an interview for Monday, April 10, or Tuesday, April 11? I would like to discuss opportunities for joining your staff.
> Sincerely,
>
>
> Mary Smith
> 777–000–1111
> smith@arnet.net

Figure 5–2　Sample Cover Letter 1.

Ending a letter with a thank you for considering the cover letter/resume may create a pleasant feeling of obligation in the reader and is a useful strategy (Morkes, 2003). A cover letter is a business letter; consequently, it contains a return address, date, a formal greeting, the job title of the addressee, the name and address of the employer, school or center, a salutation line, a letter body, a closing, and a typed signature.

Creating a succinct cover letter is a must (Kleiman, 2002). Anthony and Roe (2003) provide the following pointers for cover letters:

- Use standard 8½ × 11-inch stationery, preferably the same paper stock you have chosen for your resume.
- Use only one side of the page.
- The return address and date should appear at the top of the page.
- The inside address (name and title of the individual, name and address of the institution) should appear at least three spaces below the date and be flush with the left margin.
- The body of the letter should be single-spaced, with double spacing between paragraphs.
- The paragraphs may begin at the left margin or a half-inch to the right.
- The complementary close should appear two spaces below the last line of the letter.
- Leave four spaces between the complementary close and your name to allow for your signature.
- The word *Enclosure* appears two or more spaces below your name when you include additional items, for example, resume, transcripts, or application form.

123 Birch Street
Any town, CA 12345
March 21, 0000

Dr. Marlow Green
Principal
Blossom Hollow School
Any town, CA 12345

Dear Dr. Green,

Please consider me as an applicant for the kindergarten teacher opening at Blossom Hollow. I learned of this opening from the Career Center at State University and will complete my bachelor's degree and receive my teaching credential in May of this year. My college minor in English prepares me to promote children's literacy and early reading skills. I believe a varied research-based curriculum offers children growth opportunities.

I am currently student teaching in a diverse multicultural kindergarten in an urban school district with many children learning English as a second language. Working with small groups, I've developed a tracking system to assess each child's weekly growth and proficiency. I enjoy developing new teaching methods and aids to promote each child's progress.

I have submitted the district's online application form. My resume is enclosed, and the university's Career Center staff is sending my letters of recommendation. Transcripts are available upon request. The opportunity to be interviewed would be much appreciated. Thank you for your consideration.

Sincerely,

[Graduating teacher's name]

Enclosure

Figure 5–3   Sample Cover Letter 2.

Introductory Openings

The following cover letter introductions could create interest:

- Use the name of someone known to the employer.
  "Meg Dowing, your educational consultant, suggested I forward my resume."
- Mention your present occupation.
  "My present position as an early childhood teacher qualifies me for a similar position with your agency."
- Cite your experience and education.
  "I believe my three years teaching experience and Associate of Arts degree in Child Development may be the qualifications you are seeking."
- Show knowledge of their operation.
  "Being well-acquainted with your innovative approach to cognitive learning through workshops presented by your staff, I am including my resume and would like to discuss the possibility of my employment as a teacher."
- Introduce a specific skill.
  "I have developed a specialty in presenting drama to young children."

- Mention recent graduation and availability.
  "In June, I will graduate with a bachelor's degree and would like to discuss the possibility of a position."

Other lines that might introduce resumes follow.
"The enclosed resume describes. . . ."
"I have attached a resume so you may judge my. . . ."
"As my resume shows. . . ."
"After reading my resume, I hope you believe, as I do, that I will be an asset to your center."

Interview Queries

A request for an interview can take the following forms:
"I would like to talk with you about my interest in employment and will telephone within the next few days."
"I would appreciate an interview at your earliest convenience."
"Let me discuss this with you. I will be available for an interview. . . ."
"I will call for an appointment in the next few days, unless I hear from you sooner."
"I feel an interview within the next few days would be mutually advantageous."
"I will be available for an interview. . . ."
"When could we meet to discuss my qualifications?"
"An interview would allow you to probe what I have to offer and would give me a chance to display my sincere interest in the position."

In addressing your letter and envelope, try to identify the director or personnel manager by name with the correct job title, or use a formal greeting. If you plan to e-mail an inquiry letter, see Figure 5–4 for tips. Figure 5–5 is an example of a cover letter used as a follow-up to a job fair contact.

TIPS FOR SENDING E-MAIL INQUIRY LETTERS

1. On the subject line, specify "Early childhood teacher/educator job applicant" (job candidate) or "Interested in teacher position" to distinguish yourself from junk e-mail.
2. If you don't know the hiring individual's name, address to Personnel Manager or Director.
3. Include your signature, typed name and address, telephone number, message telephone number, e-mail and fax at the end of your letter.
4. Proofread carefully, checking neatness, grammar, spelling, and punctuation.
5. Exclude graphics that embellish or decorate; exclude photographs.*
6. Mention you will send a resume upon request, or attach your resume.

*Commercially decorated computer papers that picture children, play objects, and aesthetic backgrounds, exist. Some experts feel appearing "unbusinesslike" may not be a problem for early childhood educators.

Figure 5–4   Tips for Sending E-Mail Inquiry Letters.

000 White Ave.
Sand Point, CA 00000
March 15, 2004

Roberta Smith
Personnel Office
Child Development Centers
000 Elm Street
Sand Point, CA 00000

Dear Mrs. Smith,

I enjoyed meeting you yesterday at Central University's Job Fair. I am interested in the teaching position we discussed and have enclosed an additional copy of my resume for your review.

My skills would be a good match for Child Development Centers because ....

I have written a handbook for ....
My organizational and computer skills helped me to prepare .... In addition to my student teaching, I have been a teacher for ....

I would like to meet with you again to discuss my interest in Child Development Centers. I will call you next week to schedule an interview.

Your consideration is appreciated.

Sincerely,

Marion Brown
000–000–0000
Enclosure

Figure 5–5   Job Fair Follow-Up Cover Letter.

Resume Writing

Writing your resume may be one of the most difficult aspects of a job search. It may take the prospective employer only 20 seconds to scan it and decide if an interview is granted or to put the resume aside with the rest. It is easy to find books on the subject of resume writing and Internet advice, as well as commercial computer programs. Each may provide a different slant on what a resume should look like.

Anthony and Roe (2003) discuss the difference between resume examples:

An educator's resume is only superficially like resumes in the business sector. Not only is the vocabulary of a teacher's resume different from that of other occupations, even within the profession there is considerable variation from state to state and from region to region. Similarly, a teacher's achievement is not measured in quite the same way.

You will want your resume to capture attention, display your skills, and make you competitive for the position. Consider format, content, and layout. It is possible that you will spend more than a few hours on the project and that you will revise frequently.

A resume does not get you a job. What it does is open doors for you, so you'll have to prepare the most effective resume that you can (Kleiman, 2002). Kleiman believes she knows what employers and human resource professionals want when they sit down with a stack of resumes. Here's what employers tell her:

> *Keep your resume as brief as possible. Hiring officers aren't interested in your personal life or activities. You can talk about them in the job interview that your short resume will get you. Put the vital information, such as your title, accomplishments, and work experience up front so the reader can get it in one brief glance. And, as quickly and concisely as possible, include the names of former employers, your length of stay at each company (school), and your shining moments at each of them.*

Stern (2005) advises you to "get ruthless" with your resume, and eliminate the "fluff" many people add to resumes to make them appear self-motivated and people-oriented. She recommends sticking to specific tasks you've accomplished and specific skills. The authors remember being impressed with candidates whose resumes included leisure time pursuits, and volunteer and other job interactions with children and families. In early childhood employment, there may not be a stack of resumes or much competition for some jobs, but the really good jobs, the ones you are aiming for, may be quite competitive.

Preparation of your resume entails skill, honesty, and attention to detail. Since your resume represents you, proceed carefully in its development. Your resume should reflect a strong positive self-image and communicate that image to the employer. Consider the typeface carefully. It creates an impression in the reader. Readable typeface is a must: swirling letters won't do. Burmark (2002) points out that type style creates an emotional reaction. Certain fonts are out of place on a resume. Type can be beautiful and decorative, yet inappropriate because the type calls undue attention to itself or because the type style has a distinct personality that does not suit the resume's purpose or the personality of the person it represents. Some computer printing programs have hundreds of type styles. Think about which style will best represent you. A well-written and formatted resume adds a professional touch. Doing an adequate job of fact-finding pays off now. A resume that is tailored to an employer's needs gains special attention.

Educators at both early childhood and the primary level need to understand how the *No Child Left Behind Act* may be changing what elementary schools are looking for in their new hires. Language arts, pre-reading, reading development, and early math development are specified in the legislation. So, schools may be under pressure to show adequate improvement in these areas, and they may scan resumes differently. However, we want to alert you to the fact that a number of educators are not in accord with what they feel is an undue emphasis on assessment and pushing down curriculum from higher grades.

Certain words in resumes can alert employers to your special preparation or experience. Current terminology that may pique an employer's interest can include—documentation and assessment, research-based instruction, systematic and specific instruction, developmentally appropriate instruction, individual learning plans, phonetic and phonemic awareness, alphabet principle, print-rich environments, print awareness, theme and project instruction, child portfolios, or other currently used terms. If your background or preparation includes expertise in these or other activities that help children succeed and learn to read easily and with comprehension, it may be foolish not to include this information in your resume. Study Figure 5–6. It presents a "bare bones" resume outline with helpful directions.

Name
Address
Telephone, Message telephone
E-mail address
Fax

1. <u>Availability</u>
2. <u>Position Sought or Applying for</u>
   Title of position

3. <u>Education</u>
   Dates—Description
(List most recent education first.)
(List degree, school, address, date graduated.)
(List GPA if over 3.0.)

4. <u>Experience</u>
   Dates—Description
(List present or latest work, then others back in time.)
(List any work experiences and dates, and the names and addresses of your employers, such as practicum/student teaching, field experiences, internships, and part-time and full-time jobs.)
Related Experiences and Related Training
   Dates—Description
(List hobbies, travel, volunteer work, training programs, musical talent, memberships, arts and crafts, religious school teaching, and conferences.)

5. <u>Personal</u> (optional)

6. <u>Special Skills</u> (optional)

7. <u>Professional Affiliations</u> (optional)

8. <u>References</u> (optional)
References (on a separate sheet)
(List at least three good references. Try to list people who have seen your work. Omit relatives. Employers, teachers, clergy, and parents of children you have cared for are especially good references. List their names, addresses, occupations, and telephone numbers.)

Figure 5–6   Resume Outline with Pointers.

The Career Center of San Jose State University (2003) points out that when you attempt to highlight qualifications, accomplishments, and skills, these may be organized on a resume using different categories and/or headings. Choose headings that best display your level of experience and background. The Career Center suggests selecting from the following headings, which are not any particular order—objectives, education related coursework, projects, experience, skills, activities, awards/honors, related experience, other employment, military experience, volunteer work, community service, an employment summary, accomplishments, summary of qualifications, leadership activities, affiliations, publications, and presentations.

Filling in a Resume Outline

When creating a resume, you should not use headings such as "Resume for Mary Jones." This information is self-evident. It is important to list both your home telephone number and a message telephone number in the *heading* . You will want to receive every employer call. *Availability* lets you identify exactly what date you can begin working. You need to be clear about the *position sought*. You may be interested in more than one position with the same employer; if so, apply separately for each. *Educational background* is listed beginning with your highest formal degree, then informal training. Include each school's name and address, mentioning current enrollment. Dates can follow the award of degrees or be mentioned consistently to the left-hand side of an item. A GPA of 3.0 or better goes here. Professional conferences, workshops attended, or additional informal training can be listed separately under the heading "Other Training." A statement such as "numerous college training conferences, workshops, adult night school, including. . . ." can lump all of this type of training together.

When listing your *experience*, begin with your most recent job and proceed backward to your earliest job. Make your experience summary interesting or list job tasks and/or accomplishments. Former employer's names and addresses should be provided, and your job title, dates of employment or student teaching, or other field experiences. Include important responsibilities and a range of job duties.

Anthony and Roe (2003) state that a resume is simply a summary of experiences where you decide what is most important, what you will highlight, and what you'll not want to call to the reader's attention. Personal computers can make resume preparation easier, and a letter-quality printer adds to attractiveness. Computers also help with updating and creating different versions for specific positions. Anthony and Roe caution individuals not to use the language of other occupations. Research the terminology that is appropriate to describe teaching functions in your desired position's geographic location, or the terms that describe a teaching specialty.

Morkes (2003) suggests going back in your memory and brainstorming each of your past experiences. Visualize what you did in your work and write a step-by-step list describing your actions. Following is a description of tasks completed at a classroom opening:

- Checked lighting and heating.
- Checked inventory supplies in various room areas.
- Referred to the daily schedule.
- Rearranged furnishings for planned activities.
- Cared for class pets and/or animal's needs.
- Made room attractive and inviting with displays, flowers, child photos, musical background, etc.

Use phrases instead of full sentences. See Figure 5–7 for words that focus on skills. Include volunteer work experience. Charles Stanley, an outplacement firm consultant, states:

> *Anything you can do to add to your resume—even a couple of weeks of volunteering at a community center—illustrates a sense of service to others (Stanley, 2002).*

List unrelated part-time and summer jobs if you feel they may enhance your image. It is not necessary to cite salaries, reasons for leaving, or supervisor's names at this point.

Accomplished	Controlled	Facilitated	Linked	Publicized
Acted	Cooperated	Focused	Maintained	Published
Adapted	Coordinated	Formulated	Managed	Recorded
Administered	Counseled	Fund raised	Monitored	Reported
Advised	Created	Generated	Motivated	Represented
Analyzed	Defined	Guided	Negotiated	Researched
Anticipated	Delegated	Handled	Observed	Resolved
Applied	Demonstrated	Hired	Obtained	Reviewed
Arranged	Designed	Identified	Operated	Revised
Assembled	Detailed	Implemented	Ordered	Scheduled
Assigned	Determined	Improved	Organized	Screened
Assisted	Developed	Increased	Originated	Selected
Authored	Devised	Individualized	Oversaw	Served
Budgeted	Directed	Influenced	Participated	Staffed
Built	Distributed	Informed	Performed	Stimulated
Calculated	Drafted	Initiated	Persuaded	Summarized
Catalogued	Edited	Innovated	Planned	Supervised
Collaborated	Educated	Inspected	Prepared	Supplied
Communicated	Empowered	Installed	Presented	Supported
Computerized	Enlarged	Instituted	Presided	Systemized
Conceived	Established	Integrated	Problem	Taught
Conceptualized	Evaluated	Interpreted	solved	Teamed
Conducted	Examined	Interviewed	Produced	Trained
Constructed	Exchanged	Invented	Programmed	Updated
Consulted	Expanded	Investigated	Promoted	Used
Contracted	Explained	Involved	Provided	Wrote

Figure 5–7   Skill Words.

The *personal section* provides an opportunity to let the employer know more about you. Try to give a conceptual overview of how you see yourself in relation to the job. You do not have to include your age or marital status. This whole section can be omitted if you feel uncomfortable with it. Mention *special competencies* and/or skills, child program planning specialties like yoga instruction, gardening, and puppetry. Taylor (2000) points out that more than 60 percent of all new jobs require some technology skills. If you have them, mention them. Listing your membership in professional associations and organizations under *activities* displays your interest in professional growth and commitment. Graduating students who have been financially unable to join such groups might give a high priority to doing so as soon as they look for work or secure a position. Student membership fees are usually below regular rates, so joining while still a student can be a good idea. If you have traveled extensively, or have hobbies which relate directly to the job, mention them here. If *references* are listed, give each person's name, address, and updated telephone numbers. Job titles and places of employment are included when references are professional rather than personal. An alternative statement, "Written references available upon request," is often substituted. Toward the end of a student teaching placement, it is wise to ask your cooperating teacher for a letter of reference. It becomes difficult to trace past employers and/or supervisors for references as years go by. Remember, a resume is an individualized

Content

- Keep comments brief, relevant, and to the point. Make the resume two pages if necessary but one page is best.
- Most employers prefer hiring people who are presently working.
- Use descriptive action phrases.
- Include beginning and ending dates, job titles, and ages or grade level of children/students.
- List past responsibilities, accomplishments, and a variety of job duties. Mention those relevant to the position you are seeking first, then others.
- Omit past salary, reasons for leaving former jobs, photograph, and personal pronouns when describing education or experience.
- Write and rewrite for clarity.

Format

- Be consistent with italics, boldface, and underlining.
- Make your resume uncluttered and easy to read.
- Use a big enough print font so it can be faxed if necessary.
- Arrange headings and dates to attract attention.
- Give an impression of a good use of space, neatness and orderliness.
- Use a good quality paper stock (quality bond) in white or a subdued color.
- Omit artsy or cutesy graphics.

Figure 5–8   General Resume Tips.

document. It's your decision as to what's included. Hopefully, your resume will clearly and unmistakably say to the employer, "Call me for a personal interview." General resume tips from many sources are found in Figure 5–8.

Do I Create More than One Resume?

Yes. It is best to suit the resume to the employer. While most resume sections won't need tinkering, the skill description section and the experience section most likely will. After fact-finding and studying the employer's ad or job announcement, you will want to emphasize certain skills and experiences prominently. Often, you'll find you overlooked or played down some skill or experience this particular employer is seeking. Each resume has to be specifically tailored. Consider the words in the job description in Figure 5–9 that indicate a need for specific candidate skills and abilities that should be part of a candidate's resume. See Figures 5–10 and 5–11 for completed resume examples. You will note that each differs in format style. In addition to closely proofreading your resume, ask objective friends for comments. Then ask yourself the questions in Figure 5–12.

Posting a Resume on the Internet

Some job candidates are reticent about publishing their resume on the Internet. Job boards may allow anonymous posting with selected contact information such as a cell telephone

---

XYZ LEARNING CENTERS

A dynamic expanding organization is seeking executives, site managers, and directors. Well prepared, highly motivated, and talented individuals to oversee our growing operations, districts, and learning centers are sought.

Successful job seekers should display leadership abilities in order to attract, recruit, hire, train, and supervise staff. They must possess marketing skills, encourage enrollment, retain families, interact with children, and promote our operation to community groups and the community at large. Experience in fiscal duties, budget management, and working with local, state, and federal regulatory entities is desired. Directors must have their degrees in Child Development, have administrative and supervisory coursework, and at least two years experience. Salary and benefits are commensurate with experience. To apply, contact us at: XYZ learning Centers, 145 Walnut Drive, Anyplace, NY 12345.

Figure 5–9 Job Description.

number or an e-mail address. This prevents an employer from discovering that the employee is searching for another job. Before posting your resume on the Internet, question the job board's policy on this issue if you wish to protect your privacy and security.

Resume Resources

Most college career and placement centers provide assistance and reference material valuable in resume preparation. You can also pay an expert to develop and type your resume, but few educational professionals do so except those seeking administrative or college/university jobs. A number of Web sites post early childhood resumes, including the Helpful Web Sites listed at the end of this chapter.

Contacting References

When you contact your references and alert them that they may be contacted, Kleiman (2002), an award-winning columnist and respected career specialist, has the following advice:

> *When the people you choose to be your references agree to do it, ask exactly what they plan to say. Listen carefully. And then tell them what you want them to say. You can't leave this to chance. And make sure they understand how important it is for you to get the job. When a potential employer asks you for references and you give them, call the people involved and tell them to expect a phone call. Tell them about the company and the job you're applying for—and once again, tell them what you want them to say.*

You may not feel this is appropriate advice if your reference is your former supervisor, college instructor, or religious advisor, but you could tell them about what particular skills, abilities, talents, and experiences are important to the employer. Some reference providers may prefer to be contacted only at their e-mail address, thereby protecting their privacy and safety.

Eva Wright
111 Cherry Lane
Anyplace, ID 80000
208–000–0000
evight@sbac.net

OBJECTIVE	A teaching position at the elementary school level
EDUCATION	Credential, Central University, Boxwood, Idaho Overall GPA: 3.531 B.A. degree in Education: Minor in Art, 6/05 Overall GPA: 3.52 Member, Central Honor Society Graduated with Distinction
EXPERIENCE	Student Teacher, Wood School, 1/05–Present Elementary School District, Cover, Idaho

EXPERIENCE (continued):

- Developed and implemented lesson plans for first grade class of 25 ethnically diverse students
- Designed and taught a 4-week thematic unit on Indian history and culture
- Participated in parent conferencing and Back-to-School Nights
- Organized field trips to the Nez Perce Native American Basket Weaving Center
- Scout Leader, City of Forest Glen, 6/04–8/04
- Developed and supervised an instructional program on scouting skills for children 7 to 12 years of age
- Assisted in a combination second grade class and tutored below-level reading students

SKILLS & INTERESTS

Bilingual in Spanish and English
Proficient in PC and Mac, Microsoft Word, MS Excel,
 MS PowerPoint, and Internet research
Play piano, interested in water color painting
Have traveled throughout the United States, Europe, Asia, and
 South America

OTHER EXPERIENCE

Camp swim instructor, 6/01–8/01

- Worked an average of 8 hours weekly with special education children 9 to 12 years of age at Oak Hill Camp, Creekbend, Idaho
- Vice President, Central University Student Association, 8/03–Present
- Volunteer, Sunday School Teacher (ages 6 to 8), 1/99–5/03

REFERENCES   Available upon request

Figure 5–10   Resume 1.

Lionnel Dixon
15 Main Street
Anytown, CA 90000
(444) 555–6666 Cell: (111) 222–3333
ldixon@server.net

AVAILABILITY

June 2005

TEACHING INTERESTS

Teacher: Early Childhood Education; Preschool Education

DEGREE

May 2005   Associate of Arts: Early Childhood Education
Community College of Oakland, Anytown, CA
GPA 3.85

EXPERIENCE

January–June 2005, Student Teacher
Community College of Oakland Child Development Center, Anytown, CA

Responsibilities
- Instructed three- and four-year-olds in a multicultural and multilingual classroom in an urban setting
- Created and presented developmentally appropriate activities in language arts, music, science, art, early number and measurement, motor development, and other subject areas
- Completed an observational study with an English language learning child and individualized his learning plan
- Documented children's progress using a commercial assessment instrument
- Coordinated theme learning activities
- Constructed a classroom puppet theater and performed with the supervising teacher
- Presented language activities that emphasized phonemic and print awareness
- Developed daily lesson plans and organized group times
- Arranged classroom learning centers to augment weekly projects
- Planned one parent meeting that focused on homemade games

July 1999–November 2004, Assistant Teacher
Maple Grove Preschool, Anytown, CA

Responsibilities
- Assisted teacher in planned activities and playground supervision
- Presented songs, games, stories, and prepared and led small group activities
- Created flannel board activities
- Introduced computer programs and supervised child computer use
- Worked productively with staff, children, and parents

RELATED ACTIVITIES

2003–present   Member, Anytown Association for the Education of Young Children
2003–2004   Hospital volunteer, Anytown Hospital, Anytown, CA

REFERENCES

Available upon request

Figure 5–11 Resume 2.

Is your resume ready for the tough scrutiny of a potential employer? It is if you can check each of the following qualifications.

- Are all of my resume statements supportive of my job objective?
- Is the organization of my experiences immediately obvious and meaningful?
- Can the reader scan all key points in seconds?
- Did I describe all of my experiences with convincing examples or details?
- Did I emphasize all of my most important experiences—the experiences closest to the job I want? Have I conveyed my personality and individual strengths and interests?
- Does my enthusiasm shine through?
- Did I delete all unnecessary words? Do action words begin sentences when possible?
- Are my margins at least one inch on all sides?
- Did I capitalize, underline, or type important headings and subheadings in bold letters?
- Is my grammar correct and consistently applied?
- Is there too much irrelevant information?
- Is there incomplete data?
- Is there exaggeration of responsibility?
- Is the resume outdated?
- Are there misleading statements?

Figure 5–12   Resume Checklist.

Resume Fraud

Steingold (1997) believes employers should alert job applicants to the consequences of resume fraud. It is a legal reason for immediate firing. Lying or giving incomplete information or using creative and deceptive writing falls into this category. Some employers ask for a signed accuracy statement on both application forms and resumes.

Common resume inaccuracies can occur in dates of employment, job titles, and accomplishments due to a person's memory (Ito, 2004). Technology has made it easier to verify information. A job screening service for employers can cost $10 to $20. It verifies an applicant's education and credentials. For $20 to $35 an applicant's background can be checked and for $5 a Social Security number can be verified (Ito). Yamanouchi (2004) states most resume errors result from inadvertent mistakes and incomplete information.

Summary

A cover letter and a resume can influence an employer. You have been given many hints and tips for developing a cover letter and resume. Many resume styles and formats are possible, but they include the same categories of basic information. They market your skills. Introductory lines on cover letters and your interview queries may, if successful, get your resume read and result in an interview. You were urged to compose carefully and give attention to details. Your fact-finding activities pay off when you attempt to match an employer's needs or desires with your resume. Resources concerning resume construction are mentioned, and you were alerted to the consequence of untrue statements.

**Helpful
Web Sites**

Career Net Graduate INET
http://www.careernet.com
designed for college students and grads; free resume listing

Skill Search
http://www.skillsearch.com
100 university alumni associations include resumes in a database (fees involved)

America's Job Bank
http://www.ajb.dni.us

4Work.com
http://www.4work.com

America's Employers
http://www.americasemployers.com

Best Jobs U.S.A.
http://www.bestjobsusa.com

Black Collegian
http://www.black-collegian.com

Career Cast
http://www.careercast.com

Career.com
http://www.career.com

CareerMart
http://www.careermart.com

CareerSite
http://www.careersite.com

Careers.wsj.com
http://www.careers.wsj.com

College Central
http://www.collegecentral.com

Hot Jobs.com
http://www.hotjobs.com

Best College Resumes
http://collegegrad.com

e Resumes and Resume Writing Services
http://www.eresumes.com

How to Write a Masterpiece of a Resume
http://www.rockportinstitute.com

Top 10 Resumes
http://careers.building.com

Resources

Anthony, R., & Roe, G. (2003). *102 Grade A resumes for teachers*. Hauppauge, NY: Barron's Educational Series.

Echaore-McDavid, S. (2001). *Career opportunities in education*. New York: Checkmark Books.

Enelow, W. S., & Kursmark, L. M. (2001). *Expert resumes for teachers and educators*. Indianapolis, IN: Jist Works.

Fry, R. (2002). *101 great resumes*. Franklin Lakes, NY: Career Press.

Jackson, T. (1981). *The perfect resume*. New York: Doubleday-Anchor Press.

Rosenberg, A. D., & Hizer, D. V. (2003). *The resume handbook: How to write outstanding resumes and cover letters for every situation*. Adams Media Corporation.

References

Anthony, R. & Roe, G. (2003). *101 Grade A resumes for teachers*. Hauppauge, NY: Barron's Educational Series.

Burmark, L. (2002). *Visual literacy: Learn to see, see to learn*. Alexandria, VA: Association for Supervision and Curriculum Development.

Ito, D. Quoted in Yamanouchi, K. (2004). Resumes getting more scrutiny. *The Idaho Statesman*, p. 2CB.

Kleiman, C. (2002). *Winning the job game: The new rules for finding and keeping the job you want*. Hoboken, NJ: John Wiley & Sons, Inc.

Knowdell, R. L. Quoted in the *San Jose Mercury News* (2002, Sunday November 17). The write approach: Good cover letters call attention to job seeker's skills. Author, p. 1PC.

Morkes, A. (Ed.). (2003). *Encyclopedia of careers and vocational guidance*. (Vol.1). Chicago, IL: Ferguson Publishing.

San Jose State University Career Center. (2003). *Job and internship guide 2003–2004*. Chicago, IL: Career Recruitment Media, Inc.

Stanley, C. (2002, November 17). Quoted in "Volunteer Effort," *San Jose Mercury News*, p. 1PC, Author.

Steingold, F. S. (1997). *The employer's legal handbook*. Berkeley, CA: Nolo Press.

Stern, L. (2005, January 17). The tough new job hunt. *Newsweek*, CXLV (3) 73–74.

Taylor, H. (2000, February). Technology: A key to the future. *Head Start Bulletin (66)* 1, 13–14.

Yamanouchi, K. (2004, July 25). Resumes getting more scrutiny. *The Idaho Statesman*, p. 2CB.

CHAPTER SIX

Applications and Interviews

*Courage is being scared to death
and saddling up anyway.*

John Wayne

Oops

Petra had many years of experience working with children, and she possessed considerable skills including an ability to create an interesting science curriculum. She was justly proud of instilling a sense of inquiry, observation, and recording in the preschoolers in her classes. She entered the interview room with confidence.

The interview went well until the end, when one interviewer asked "What do you think of Reggio Emilia?" Never having heard of it, Petra took a stab at an answer with "Sounds like an Italian restaurant."

QUESTIONS TO PONDER

1. As her own career manager, what should Petra have done?

2. Is it better to admit ignorance than to guess during an interview?

3. If Petra's remark was an attempt at humor, was it appropriate?

Applications

Application forms need to be clean, neat, legible, professional, and completed without misspellings or omissions. They reflect an applicant's honesty, history, and attention to detail. It is best to take job applications home. Typed applications are preferred by many employers. Applicants can ask to take the application home and return it later, rather than filling it out immediately. In case this isn't possible, it is wise to carry a personal organizer with names, addresses, telephone numbers of past employers and supervisors, in addition to dates of employment, former job titles, and descriptions of duties. You can also carry along a previously completed generic application form, like the one in the Appendix, to use as a reference.

Employers may be interested in why an applicant left former employment. Negative comments about a school, staff, working conditions, or supervisors give most employers cause for concern. A sincere answer doesn't have to be negative: "left to find a challenging position with more responsibilities," or "searching for an accredited program that allows greater professional growth potential," or "left to pursue further education" suffices.

Many job seekers underestimate the value of the appearance of their job application form. See Tips in the boxed area on the next page. It presents an image of the applicant to the employer; see Figure 6–1. Resumes can be attached, giving a professional aura to an application. A sample job application form with typical data requested is available for study in the Appendix.

Written Job Descriptions and Applications

A written job description should be obtained. If available, study it closely before your job application is completed, so that your application can show how your experience and training reflect the needs of the position.

Courts overwhelmingly have ruled that applicant misstatements on applications are excellent reasons for not hiring or for immediate firing. Employers who do not check a prospective employee's answers on an application or their references can be deemed by the courts to have negligently hired if that employee hurts or damages others on the job (Morton, 1997).

Most employers are knowledgeable about questions that legally should *not* be found on application forms. These are questions that have no relationship to an applicant's ability to perform job tasks and can include disabilities, marital status, living with partners, pregnancy plans or possible pregnancy, group affiliations, off-duty pursuits, hobbies, and height or weight.

"*When I filled out the application did I mention that I learned to walk at seven months, wrote my name at 18 months, and memorized the Declaration of Independence at age three?*"

Figure 6–1   The Job Application Form Presents an Image of the Applicant to the Employer.

TIPS FOR FILLING OUT APPLICATION FORMS

1. THE JOB APPLICATION IS A DEVICE FOR SELLING YOURSELF!
   Sometimes many people apply for the same position. The application is the single most important item that determines whether the applicant gets past the screening committee to the interview.

2. TAKE TIME TO DO IT RIGHT.
   An application that is dashed off at the last minute is usually incomplete and often looks careless.

3. MAKE IT LOOK GOOD AND EASY TO READ.
   The appearance, clearly identified categories, short concise sentences, effective use of spacing, capitalizing, underlining, italicizing, and numbering are all important parts of an attractive application.

Tests or essay questions can be part of an application form (see Figure 6–2.) Ask to fill out this application form at home. A sample application screening form is found in the Appendix. Screening forms are used by employers to narrow a field of candidates.

Express what you feel is best and right for children /students.
Share your values and teaching standards.

Finish the incomplete sentences below.

1. Children/students need _____

_____

_____

_____.

2. Children learn by _____

_____

_____

_____.

3. A teacher's most important task is _____

_____

_____

_____.

Figure 6–2 Sample Essay Questions.

4. My classroom will be _____

   _____

   _____

   _____.

5. In guiding child/student behavior I believe _____

   _____

   _____

   _____.

6. Parents are _____

   _____

   _____

   _____.

7. Which teacher characteristics are the most important? Choose 10 and number them in priority order from 1–extremely important to 10–important. If you wish, add characteristics to the list.

maturity	sensitive	relaxed
team player	sympathetic	self-contained
articulate	communicator	empathetic
sense of humor	caring	organized
enthusiastic	affectionate	creative
unselfish	risk taker	inquisitive
persistent	lifelong learner	resourceful
knowledgeable	industrious	independent
punctual	originator	open-minded
listener	confident	
honest	energetic	
opportunist	playful	

8. Explain your 10 choices as briefly as possible.

Figure 6–2   *(Continued)*

Interviews

Interviews vary as much as individual schools and centers. In general, an interview is simply a formal or informal question-and-answer session between the applicant and the prospective employer or employer representatives; see Figure 6–3. The interviewer tries to evaluate a

Figure 6–3 In an Interview, One Listens Closely.

candidate's appearance, manner, English usage, professionalism, and the quality of responses. The applicant's goal in the interview is to appear qualified in addition to being well-dressed, well-groomed, well-mannered, and well-spoken.

In early childhood interviews, particularly in large centers and in large publicly funded programs, you will probably be interviewed by a group comprised of supervisors, teachers, school board members, administrators, community representatives, and parents. The interview may last one to two hours. This type of interview may also take place for kindergarten, elementary, middle, and secondary school job candidates. When notified for an interview, you will find out where it is to be held, time of day, date, interview length, and sometimes you will receive an agenda and be told who will be present.

Portfolio—Yes or No?

If you developed a professional portfolio while in training, you probably spent considerable time on it. Since its purpose was to display your occupational competence and your training growth, you prepared it carefully and documented your progress by including items such as photographs and ratings by others. If the portfolio needs updating, do so. Portfolios are usually impressive, and most employers enjoy reviewing them. In fact, many students carry them to interviews and may be asked to leave them with the employer overnight or for a longer period. Ask if you can drop your portfolio off before an interview. Since it takes time to go through a portfolio, it is awkward to sit while an interviewer examines it. Interesting activities with children may capture an interviewer's attention. Some colleges recommend electronic portfolios that can be sent before interviews. Or, create a shortened version of a portfolio that contains a representative sampling.

It is prudent to review the portfolio to refresh your memory because an interviewer may ask about specific items.

The key to deciding to show your professional portfolio is its *quality* and whether it represents you in a professional manner. Some students prefer to discuss their competence orally without a portfolio. Others may feel their portfolio is dated, too bulky, or does not represent them sufficiently. Keep copies or photographs of original and irreplaceable portfolio items in case originals are lost or become damaged.

Interview Preparation

Interviewing skills can be acquired through the experience of being interviewed a number of times or through practice. Job counselors suggest that interviewing for a number of positions with different employers affords opportunities to evaluate your interviewing behaviors.

What are your feelings before an interview? Fear, negative self-talk, anxiety, apprehension, excitement, confidence, and a sense of adventure are mentioned most often. Slack (2004) believes that being articulate, confident, and clear about your skills and abilities is necessary. Quinn (2004) suggests that the key to successful interviewing is arriving at an interview feeling empowered and displaying vitality. Carlson (2004) points to self-esteem as critical. Visualizing good fortune before job interviews rated high with Wiseman (2003):

> *When faced with an important opportunity such as a job interview, sit quietly, close your eyes, and imagine yourself in the situation. Think about the surroundings . . . the people likely to be there . . . the sights and sounds you'll encounter. Imagine yourself lucky, fielding the questions with assurance and conviction. Focus on how it will feel to achieve your goals.*

Some experts recommend facing fears and thinking about worst case scenarios. The strategy is to then conquer and dispell fears.

1) List these "worst things."

2) Describe the consequences of each.

3) Let go, and remember that nothing will lead to physical injury even if some things may be embarrassing.

4) List how you would handle each consequence.

Both Carlson (2004) and Slack (2004) believe good interviewees sell their talents as a salesman sells his products. This is accomplished by providing detailed, convincing descriptions of how you overcame work problems or created solutions in past work situations. Slack believes that it is not what you did but how well you did it that matters. Later on, on the job, the reality of your talents will need to be displayed.

Kleiman (2004) believes that if you are not prepared to answer the request "Tell me about yourself" or the question "Why should I hire you rather than the next candidate?" it may be the end of your chance to get the job. This is the time to concisely convey (in 30 to 60 seconds) your interests, abilities, character, personality and what you are looking for (Karras, 2004). Karras also encourages job seekers to emphasize in opening comments their "soft skills" (defined as personal points of marketability) that define them as people rather than their job experience. He suggests the following as examples:

"I'm kind to my parents."

"My dog loves me."

"I help people across the street."

"I'm someone who really needs a job!"

You can probably think of better responses! But these should bring a smile.

Lindgren (2003) notes the best way to knock the socks off an interviewer is to know something about the place where you hope to work. Richter (2003) is convinced that job candidates do themselves a terrible disservice by not preparing more fully for important interviews. This includes knowing industry trends, innovations, the latest education fads, and current professional issues—in other words, being up on what's going on in the education field, and also with this particular employer.

Interviewers usually give an interviewee the opportunity to discuss the significance of education and the trained professional's ability to provide quality services to students and families. Practice how you would express this to an interviewer. Try to persuade your interviewer that you would be an invaluable addition to their school or center:

- Clearly convey career goals.
- Express your enthusiasm and intelligence by asking well-prepared questions. (Questions you have a real desire to know the answer to.)
- Reveal essential job traits such as poise, thoughtfulness, and the ability to speak well and listen carefully.

Appearance

Concentrating on your interview appearance and dress is important. Feeling well-dressed, attractive, and well-groomed boosts your spirits and your confidence. Morkes (2003) states that employers hire people whose appearance matches that expected of employees. Traditional, conservative, classic, and comfortable styles are usually preferred. Make-up and jewelry should be understated and subdued. Johansson (2004) identifies how to look professional at an interview without spending a lot of money. She suggests avoiding short skirts, low necklines, and tight clothes. Wear the best quality you can afford, and spend more on shoes and accessories. Choose subtle, sophisticated colors, or black or bright colors if they become you. Wear a few jewelry pieces that make you feel unique. Men's fashion, Johansson believes, is moving away from casual and toward a suit. Dockers and polo shirts are second best. Johansson recommends wearing the interview attire appropriate in the business world. Since clothing worn by staff members in early childhood centers is often casual, interview attire can be more informal. Interviews for elementary school, middle school, high school, and university and administrative positions are another matter.

Preparation Strategies

Consider the following interview preparation exercises.

1) Role-playing and using the following alternatives and questions may give critical insights concerning the image you project.
   While role-playing, play the part of an interviewer and look at yourself in the mirror. You become your own alter ego. Watch and monitor body language closely to gain insights.
   Eye contact—Do you look at yourself without staring or do you find yourself looking at the floor or somewhere other than the interviewer?
   Posture—Are you fairly relaxed with hands in your lap or are you slouched or stiff and uncomfortable? Try to be at ease. Practice relaxing. Deep inhaling should help you to relax. Morkes (2003) suggests relaxation techniques can quiet tense muscles and shaky hands.
   Body language—Learn to read some of the simple cues. Are your arms folded, or are you twisting a piece of paper? Relax and visualize yourself to be a warm, charming, positive, and unstressed person. Experiment with positions.

2) Audiotape recording—Record a mock interview and critique it.

3) Video recording—This is a very realistic medium. You can hear yourself and also view body language, gestures, posture, quality and tone of voice, eye contact or absence of it.

4) Visualization lets you shape your interview conduct mentally beforehand. This exercise is a mental rehearsal where you envision entering an interview room, imagine confidently fielding questions, asking your own questions, and tactfully concluding the interview and exiting.

5) A further preparational activity involves practicing answering the following common interview questions.
   a. Why do you want the position?
   b. What can you do for the employer?
   c. What kind of person are you?

Practice the answers to as many interview questions as possible. Figure 6–4 lists additional interview questions for a teaching position.

General

- What can you tell me about yourself?
- Why are you interested in this position?
- Why do you feel qualified for the job?
- What caused you to enter this field?
- What would you like to be doing five years from now?
- Why did you leave your last job?
- What is the minimum pay you will accept?
- What are your three greatest strengths and limitations for this job?
- Why should I hire you?
- How would you improve our operation?
- What is your greatest accomplishment to date?
- Of your past duties, which have you liked the best and least? Why?
- What is the ideal job for you?
- What attracts you to this center?
- What can you tell me about your experience?
- Do you have special training for this job?
- What kind of people appeal most and least to you as work associates?
- Could I see some samples of your work?
- Whom can we check as references?
- Do you prefer to work with two-, three-, four-, or five-year-olds? Why?
- What are your talents or skills?
- Can you describe how children best learn?
- What are important services that centers can provide for parents and a community?
- Can you describe a quality morning program for preschoolers?
- What is a typical morning schedule in your classroom?
- How could you provide young children with multicultural, nonsexist, developmental, creative, and physical development activities?
- What teaching strategies would you use during one of your planned activities?
- What do you feel promotes a spirit of teamwork between teachers working in the same classroom?
- What experiences have you had in working with parents?
- What guidance techniques work best for you?
- Briefly describe your philosophy concerning appropriate goals for an ideal early childhood center enrolling four-year-olds.
- How do you handle constructive criticism?
- Describe yourself as other teachers and supervisors have described you.
- What type of activities do you offer with great enthusiasm to children?
- Why did you choose a career working with young children and their families?
- Pick a theme and describe how you would offer that topic to young children.
- What well-known early childhood educator has made a lasting impression on you?
- Do you belong to any professional early childhood organizations or associations?
- In what way would you be an asset to our program?
- Describe events, program, activities you've developed or initiated that were important and successful for enrolled children.

Figure 6–4   Possible Interview Questions.

- Have you developed an IEP (Individual Education Plan) for a special needs child? What goals were accomplished?
- Could you briefly describe your own theory of education?
- What methods or strategies would you plan to increase English usage in a bilingual child?
- What do the words "developmentally appropriate" mean to you?
- What are the best ways for children to learn?
- What will be your most important goal in working with young children?
- What will young children need most from you as their teacher?
- What relationships do you expect to have with your attending children's parents?
- What specific talents do you bring to the teaching profession that will benefit students?
- How do you think students learn? How do you stimulate their thinking?
- How would you go about maintaining discipline and creating an environment conducive to learning?
- How prepared are you to work with diversity among learners?
- What resources have you used effectively in the classroom?
- What types of student assessment have you used? What were the results?
- How would you get parents involved in their child's learning?
- What is your philosophy of education?
- What are your greatest strengths? Is there any room for improvement?

Situational

- How would you react to a parent who angrily said, "This school's much too rigid!"?
- If your co-teacher does not help enough with the activity planning, what would you do?
- A child just said, "You're an ugly witch!" How would you deal with it?
- A child just kicked you; how would you handle it?
- A fellow teacher said, "The principal is so unfair!" What would you do?
- You spotted an abused child in your class. What should you do?
- If you could choose only three picture books for a group of four-year-olds, what would they be? Why?
- Tell us about a problem you solved at your last job.
- Imagine your classroom; describe what would go on between 9–12am.
- If you were choosing a center for your own child, what would you look for?
- Describe your best day at your last job.
- Give an example of how you organize your professional life to get everything done.
- If I were to encounter you three, six, and nine years from now, what would you be doing?
- To what extent are you willing to explore and share new ideas with others?
- In what ways have you integrated technology in your teaching?
- Describe any opportunities you have experienced to develop unit and/or interdisciplinary teaching.
- What can be learned from observations by supervisors and principals?
- What is the most important quality you have to offer children?
- Describe your special talents and skills.
- What professional accomplishment are you most proud of?
- What was your worst work experience? Why?
- How would your co-workers at your last job describe you?
- If a parent asked you to suggest a good children's book, what would you recommend? Why?

Figure 6–4   *(Continued)*

Don't forget to review your resume before your interview, especially if you made changes to it to match the employers' needs. Kleiman (2002) advises the following:

Study every item you so painstakingly put on your resume. Make sure you know every detail of every job you listed and when you worked there. You don't want to be taken by surprise when the interviewer asks, "When did you work at XYZ Auto Supply Store?" and you don't want to have to respond, "When did I do that?" Not in this job market.

When you are on top of what you've done, you can talk about it more easily. And talk is what you will have to do. Be prepared to tell anecdotes or stories about your past accomplishments.

You can make a good impression without words. Behaviors you may need to practice include facial expressions, tone of voice, rate of speech, and gestures. Speak slowly, distinctly, and as an equal to the interviewer(s). Exude confidence, energy, self-empowerment, but not arrogance or conceit.

Want to "ace" a job interview with an individual interviewer? R. Medich (2003) advises using what he calls insider tricks.

For the first 2 minutes of your interview

1) Arrive no more than 5 minutes early.
2) Remain standing while waiting for the interviewer to greet you.
3) If you have carried a briefcase, purse, or other carrier with papers, carry it in your left hand so the right is ready to shake a hand if offered.
4) If an assistant, receptionist, or secretary greets you, introduce yourself, and learn the assistant's name so when exiting you can say, "Thanks, Mary."
5) Choose the right seat. If the interviewer hasn't taken a seat, rest a hand on one of the chairs and ask, "Is this a good place for me to sit?"
6) Sit straight in the middle of the chair with one arm resting on the table.
7) When you are asked, "Tell me about yourself," prepare a "60-second commercial spot" that summarizes the responsibilities at your last job and the reason for pursuing this position. Don't go on at length.

Three rules for breaking the ice

8) Ask about photos or memorabilia on the interviewer's desk. Avoid assumptions about who is pictured. Instead, ask where a photo was taken.
9) Avoid jokes.
10) Don't talk about traffic, sports, or the weather.
11) If the interviewer asks more than once if you have any questions, create a diversion. Asking for a glass of water will give you time to remember your prepared questions.
12) If you draw a blank on a question, ask the interviewer to rephrase it, or say, "I'm not sure what you are asking. Which point would you like me to answer?"
13) If you catch yourself rambling, ask "Have I answered your question?"

Five deal breakers

14) Avoid excessive note taking. Jot down only key points to which you want to respond.
15) Never say anything you don't mean.

16) Avoid cliched responses. "I pay too much attention to detail" is the response of too many people when asked to describe a fault.

17) Not looking professional is a deal breaker.

18) Other deal breakers include not taking the interviewer's business card, if offered, and misspelling an interviewer's name on a follow-up thank you letter.

Although some of Medich's tips seem more appropriate to the business world, they may be helpful to education majors who intend to work for large companies or nonprofit organizations providing indirect services to children, families, or other businesses. During interviews, others will attempt to measure you. Your tact, maturity, courtesy, and professional knowledge give interviewers an idea of how you will represent their organization or center. For additional interview tips and hints, see Figure 6–5.

- Go to an interview alone.
- Shake hands firmly.
- Walk through the door smiling confidently. Scan all eyes in the room.
- Wait briefly to ascertain where you will sit.
- Take special note of interviewers' names and job titles.
- Do not volunteer something that can be construed as negative.
- Direct your conversation toward the interviewer's special enthusiasms and job needs if you know them.
- Be memorable.
- Listen attentively.
- When you don't understand, ask questions to clarify.
- Pause and think before you answer.
- Don't guess; admit you don't know.
- Mention the skills and interests you possess which best fit the job you are seeking.
- View the interview as a learning experience.
- Bring extra copies of your resume.
- Answer situational questions with "One of the things I might consider would be . . ."
- Avoid overeager discussions of what is in store for you in the next three to five years.
- Avoid tension in your voice.
- Ideally, salary isn't discussed before a firm job offer is in hand.
- When asked about weaknesses, mention those that are possible strengths, e.g. "I'm hard on myself when. . . ."
- End on a cordial note.
- Avoid vagueness; make your point and move on.
- Be assertive rather than pushy.
- Sleep well the night before.
- A fast heartbeat is natural; ignore it.
- Be alert.
- Do not interrupt.
- Avoid becoming defensive.

Figure 6–5 Interview Tips.

"I see your experience is limited, but I admire the way you've given the impression that you're an old pro!"

Figure 6–6   Humor Is a Powerful Communication Tool When Used Appropriately.

Dean (2004) suggests adding a touch of humor (rather than a joke) to an interview might work very well. He believes humor is a powerful communication tool when used appropriately to defuse prickly situations with clients, co-workers, and/or family; see Figure 6–6. A shared laugh improves relationships. To some prospective employers humor can indicate a creative mind and being good-natured. It may also indicate good health and stability.

The *San Jose Mercury News* (2002) points out that job seekers should realize employers are looking for team players, not complainers. You gain little if you degrade a former employer or past co-workers. If anything, unnecessary criticism is a red flag. Many times, if a number of candidates are interviewing for the same position, interviewers will take notes. They may also fill out checklists or rating forms immediately following your departure. It is an advantage to be memorable, especially as a dedicated professional who works well with others. Don't let their note taking distract you.

Most interviewers are careful not to ask illegal, discriminatory questions such as those listed in Figure 6–7. Peppard (2003) suggests that if you are asked an inappropriate or invasive question, dodge it with a positive and professional tone and draw the conversation back to your skills and experience. For example, when asked about your own child care arrangements, respond with "I'm happy to discuss my qualifications and experience and provide references citing my work attendance record."

It is expected that you will want to ask questions. Time is usually provided near the end of the interview. Read over your notes beforehand; they will help jog your memory. It is best to keep your list of questions short. Here are some questions interviewees ask:

- Is there anything else I can tell you about my qualifications?
- How soon will I know the outcome of this interview?
- Do you notify candidates by mail or with a telephone call?
- Is there any additional information you would like me to provide?

Have you

1) had a serious medical condition or disease in your lifetime?

2) been hospitalized?

3) seen a mental health professional?

4) had many absences at work or school because of a health problem?

5) taken prescription drugs?

6) filed for Worker's Compensation Insurance?

7) been married?

8) lived in the United States your entire life?

9) applied for U.S. citizenship?

10) attended church frequently?

11) ever weighed over 150 pounds?

12) a height measurement under 5'1"?

13) applied for Social Security benefits?

14) had pregnancies?

15) been arrested?

16) visited relatives who lived in another country?

17) you listed all clubs, associations, societies, and lodges to which you belong?

18) had problems finding someone to watch your children when you are at work?

Figure 6–7 Questions Prohibited by the *Americans with Disabilities Act.*

Ask questions you truly want an answer to! Kleiman (2003) believes quickly pulling out a short list might favorably impress interviewers. Note cards can also be reviewed quickly, if you've prepared them and have them handy.

Male Job Seekers

Although highly sought and in short supply, male job applicants may face suspicion and a pervasive belief that men are less able to care for and educate young children. Fortunately, in most instances, male early childhood educators will be eagerly welcomed and recruited. Males are often valued as assets who may add balance to an all female staff, provide male role modeling, offer new points of view, use new techniques and skills, and possess unique male-related teaching strengths and strategies.

At job interviews, males will usually probe for specific information about employer's attitudes and policies concerning teacher-child physical contact and toilet supervision in early childhood classrooms. Sargent (2002) points out that men must sometimes employ different teaching tactics because limits may be placed upon them in some school situations. He notes that actions considered natural for female staff may be evaluated differently for males. One of the conclusions Sargent draws from his research on a small group of employed male teachers is that men and women do not necessarily have different styles of teaching.

Post-Interview Analysis

After an interview, assess your conduct and performance. Take note of your strengths and possible growth areas. You can learn immeasurably from the interview experience and become more polished and relaxed during succeeding interviews. A post-interview questionnaire is provided in Figure 6–8. Some personnel departments will share interview ratings with applicants; this can be a valuable aid.

1) Was I relaxed, confident?
2) Did I control my part of the interview with good, solid answers?
3) Did I listen and pause thoughtfully before answering?
4) Was my knowledge of the center/agency adequate?
5) Was my personal appearance appropriate? Was I self-confidant?
6) Were my remarks clear and concise?
7) Did I jump to answer questions too quickly?
8) Was I convincing?
9) Did I relate the prospective job to past jobs or skills used in a previous job?
10) During the interview, did nervousness or tension immobilize me?
11) Was I able to justify my background in terms of the job requirements?
12) Did I demonstrate that I really wanted the job?
13) Did I do well overall?
14) List the areas that went well.

    a. _____   b. _____

    c. _____   d. _____

15) Did I forget to mention anything about my background that would have helped me?
16) Did I come on too strong? Did I not come across strong enough?
17) Did I have all the information I needed about the job?
18) Did I neglect to ask the right questions? What, if anything, did I leave out?
19) Am I clear on the duties and responsibilities of the job?
20) Where did I make the biggest mistake during the interview?
21) Where did I appear to make the most favorable impression?
22) Did I talk too much? Did I talk too little?
23) List the interviewing skills that need improvement.

    a. _____

    b. _____

    c. _____

    d. _____

Figure 6–8   Post-Interview Questionnaire.

Other Possible Screening Techniques Employers Use

In addition to a first interview, other screening techniques may be designed by a prospective employer. These can include second interviews, peer or co-worker interviews after an applicant has observed their classroom, professional portfolio review, demonstration or participation teaching, writing samples, and take-home essay questions or essay questions completed at the job site.

A new twist in interviewing includes showing the job applicants a series of classroom video scenes and asking for an applicant's analysis of whether the scene reflected quality and/or professional teaching practices. Some scenes may be stopped during play and the applicant asked to describe how the situation should be handled or how teacher actions could promote student's growth and development. Applicants may also be asked if their comments can be recorded. To prepare for this type of interview job seekers need to express themselves in a confident, articulate manner and provide the reasoning behind their decisions. Applicants' comments about the video scenes should take into account that the scenes are discrete episodes that may have followed actions or events not in that portion of the video viewed. Teacher actions in the video may also be based upon the viewed teacher's intimate knowledge of a particular child's unique and individual developmental needs, which an applicant may not be able to consider in discussion.

McDorman (2004) identifies two "sneaky tricks." The first may seem like small talk during or immediately after an interview. This trick involves the interviewer making a negative comment about a candidate's previous employer, supervisor, or co-worker, such as "I've heard that teacher has a questionable reputation," or "I've heard many complaints about that employer." Do not fall into the trap of also being negative. The second trick is the question "What do you do for fun?" This may not appear to have any relationship to job skills, but probes your socializing ability. McDorman suggests giving a response that displays you can work well with others.

Stern (2005) notes that interview brain teasers such as "How would you test a salt shaker?" and "Why might your best friend get angry with you?" are asked in some employment sectors. Stern recommends answering but avoiding a fast answer or getting flustered because there is no one right answer to these open-ended brainteasers.

After the Interview Thank-You Letter

A brief note, like the one in Figure 6–9, emphasizes your desire to work for the employer and allows another chance to market skills and abilities. Even if a job isn't offered, you can still make a favorable impression and may be contacted if there is another opening. You'll have a definite advantage if no other competing candidate sends one! Again, edit what you send so that it is perfect. Try your hand at writing a thank-you that is less businesslike and softer in tone than Figure 6–9.

After a Job Offer

If you receive a second interview, an oral job offer, or an employment letter, there should be a statement asking if you have any additional questions before formally accepting the employer's offer. This is the time when you are in the strongest negotiating position

```
                                                   Lila Hunter
                                                   14 West Ave.
                                                   Anytown, CA 95101

Mrs. Sue Williams
Director
Bird Hollow Preschool
12 Main Street
Anytown, CA 95101

Dear Mrs. Williams,
     This is to express my appreciation for your courtesy in granting me an interview
yesterday for the position of Early Childhood Teacher.
     I am very interested in this position and feel confident that my training and
experience will enable me to competently perform the duties which you described. I
feel particularly qualified to handle the curriculum planning.
     I look forward to hearing from you.

Sincerely,


Lila Hunter
```

Figure 6–9   Interview Follow-Up Letter.

(Whitaker & Austin, 2003). Hopefully, you reviewed the employer's salary schedule and you have knowledge of the salary range. If not, some employers will ask the prospective employee to name a figure. Be strong and ask for above what you think you'll be able to get.

Many factors can help you to determine the level of salary that feels acceptable. Web sites such as http://www.salary.com will provide an estimate of pay for any job. You can receive a free basic salary report or, for a fee, a more detailed one. Keeping career and personal life in balance may mean more than getting the salary you know you deserve. If the job serves a purpose, moves along career goals, or is a step in your career direction, salary can be secondary. Many individuals have taken a low-paying job just to learn a particular skill or to learn how a business operates.

Slack (2004) suggests viewing yourself as a product for sale to the highest bidder. He believes that negotiating for pay and benefits scares many job seekers because they fear the job offer will be withdrawn. According to Slack, a resource development specialist, this rarely happens. He reminds job seekers that after the selection process most employers have made a final decision. Before negotiating salary, Slack warns that it's important to receive a *written* offer, which makes an offer *legitimate*. View negotiation as a way to get a raise before you are actually employed; it is well worth the effort.

Think of employers as having a need, seeking help, or looking to have a problem(s) solved with a new hire. Usually something in the interview has given them the idea that their chosen candidate could succeed in these areas. Almost everything about a job can be negotiated including salary, benefits, vacation days, sign-on bonuses, and a worker's particular desires such as starting time (when the applicant depends on public transit or needs certain necessary days off). Public sector employers may have a very narrow range of salary they can offer, but large companies and private businesses, Slack points out, are another matter. When negotiating salary, Garber (2004) suggests that you need to know the average salary in the area for the same job, the national average, and costs of rent or housing.

Slack (2004) mentions that there is a tendency apparent in the marketplace for women to get lower pay than men who have the same job position. He conjectures this may be attributed to women's hesitation to negotiate.

Employers prefer to know the salary and the benefits received at an applicant's last place of employment. They sometimes probe by asking, "What was your salary in your last position?" or "What salary are you seeking?" An applicant can dodge the second request by saying, "I would like to hear more about job specifics and the work environment before I come up with a figure." The first question could be answered, "While we are talking about salary, what is your salary range for this position?" Many employers clearly state a salary figure on their job announcements; if so, negotiation may not be appropriate.

Employment Contracts

A few private schools and centers may ask an applicant to sign an employment contract that ensures a term of employment, often one year. Contracts usually specify termination procedures, the scope of employee duties, compensation, a "competing" covenant clause, and a confidential information section. Faucher (2002) suggests that a prospective employee thoroughly understand these legal documents before signing. Signing gives you "independent contractor tax status." You become a self-employed worker. Of particular interest in contract work is what happens if you are forced to move, exactly what work duties are required, and at what time of the day or week you must work. Kleiman (2002) advises an employment contract doesn't have to be signed right away, even if it is a condition of employment. She urges consulting an employment lawyer.

Checking Credibility and Eligibility

Employers routinely check references, verify credentials, and contact former employers. Before verification begins, an employer may require photocopies or certified copies of documents such as degrees, certificates, clearances, fingerprints, criminal background checks, and credentials. All employees are required to prove eligibility to work in the United States. You can be required to sign a declaration that you have no prior criminal arrests or charges relating to child sexual abuse. Interviewers may not ask questions regarding an applicant's health or medical history, and they avoid questions violating the *Americans With Disabilities Act* (ADA), but a job offer can be conditional on the applicant's passing a medical exam. Some employers checking references ask former employers if they would rehire the person.

Summary

Application forms may eliminate you immediately, if the application is not complete, neat, accurate, and detailed. Typed applications are preferred. You can prepare yourself by filling out an application form beforehand and taking it with you when you visit possible places of employment, or by taking a personal organizer with dates and addresses. Your updated professional portfolio will be valuable now. Many people condense their portfolio and add photos or copies so that original items are secure. Some candidates develop electronic portfolios. These can be submitted with resumes prior to interviews or at interviews. Prepare and practice your interview skills. Many tips and hints were provided. Seeing an interview as a learning experience is prudent. Help was offered on appropriate interview questions to ask at an interview, and you were urged to negotiate salary and benefits when possible.

Helpful Web Sites

America's Career InfoNet
http://www.acinet.org
supplies salary ranges and personalized reports

Career Builder
http://www.careerbuilder
use key word "interviewing techniques"

Hoover's Online
http://www.hoovers.com
research large companies

Sharing Board for Males in Early Childhood Education
http://www.earlychildhood.com
provides a message board for discussion

U.S. Department of Labor, Bureau of Labor Statistics
http://www.bls.gov
detailed job descriptions

Resources

Adams, B. (2001). *The everything job interview book: Answer the toughest job interview questions with confidence.* Avon, MA: Adams Media Corporation.

American Association for Employment in Education. (2002). *Educator supply and demand in the United States: 2001 research report.* Columbus, OH: Author.

Babcock, L., & Laschever, S. (2003). *Women don't ask: Negotiation and the gender divide.* Princeton, NJ: Princeton University Press.

Canfield, J. (1998). *How to build high self-esteem.* Niles, IL: Nightingale-Conant Corp.

Education Research Service. (2002). Salaries paid professional personnel in public schools, 2001, 2002, Part 2. *National survey of salaries and wages in public schools.* Arlington, VA: Author.

Haberman, M. (1995). *Star teachers of children in poverty.* West Lafayette, IN: Kappa Delta Pi.

References

Carlson, T. (2004, June). The graduation advice I never got ... but wish I had. *Reader's Digest,* pp. 153–156.

Dean, S. (2004, September). The last laugh. *Reader's Digest,* pp. 100–107.

Faucher, R. (2002, May 26). Learn what to look for when signing an employee contract. *The Idaho Statesman*, p. 3B.

Garber, R. (2004, August 15). How to negotiate your first salary: Play it smart. *The Idaho Statesman*, p. CB1.

Johansson, C. (2004, August 29). Longer skirts and suits are the trend for looking all business: The new business fashion hints at femininity but shuns sexiness. *The Idaho Statesman*, p. CB1.

Karras, J., Quoted in Kleiman, C. (2004, September 26). How to answer "Tell me about yourself." *The Idaho Statesman*, p. CB1.

Kleiman, C. (2002). *Winning the job game: The new rules for finding and keeping the job you want*. Hoboken, NJ: John Wiley and Sons, Inc.

Kleiman, C. (2004, September 26). How to answer "Tell me about yourself." *The Idaho Statesman*, p. CB1.

Lindgren, A. (2003, August 31). Research the key to successful interviews, CEO says. *The Idaho Statesman*, p. 2CB.

McDorman, J. (2004, September 15). Job interviewers' sneaky tricks. *Bottom Line. 25* (18) 5.

McMullen, M. B., Alat, K., Buldu, M., & Lash, M. (2004, March). A snapshot of N.A.E.Y.C.'s preschool professionals through the lens of quality. *Young Children. 59* (2) 87–92.

Medich, R. (2003, May). Ace that job interview: 18 insider tricks. *Bottom Line. 24* (9) 11.

Morkes, A. (Ed.). (2003). *Encyclopedia of careers and vocational guidance*. (Vol. 1). Chicago, IL: Ferguson Publishing.

Morton, J. (1997, June 17). *Fundamentals of personnel law for managers and supervisors*. SkillPath Seminar, Boise, ID.

Peppard, K. (2003, March 4). Illegal or just inappropriate? Know your rights when it comes to interview questions. AOL Careers and Work. Retrieved April 6, 2003 from http://interview.wworkplace.aol .monster.com/articles/illegalqs.

Quinn, G. (2004, May 29). Living in the spiritual zone. [Presentation.] Sun Valley Mountain Wellness Festival, 7th Annual Conference. Ketchum, ID.

Richter, S. Quoted in Lindgren, A. (2003, Sunday August 31). Research the key to successful interviews, CEO says. *The Idaho Statesman*, p. 2CB.

San Jose Mercury News. (2002, November 17). No comment, p. 1PC.

Sargent, B. (2002, November). Under glass: Conversations with men in early childhood education. *Young Children. 57* (6) 22–30.

Slack, J. (2004, February 10). How to successfully negotiate your next job contract—The "real" art of the deal. *Mercury News Career Fair*. Santa Clara, CA.

Stern, L. (2005, January 17). The tough new job market. *Newsweek*, CXLV (3) 73–74.

Whitaker, L., & Austin, E. (2003, September 28). Don't ask about your salary until an offer is made. *The Idaho Statesman*, p. 1CB.

Wiseman, R. (2003, October). Change your luck, change your life: Anyone can do it. *Bottom Line, 24* (20) 1.

CHAPTER SEVEN

Workplace Skills

*Even if you're on the right
track, you'll get run over
if you just sit there.*

Will Rogers

New to the Community

Claire, an educator, was new to the area and curious about the neighborhood shopping center schools. She noticed these schools on the Saturday she was scouting for housing. In a three-block radius, she found signs for an art school, music school, children's gym, a "clayground" (a school), swim school, tennis school, and a children's computer center. They all seemed to be successful enterprises with children coming and going. She didn't feel like she fit in with most of the neighborhood population. They were affluent professionals (new and luxury cars), ethnically diverse, and many who walked by her were speaking in another language. Welcome to Silicon Valley, she thought. Her husband's company had transferred them, and considering housing costs she knew she would have to seek work.

QUESTIONS TO PONDER

1. When Claire takes a position in this area, which of her acquired skills are likely to be appreciated by parents?

2. What are the chances that elementary schools in this area will be struggling to meet state grade performance standards in lower elementary school classes?

3. No matter where Claire works, what three workplace skills will be most important?

Entering the Workforce

Many well-managed educational facilities provide an orientation that aids a new worker's transition into the job. Since teachers have many job functions, new teachers usually target some job functions first. Most often protecting child health and safety is a top priority, and other job priorities follow. The National Research Council (2002) describes the challenges that graduating teachers face when they enter the workforce:

> *Even teachers who attend institutions that provide a strong preparation for teaching face major challenges after they graduate. They need to make the transition from a world dominated primarily by college courses, with only some supervised teaching experiences, to a world in which they are the teachers; hence they face the challenge of transferring what they have learned.*
>
> *People often need help in order to use relevant knowledge that they have acquired, and they usually need feedback and reflection so they can try out and adapt their previously acquired skills and knowledge in new environments.*

This kind of challenge was also faced in your student teaching classes. New employment may not offer you any supportive assistance! If an orientation isn't provided by your employer, you may be on your own from the first day.

Probation and Trial Periods

Some employers are required to have a probationary period for new employees. If so, the new workers are informed, and their work is evaluated over a specified period of time. If a probationary employee exhibits satisfactory performance, then he or she is retained. Morkes (2003) notes that probationary employees have better protection against being let go or fired than workers whose employer does not offer probationary status. Their employment is "at will," meaning their employer may dismiss them without following any formal procedure. This will be discussed further in Chapter Nine.

Ethical Conduct

The National Association for the Education of Young Children initially approved a *Code of Ethical Conduct and Statement of Commitment* in 1989. It serves as a guide for the professional decisions early childhood educators make on a daily basis. Stephanie Feeney and Kenneth Kipnis (1989) conducted extensive research and prepared the original draft code. A revised edition is available in a brochure from NAEYC (http://www.naeyc.org) and is widely recognized in early childhood education as professional practice. The NAEYC's code section that deals with ethical responsibilities to colleagues is presented in Figure 7–1. Having character involves working with high personal standards of honesty and dependability (Morkes, 2003).

Worker Skills

Most employees don't get dismissed because of work performance but rather because of their inability to get along with others—their social and communicative relationships. Figure 7–2 displays the skills that employers rate as important. Note that interpersonal skills are given the highest priority. So let's discuss skills that enhance personal relationships.

Section III: Ethical responsibilities to colleagues.

In a caring, cooperative workplace, human dignity is respected, professional satisfaction is promoted, and positive relationships are modeled. Based upon our core values, our primary responsibility in this arena is to establish and maintain settings and relationships that support productive work and meet professional needs. The same ideals that apply to children are inherent in our responsibilities to adults.

A—Responsibilities to co-workers
Ideals:

I-3A.1—To establish and maintain relationships of respect, trust, and cooperation with co-workers

I-3A.2—To share resources and information with co-workers

I-3A.3—To support co-workers in meeting their professional needs and in their professional development

I-3A.4—To accord co-workers due recognition of professional achivement

Principles:

P-3A.1—When we have a concern about the professional behavior of a co-worker, we shall first let that person know of our concern, in a way that shows respect for personal dignity and for the diversity to be found among staff members, and then attempt to resolve the matter collegially

P-3A.2—We shall exercise care in expressing views regarding the personal attributes or professional conduct of co-workers. Statements should be based on firsthand knowledge and relevant to the interests of children and programs

B—Responsibilities to employers
Ideals:

I-3B.1—To assist the program in providing the highest quality of service

I-3B.2—To do nothing that diminishes the reputation of the program in which we work unless it is violating laws and regulations designed to protect children or the provisions of this Code.

Principles:

P-3B.1—When we do not agree with program policies, we shall first attempt to effect change through constructive action within the organization.

P-3B.2—We shall speak or act on behalf of an organization only when authorized. We shall take care to acknowledge when we are speaking for the organization and when we are expressing a personal judgment.

P-3B.3—We shall not violate laws or regulations designed to protect children and shall take appropriate action consistent with this Code when aware of such violations.

C—Responsibilities to employees
Ideals:

I-3C.1—To promote policies and working conditions that foster mutual respect, competence, well-being, and positive self-esteem in staff members

I-3C.2—To create a climate of trust and candor that will enable staff to speak and act in the best interests of children, families, and the field of early childhood care and education

I-3C.3—To strive to secure equitable compensation (salary and benefits) for those who work with or on behalf of young children

Principles:

P-3C.1—In decisions concerning children and programs, we shall appropriately utilize the education, training, experience, and expertise of staff members.

P-3C.2—We shall provide staff members with safe and supportive working conditions that permit them to carry out their responsibilities, timely and non-threatening evaluation procedures, written grievance procedures, constructive feedback, and opportunities for continuing professional development and advancement.

P-3C.3—We shall develop and maintain comprehensive written personnel policies that define program standards and, when applicable, that specify the extent to which employees are accountable for their conduct outside the workplace. These policies shall be given to new staff members and shall be available for review by all staff members

P-3C.4—Employees who do not meet program standards shall be informed of areas of concern and, when possible, assisted in improving their performance

Figure 7–1   Ethical Responsibilities to Colleagues.

P-3C.5—Employees who are dismissed shall be informed of the reasons for their termination. When a dismissal is for cause, justification must be based on evidence of inadequate or inappropriate behavior that is accurately documented, current, and available for the employee to review.

P-3C.6—In making evaluations and recommendations, judgments shall be based on fact and relevant to the interests of children and programs.

P-3C.7—Hiring and promotion shall be based solely on a person's record of accomplishment and ability to carry out the responsibilities of the position.

P-3C.8—In hiring, promotion, and provision of training, we shall not participate in any form of discrimination based on race, ethnicity, religion, gender, national origin, culture, disability, age, or sexual preference. We shall be familiar with and observe laws and regulations that pertain to employment discrimination.

Source: NAEYC. 1998. Position statement. *Code of Ethical Conduct and Statement of Commitment.* Washington, DC: Brochure.

Figure 7–1 *(Continued)*

Employers rate the importance of candidate qualities/skills	
(5-point scale, where 1 = not important and 5 = extremely important)	
Communication skills (written and verbal)	4.7
Honesty/integrity	4.7
Interpersonal skills (relates well to others)	4.5
Strong work ethic	4.5
Teamwork skills (works well with others)	4.5
Analytical skills	4.4
Motivation/initiative	4.4
Flexibility/adaptability	4.3
Computer skills	4.2
Detail-oriented	4.1
Leadership skills	4.0
Organizational skills	4.0

Figure 7–2 Skills Employers Want.

Reprinted from *Job Outlook 2005,* with the permission of National Association of Colleges and Employers, copyright holder.

Active Listening

A good listener maintains eye contact, doesn't interrupt, maintains focus by facial, verbal, and body signals to the speaker. Nodding "yes, oh, okay, uh-huh, really," or leaning in toward the speaker lets the speaker know that you are listening. We all seek out and remember good listeners. They are the ones who affirm that our thoughts are important. Listening ability is an important job skill. Educators focus daily on what children say; in fact, they try to give total attention to them.

In adult-to-adult staff conversations when we use focused listening we have a better understanding of the speaker's intent, feelings, and ideas. Close listening acknowledges the speaker, validates the speaker, and creates a feeling of connection. Good listeners are great at building relationships. Shafir (2003) believes when we listen to another's story, we overcome our internal distractions, which includes self talk, judgment, bias, and getting to our own agenda.

Clarifying Questions

Co-workers who are not sure of another's message should ask for clarification.

What you are saying is . . .

You are saying that . . . , right?

What do you mean by. . . ?

This strategy is good for catching your listening errors, or may prevent jumping to conclusions.

Receiving Constructive Criticism or Other Comments

Feedback of your job performance may be difficult to take without an emotional response. If it is perceived as a negative comment or a criticism, it can be difficult to remain calm. The best way to handle such a situation is to pause, breathe, and answer slowly and deliberately. Ask for specific examples, and squelch defensive responses. If your emotions are high, ask for time to think about it. "I appreciate your feedback or concern. Can this be discussed later after I've thought it over?" Then formulate a response. It is best to be open, pleasant, neutral, and relaxed for the follow-up discussion.

Not Comparing Yourself with Others

Comparing yourself with others is destructive to your self-esteem. You've heard of apples and oranges; it's the same with people and people! Remember you are a unique and one-of-a-kind individual. Think positively.

Victim or Whiner

Victims and whiners can be found in many workplaces. Someone else causes most of their problems, they will tell you. It is always "poor me." Stick around the productive, dedicated, professionals who are still entranced with the fun, joy, and challenge of their work. Look for solutions rather than blame. Robin (2003) suggests the best way to deal with disgruntled co-workers is staying out of the fray. She goes on to recommend the following:

"Remember that they're stuck in the blame frame—

they're focused on a problem."

"You don't want to argue with them. They're trying to

drag you into their misery."

"At the very least, they may just want to hear some

acknowledgment of their feelings."

"Sometimes it works to just say, 'That's awful'"
"Sometimes they'll solve it for themselves, if you acknowledge there's a problem."

Dougherty (2004) suggests using written, e-mail, and telephone messages when possible in communicating with co-workers who aggravate. When meetings are unavoidable, he believes you should say less. Workplace resentments, rivalries, and conflict are often the result of an individual's innate inability to stop talking.

Combating Stress

Breathe, enjoy the wonder of children, see the humor in everyday situations. Use relaxation techniques and focus on healthy living, including nutrition, exercise, and rest.

Analyzing Your Communication Style

So much has been written about assertive versus passive or aggressive behavior. Norma Carr-Ruffino (1997), the author of *The Promotable Woman*, offers nonverbal comparisons in Figure 7–3. Find your style. Often others "read" your nonverbal signals instead of your words.

Nonassertive Behavior	Assertive Behavior	Aggressive Behavior
Facial Smiling often, broadly; relatively animated, expressive	Relatively impassive; less smiling	Tight with anger; jaw and brow tense; sneering or scornful; patronizing, come-on, smiling, manipulative
Voice tone Relatively expressive, sometimes apologetic, tentative, meek, prissy	Relatively impassive, objective, self-confident, firm, decisive	Angry, sarcastic, sneering flippant, nagging, scolding, or scornful; extremely loud or menacingly low
Voice pitch High, little-girl quality	Relatively low, forceful	Menacingly low or yelling
Hands Playing with hair; nervous; folded in lap primly	Still or purposeful, smooth movements; hands at sides	On one or both hips; pointing or shaking finger
Eyes Cast downward: little contact while speaking; watching speaker intently; avoiding direct contact	Frequent eye contact while talking, steady, firm; casual, relaxed observation while another is talking	Staring; angry, challenging; or cold, expressionless

Figure 7–3 Nonverbal Behaviors and the Range of Assertion.

Nonassertive Behavior	Assertive Behavior	Aggressive Behavior
Head Titled, moving from side to side, up and down; ducked	Still, straight	Stiff, erect
Posture Slumped, stooped, but tense; or ramrod tense, at attention, nervous	Almost military but relaxed; head and spine straight; feet slightly apart, well-grounded; arms at sides	Tense—knees locked; feet spread widely apart, firmly planted; fists clenched
Positions Hesitantly standing, sitting forward tensely, knees and feet together; arms folded tightly in lap; other balanced, tense positions; vigilant	Asymmetrical, expansive positions: arms on sides of chair, sometimes leaning to one side in relaxed way; leaning back, clasping hands behind neck; males: turning chair around and straddling it or putting feet on desk; casually turning one's back on another to get something	Tensely, forcefully leaning forward; pointing fingers; pounding desk
Movements Small, controlled, tense; covering face with hand; fiddling with an object; rhythmic shaking of leg/foot	Expansive, relaxed, free; pressing fingertips together in a steeple; free of nervous mannerisms	Waving arms angrily; closely towering over another; invading another's personal territory

Figure 7–3   *(Continued)*

Permission of Career Press Inc.

Apologizing

This may be a lost art. Apologies can soothe staff relationships. Here are some good apology hints.

Hints for making a good apology:

- Look someone in the eye.
- State what the apologizer did and that it was wrong.
  "I was late and that caused other staff to cover for me."

- State how this hurt or disappointed.
  "I've hurt my image of dependability."
- Present an idea to prevent it from recurring, and suggest what repair might be done.
  "I plan to take another route to work and start earlier. I'll stay late today and help parents taking children home. I'll offer an apology for not being here on time."

Being Resilient

Resiliency can be described as going with the flow, thriving under pressure, and keeping on task. Webster's dictionary adds that resiliency is rapid recovery from change, misfortune, or illness, and also buoyancy and elasticity. Noble (2004) defines resiliency as the ability to bounce back from difficulties, to manage pressure, and to adapt quickly to perform your work at a high level. She notes in a recent survey that only 52 percent of her survey sample believed they were able to manage the pressures of their job. Many businesses are attempting to train employees to be more resilient by promoting healthy lifestyles. This includes habits, diets, and giving time to yourself. Teachers often build fun and relaxation into their daily activities to reduce their own and students' stress. Given a chance, many of us would choose work partners that display resilience.

What a New Employee Needs to Know

Newly hired workers should know what most staff members look for and appreciate in fellow staff members. Read the tips in the boxed area on page 146.

Additional Advice from Other Sources

Based on her input from a number of employers, Kleiman (2002) suggests that employers want new hires to be productive from the first day. She believes they also want hard workers and problem solvers who are loyal, confident, committed to their jobs, eager to learn, easy to get along with, ambitious but not too ambitious, and flexible about their assignments.

Parrish-Porter (2003) shares her advice concerning job skills and career growth. Her Giant Steps to Success follow:

- Control your own public relations. Every time you speak, think of it as a press conference.
- Learn to experience criticism. Make sure you understand the feedback you are given, and act to improve accordingly. Don't take it personally.
- Be confident. Learn to act even in times of great uncertainty. This will inspire others to do the same.
- Be willing to step up to challenges. Do what it takes to deliver. Don't be afraid to ask for help when you need it.
- Establish a strong support network, both within and outside of your work site. Reach out and be open to interacting with a diverse array of people, including people who don't look like you.
- Don't be afraid to step out of your comfort zone.
- Keep a sense of humor. It will serve you well along the way.
- Stay focused on delivering results to your employer (business).
- Find your true passion. (Perfect teaching skills with the passionate conviction that the work you're doing is a contribution to children's lives.)

TIPS FOR NEW EMPLOYEES

- Park your car away from "drop off" parking.
- Be prompt.
- Realize your clothing can project a professional image. Dress comfortably. Notice the accepted style of dress others wear. Fit in.
- Watch for what needs to be done without others asking.
- Supervise the room by taking positions which allow your viewing of as many children as possible when not engaged with children.
- Pick up and return supplies. Equipment is returned in the condition it was found.
- Call in early when late or ill.
- If another teacher is leading an activity, help children to hold their attention by sitting close when you don't have other duties.
- Extended conversations with other staff during duty hours gives others the idea you aren't aware of a continual and constant need to supervise children.
- Try not to keep company with only those children who make you feel comfortable.
- Periodically clean up after yourself.
- Make an effort to learn co-workers' names and correct pronunciation.
- Be prepared. Create a collection of activities that can be used as a "backup" when necessary.
- Treat other's opinions with respect, being open minded and reflective; Figure 7–4.
- Add to the beauty of the classroom.
- Notice classroom trouble spots.
- Ask for training on equipment that is new to you.
- Share breaks and lunch in staff rooms.
- Ask questions when you don't know.

Parrish-Porter's tips, though intended for employees of companies, apply also to the education career field.

Kleiman (2002) believes all employees have a right to enjoy their work. She goes on to say, "It's up to you to create a good work environment for yourself." A positive attitude can make a difference. Kleiman describes what to do during poor economic times to make sure your present job is not your last job:

- Be proactive about protecting your job. When appropriate ask how you are doing.
- Have a personal strategy. Figure out where you want to go and then plan to get there; include your time frame.
- Ask questions whenever you have them. Carefully watch what is going on around you.
- Stay competitive in your profession. Keep up on the latest techniques and issues.
- Show flexibility at all times, from accepting new assignments in a positive manner to welcoming new employees and encouraging colleagues.
- Be friendly with everyone, even people you don't like. Avoid vicious office gossip.
- Be respectful of team members. You don't have to be best friends.
- Avoid office politics. Form friendships and alliances.
- Be part of the office grapevine or you'll miss out on valuable information.

Figure 7–4   It Is Important to Respect Other's Opinions.

- Make yourself invaluable by offering to work whenever needed. Volunteer for projects. Brainstorm about ways to reduce work problems.
- Keep your sense of humor.
- Don't ever feel your job is secure. It isn't.

According to Gustafson (2004), author of *What Color Is Your Cubicle: Everything You Need to Succeed in Your First Job*, new workers should get to work early, leave on time, be nice to everyone, refrain from telling co-workers about their latest social adventures, not try to be a superstar on the first day, and not pretend to know things they don't.

Remember the personal dynamics of your workplace are already established, and you are trying to find your place. View every assignment given to you as important, and know why it is needed. Aim to recognize job opportunities when they happen. If you are asked to do another's job, remember that you will learn about how that position fits into the goals of the operation.

Organization

Higgins (2004) alerts new and already employed workers to a new study that finds the majority of employers and supervisors consider a worker's level of organization when conducting annual reviews and making salary increases. In teaching situations, rooms of children will necessarily be somewhat messy and disorganized during work and play times. This is usually taken care of with scheduled cleanup times. The teacher's desk, supply closet, and storage areas are another matter. Storage areas in classrooms are notoriously inadequate. It's a good idea to have team and administration discussions concerning expectations in this matter. There are a few employers and supervisors that view a messy teacher's desk as a sign of a creative mind, but others only see unnecessary chaos.

Conflict Resolution and Team Building

Conflicting opinions can be viewed as a sign of a healthy, vital, growing teaching team or staff. Conflict resolution involves negotiating win-win outcomes. A person with the right skills and expertise can turn conflicts into opportunities to contribute, to lead, and to build career success. Unspoken feelings of resentment, frustration, and other stressful feelings can erode relationships and work environments. Conflict is a natural and healthy aspect of group effort.

TIPS FOR MOVING UP

- Find ways to take on new responsibilities and to volunteer for tasks.
- Learn to do lateral and supervisory staff positions.
- Appreciate and respect the work of others. If you are overly judgmental or critical of your colleagues, you will be treated likewise (CareerSource, 2003).
- Use a strong tone of voice and confident body language. Timidity just draws attention away from your message (CareerSource, 2003).
- Many people find it distasteful to toot their own horns. They (erroneously) think their work speaks for itself and that they will be rewarded in turn. The only way you and your work will be consistently recognized and appreciated is if you promote it (CareerSource, 2003).
- Negotiate for the compensation you feel you deserve.
- Keep current. Ask. Listen. Learn. Make up your mind to be a lifelong learner (Carr-Ruffino, 1997).

As an educator working with a team of others, you can become involved in the politics of a center. We recommend that you avoid taking sides and remain objective and open-minded, especially if you are a new employee. Figure 7–5 presents a "principled negotiation" model. If you feel unprepared in this area, we advise further reading to acquire conflict resolution skills. As your own career manager, only you can gauge if you need help.

Time Management

New teachers often wonder how other teachers can possibly have enough time to do all that is required. Practicing teachers usually say, "organizing, planning and prioritizing." Every teacher develops their own unique system. Here are some suggestions:

- Keep a work calendar.
- Break tasks into parts.
- Delegate when possible or appropriate.
- Set aside certain hours for prep time.
- Don't skip breaks or rest periods.

Asking for Job Reviews

Some centers rarely conduct employee job performance reviews. Reviews can help a worker understand how he/she can improve. They also document adequate job performance. If a time period is set for worker improvement, a follow-up meeting can note which job skills have been accomplished. Ask for both a written review and a follow-up meeting. Copies of meeting notes belong in an employee-maintained personal personnel file.

Employers with written personnel policies usually have formal evaluation procedures. An employee handbook spells out details and specifies raises, promotions, dismissals, and various other personnel issues. Be sure to read your employee's handbook and any other handbook dealing with the program's operation. Kleiman (2002) urges "Read the employee handbook as if it were a bible."

The Soft Touch	The Hardheaded Touch	The Principle of Negotiation Model
We're all friends.	We are adversaries.	We are all problem solvers.
Our goal is agreement.	Our goal is to win.	Our goal is to reach an outcome efficiently and amicably.
Make concessions to keep relationships with others.	Demand concessions as condition of the relationship.	Separate the people from the problem.
Work softly with others and the problem.	Be hard on others and the problem.	Be soft on people, but hard on the problem.
Trust others.	Distrust others.	Proceed independent of trust.
Easily change positions.	Dig into your position.	Focus on interest, not positions.
Make offers.	Make threats.	Explore interests.
Tell your bottom line.	Mislead your bottom line.	Avoid having a bottom line.
Adopt one-sided losses to reach agreement.	Demand one-sided gains at the price of agreement.	Invent options for mutual gain (win-win).
Search for the single answer.	Search for the single answer *you* accept.	Develop multiple options to choose from; decide later.
Insist on agreement.	Insist on your position.	Insist on using objective criteria.
Avoid a contest of will.	Win a contest of will.	Try to reach a result based on standards independent of will.
Yield.	Apply pressure.	Reason and be open to reason: yield to principle not pressure.

Figure 7–5   The Principled Negotiation Model of Conflict Resolution.

Adapted from Newton, A., Bergstrom, K., Brennan, N., Dunne, K., Gilbert, C., Ibarguen, N., Perez-Selles, M., & Thomas, E. (1994). *Mentoring: A Resource and Training Guide for Educators*. Andover, MA: The Regional Laboratory for Educational Improvement of the Northeast and Islands. With permission from West Ed., 2005.

Asking for a Raise and/or Benefits

Morkes (2003) has the following advice for newly hired workers:

Employers are not obliged to offer raises. Many employers have no schedule for raises and no policy for increasing workers' pay. Workers often have to ask for raises. Asking for a raise requires the same sort of personal marketing skills that got you the job. A record of work achievements provides a convincing reason why a raise is deserved. Before you ask for a raise, you need time on the job to accomplish achievements that show you are valuable to your employer. It is seldom wise to ask for a raise prior to having spent six months on the job.

With health care premiums rising, centers can sometimes join together and then offer a group health plan unavailable to small centers. It pays to ask.

Wearing Your Career Manager's Hat

During the first few months when you are learning the ropes, you may be just surviving day to day, but you should still attempt to identify where the job is on your long-range career path. The things you might investigate at your new work site include the following:

- Is there a role model or possible mentor among co-workers?
- Who might be a networking contact?
- Have I succeeded at becoming a valued team player?
- Have I identified possible obstacles impeding my career, such as lack of opportunity to learn new skills?
- Am I visible to people who supervise my work or those higher up? Do I come in contact with them daily? Am I the kind of worker they depend upon?
- Am I well regarded? (Workers who are well liked by supervisors and colleagues are more successful.)

As you documented your competencies during your training, start a work file describing your employment accomplishments. List dates, take photos. Keep written records of your contributions and growing teacher excellence.

Summary

New employees can possess definite workplace skills that improve their ability to stay employed and move them toward their career goal. If you are a new teacher, you may struggle to put into practice what your education directed. There may be a probationary period. You were urged to follow ethical and recognized professional conduct standards, use active listening techniques, communication techniques, conflict resolution strategies, and consider your stress and resiliency.

Tips and hints were provided, and you were urged to evaluate your progress toward becoming an invaluable employee. New employees need information and should start by reading employee handbooks, parent handbooks, and any other written material available at the work site. Examine the professional growth possibilities at your job site, begin your own personal work file, and keep track of your growing accomplishments and competencies.

**Helpful
Web Sites**

Equal Employment Opportunity Commission
http://www.eeoc.gov
employment discrimination issues

Occupational Safety and Health Administration
http://www.osha.gov
guards employee's health and safety

Resource

Oxman, M. (1997). *The how to easily handle difficult people handbook.* Corvallis, OR: SWS Books.

References

CareerSource. (2003, October 14–November 14). Work tips. Issue 147, 24. Author.

Carr-Ruffino, N. (1997). *The promotable woman: 10 essential skills for the new millennium.* Franklin Lakes, NJ: Career Press, Inc.

Code of Ethical Conduct and Statement of Commitment. (1998). [Brochure.] Washington, DC: National Association for the Education of Young Children.

Dougherty, J. Quoted in Holleman, J. (2004, July 18). Office creatures we all know and hate. *Idaho Statesman,* p. CB1.

Feeney, S., & Kipnis, K. (1989, January). Code of ethical conduct. *Young Children* 45(1) 115–22.

Gustafson, K. M. Quoted in Gilsenan, P. (2004, July 2–4). Welcome to the workforce. USA Weekend. *The Idaho Statesman,* pp. 8–9.

Higgins, T. (2004, July 25). Make sure your desk sends the right signal. *The Idaho Statesman,* p. 2CB.

Kleiman, C. (2002). *Winning the job game: The new rules for finding and keeping the job you want.* Hoboken, NJ: John Wiley & Sons, Inc.

Morkes, A. (Ed.). (2003). *Encyclopedia of careers and vocational guidance.* (Vol.1). Chicago, IL: Ferguson Publishing.

National Association of Colleges and Employers. (2005). *Job outlet 2005.* Bethlehem, PA: Author.

National Research Council. (2002). *How people learn: Brain, mind, experience and school.* Washington, DC: National Academy Press.

Noble, K. F. Quoted in Kleiman, C. (2004, September 19). Bouncing back is key skill in workplace. *The Idaho Statesman,* p. CB1.

Parish-Porter, V. (2003, October). HP's Vallerie Parish-Porter charts 10 giant steps to success. *Women of Color Conference, 3* (1) 14.

Robin, D. Quoted in *The Chicago Tribune.* (2003, October 5). Negative co-workers can be a real drag. Career Builder, p. CB1, Author.

Shafir, R. Quoted in Graham, L. (2003, October).Wanna talk? *Reader's Digest,* 157–160.

CHAPTER EIGHT

A Teacher of Teachers

> The task of a leader is to get his people from where they are to where they have not been.
>
> Henry Kissinger

The Re-entry Students

Cia's first and only child needed playmates so she enrolled her in a cooperative preschool, worked there as an assistant, and took the parenting classes required. The experience convinced her that she enjoyed the teaching role. Her college degree was in art, and she used this background to plan children's activities. Cia returned to college and obtained a master's degree in Early Childhood Education. Shortly after graduating, Cia became a community college early childhood instructor and remained so for 22 years.

Many of Cia's former community college students returned to visit her and she ran into them at professional conferences. Four of them had become Early Childhood Education college instructors. Each of them were re-entry students who, after marriage, children, and being out of school for a period of time, like Cia, decided to go back to college.

QUESTIONS TO PONDER

1. Do mature returning education college students have special characteristics that help them attain their long-range goals? Or is this probably just a coincidence?

2. Can a teacher trainer reach and benefit more children as a teacher trainer or as a children's teacher?

Where to Start

If your goal is college or university teaching, you need to obtain the necessary experience and degrees. Many educators begin this career path when they provide advice or training to fellow staff members, student teachers, interns, parents, or volunteers while they are also actively working with children. They share techniques, strategies, methods, and procedures they have found useful or effective in their own classrooms. Some practicing teachers have developed laterally by polishing and perfecting specialties such as curriculum development, children's physical development, conflict resolution, anti-bias instruction, computer use, or any other teacher skill area. Others have created new teaching aids, materials, room designs, and so on. They also may have gathered the necessary years of experience required to equip them to instruct others. Many teachers have a love of learning and have pursued training and additional education.

Almost all teacher trainers (instructors/professors) doing formal training in institutions of higher education have advanced degrees—MAs, doctorates, or Ph.Ds in early childhood education, education, or another specialty area. Some may have served as a college classroom teaching assistant, intern, or aide while working on their degrees. Their experiences beyond their own classroom might include conference or workshop presentations, various community training program activities, private preschool ownership, institute presentations, publication, and grant and/or research activities. The most competitive candidates for college and university jobs have made a name for themselves.

Nationwide, in 2002–2003, the number of 2-year public institutions in the United States was 1,081; private nonprofit institutions numbered 127; and private, for-profit institutions numbered 494. Teaching faculty salary averaged $50,837 per year at public colleges and at private colleges $33,139 (*The Chronicle of Higher Education,* 2004). See Figure 8–1 for additional salary information. College student population is projected to grow for the next 10 years. Shannon (2004) states that the biggest challenge community colleges face in the next 5 years will be hiring and retaining personnel.

Public two-year colleges have been among the fastest growing institutions in American education (Edelfelt & Reiman, 2004). Levine (2004) reports:

> *in 22 states 2-year colleges are engaged in teacher education, and in New Mexico, 2 community colleges are already turning out more school teachers than traditional 4-year colleges and universities.*

	Professor	Associate Professor	Assistant Professor	Instructor	Lecturer	No Rank
All institutions	60,803	47,967	42,667	35,421	41,687	39,685
Public	60,977	48,046	42,755	35,445	41,693	39,685
Private	52,678	46,662	42,228	34,948	38,938	NA

Figure 8–1 Average Salaries (in Dollars) of 2-Year College Professors on 9-Month Contracts (in Dollars), by Control of Institution and Rank (Where Applicable), 2002.

From "Facts & Figures: Salaries of Professors," *Chronicle of Higher Education,* April 19, 2002, available at http://chronicle.com/chronicle/ v48/4832guide.htm.

Types of Positions on College or University Campuses

Varied job titles exist for both private and public college or university educators with instructor or professor being the most common. Figure 8–2 contains a listing of additional higher education job titles. Many campuses have child development centers and/or laboratory schools connected to college and university departments of early childhood, psychology, human development, home economics, child development, or some other college department. Laboratory schools and campus child center staff members most often are not college faculty but rather classified employees.

Campus positions at many colleges are divided into instructional, administrative, or classified categories. One university president in Georgia is an administrative employee. She started her career as an early childhood teacher. Short-term, part-time, day, evening, and summer jobs are usually available on most campuses. If a college or university provides community and/or work experience coursework, jobs in this area can be scheduled on weekends and at off-campus locations. Faculty on many campuses instruct distance learning classes. Community locations may be used for regular college or university classes. One

Provost	*Dean*
Community College Instructor	*Associate Dean*
Assistant Professor	*Dean of Students*
Professor (full)	*Assistant Superintendent*
Associate Professor	*Program Director*
Visiting Professor	*Instructional Supervisor*
Adjunct Professor	*Director of Admissions*
Lecturer	*Registrar*
Vocational Instructor	*Director*
Adult Education Instructor	*Development Director*
Continuing Education Instructor	*Counselor*
Correctional Instructor	*Academic Librarian*
College Career Counselor	*Technology Specialist*
Administrator	*Department Chairperson*
President	*Instructor*
Superintendent	*Teacher*
Chancellor	

Figure 8–2   Job Titles in Higher Education.*

*not meant to be a complete list

community college is holding classes in a former shopping mall (Arnone, 2004). Working in a grant-funded position usually entails working for a specific period of time ranging from a few months to a period of years. Employment often depends on a continued source of grant funds.

Part-time college and university professors, called adjunct professors, have temporary or contingent status. There is no obligation on a college's part to hire a particular adjunct professor should a full-time position become available (Zimmerman, 2004). Most part-timers do not have full retirement or health benefits nor do they qualify for unemployment benefits even if they have worked for the same college for a number of years. Smallwood (2004) points out that some part-time professors do collect unemployment benefits regularly, especially in places where unions encourage instructors to file claims. In the state of Washington, part-time faculty can receive unemployment benefits, but these may only amount to $150 per week.

Part-time faculty are usually paid $2,200 or more per class. Colleges and universities with tight budgets often use part-timers to save money. This causes considerable ill will and increases feelings of exploitation among adjunct faculty.

Full-time college faculty members may receive tenured status meaning that they are assured a continued position from semester to semester. Most full-time faculty also receive job benefits including health care coverage and other guarantees.

Ways Some Faculty Have Landed Jobs

One successful college educator approached a college's community service coordinator with an idea for a class. He sold his idea. The educator was to be paid through student fees in this arrangement. The class would be cancelled if a certain student enrollment was not reached. The college advertised the proposed class in community mailings, and the educator distributed self-made posters to local teacher workplaces. The class attracted a large number of students who evaluated the course enthusiastically. Needless to say, this attracted the attention of the college's instructional staff. When a position opened in their department, the educator was a very competitive candidate with a proven track record. Another educator approached a department chairperson with an idea for a grant and was subsequently hired when the grant, which he helped write, was funded. In many cases, the part-time instructors or professors have a fairly good chance of eventually obtaining full-time faculty employment.

One elementary school educator bent on college teaching attained her goal by becoming well-known as a conference presenter. She expended energy and effort and developed session presentations that were very timely and helpful to attendees. Attendees took away ideas they could immediately institute in their classrooms. The conference sessions she offered needed larger and larger rooms, and she was invited to offer short paid workshops at a number of campuses. It didn't take too long for one college to recognize her talent.

Another educator entered the higher education teaching profession through her volunteer work as an employment chairperson for a large urban teacher professional association. Her volunteer job entailed listing local job openings for other association members. This put her in contact with college instructors who were looking for jobs for their college's early childhood majors and graduates, and this also put her in touch with local school administrators, owners, and directors looking for employees. The old adage "It's not what you know but who you know" worked well. A college staff member encouraged her to apply for a vacant college position. Fortunately, she had already acquired the necessary degrees.

Zimbleman (2004), a community college instructor trying to change jobs and move West, found college interview committees were asking questions about pedagogical trends, new instructional theories, various learning styles, and innovations in instruction. A prudent candidate needs to be current in their academic reading and practice in addition to knowing current concerns and innovations in their specialty field.

> **Question:** If I landed a teacher's job in a campus laboratory school, would it enhance my chances for a faculty position?
>
> **Answer:** It could, but it is not guaranteed. You would still need the required degrees and experience and the respect and admiration of the early childhood faculty—one or more of whom would probably be on the selection committee and interview panel.

Middle School and Secondary Teachers

Since middle and secondary school teachers have already majored in a core subject before being credentialed, many acquire advanced degrees in their subject field and then seek college level teaching. Instead of active involvement in education associations, they often join specialized organizations such as the National Council of Teachers of English, National Council of Teachers of Mathematics, and the National Association for Sports and Physical Education. These organizations frequently alert members to college position openings.

Fact-Finding

A wise candidate for a higher education position does considerable fact-finding and visits college and university Web sites. Each college or institution is unique. Another first step is to visit a college and/or university campus to obtain any written materials. These include the college's catalog, directory, map, and any other informative publications. During a visit, candidates take a close look at the student body, faculty and on-going campus activities. Written notes may be useful later if the intent is to interview for a position later on. If a tour of child centers is possible, collect written handouts and observe closely, looking for clues to possible needs or staff desires. College counselors, clerks, and library staff are often great sources of information. Locating the college's personnel department and inquiring how positions are advertised and whether salary schedules are available comes next. It's a good idea to visit a number of campuses, if eventual higher education employment is part of your career plan.

Another Set of Teaching Skills

Teaching adults differs in many ways from teaching younger students. Many teacher trainers, college instructors, and university professors enroll in instructional methods coursework to prepare themselves. Often, instructional theory and design, research, new technology, assessment, and communication skill are extensively targeted in these classes. Edelfelt and Reiman (2004) note the primary activity of two-year college faculty is teaching, and there usually is little pressure to "publish or perish." They also point out that about two-fifths of faculty are part-timers.

University faculty have the task of keeping current in their field and being aware of research. Echaore-McDavid (2001) states that universities and many colleges expect professors to conduct academic research and publish their results. Some universities identify themselves as research universities and serve educators and others pursuing research-based careers. Echaore-McDavid suggests that faculty duties may include writing grants, attending faculty meetings, serving on committees, and being active in community service. Faculty, like other teachers, grade papers, prepare and present lectures, consult on student projects and progress, secure or develop teaching aids and materials, and requisition supplies and equipment for their classrooms. Community college instructors also have many of the same tasks. The counseling of students is another component of a faculty member's work load.

There are many associations and unions associated with community college and university faculty. They include:

American Association for Higher Education
National Association of Scholars
American Association of University Professors
National Education Association
American Federation of Teachers
American Associate Degree Early Childhood Educators (ACCESS)
National Council for Accreditation of Teacher Education

Early Childhood Leadership Training Programs

Leadership training programs often provide financial assistance in the form of grant monies to students and working professionals. Eligibility for these programs differ and is unique to each program; Figure 8–3. Bloom and Bella (2005) note that two well-known leadership training programs are the McCormick Fellows Leadership Training Program and the Taking Charge of Change Leadership Training conducted at the National-Louis University in Chicago. Other training programs may be described as graduate, continuing studies, director, fellowship, or leadership training programs. The National Association for the Education of Young Children (NAEYC) National Leadership Program, funded by the Doris Duke Charitable Foundation in 2002, aims to prevent child abuse and neglect by offering

Figure 8–3 Teachers with Special Skills May be Eligible for Leadership Training Programs.

training opportunities to leaders in the field (Olson & Hyson, 2005). Other charitable and nonprofit groups fund leadership programs that they hope will make an impact on the quality and availability of child care, early childhood education, and those who provide supportive services to families. Many of these training opportunities are announced or advertised through education associations or college campuses.

Administrative Positions

Countless individuals switch from instructing adults to administering some aspect of the operation of a higher education institution. This can include positions that supervise departments, divisions, or schools of education. Other administrative positions can involve budget, student services, personnel, planning, facilities, grants, business services, staff development, public relations, community education, and other campus operations. A campus directory often lists all campus staff. Individuals in administrative positions overwhelmingly hold administrative or other advanced degrees.

Classified Position

Classified staff is thought of as support staff, although some work as directors of particular college support areas. On some campuses, directors of campus child centers or laboratory schools are classified staff; on others they are administrative personnel or faculty members. Preschool and/or infant/toddler teachers on college campuses who work in campus child facilities are usually classified staff.

Where to Find Job Announcements

Information on available community college instructor positions is available from the *Community and Junior College Journal's* "Positions Open" section and the Career Staffing Center, 621 Duke Street, Alexandria, VA 22314 (Fine, 2000). Web sites previously supplied in Chapter 4 will list some college and university openings but *The Chronicle of Higher Education* will list many positions nationwide. This publication is available at major libraries and can be subscribed to on the Web at http://chronicle.com. *Chronicle* supplements sometimes include community college instructor openings but the *Chronicle* mainly lists university positions. Reading *Chronicle* articles will make you aware of trends and issues important to the field of college and university teaching.

Collective Bargaining

College faculty and college administrators engage in yearly talks called collective bargaining to discuss salary, perks, benefits, and other pertinent issues. Faculty members are represented at these meetings by union negotiators and/or elected or designated fellow instructors. Faculty union membership is optional rather than mandatory.

Quality of Life

As suggested earlier, each employment location offers features that contribute to a worker's quality of life—colleges and university settings are no exception. Some campuses offer prestige and cultural amenities that draw large numbers of job applicants. Other campuses are special to other candidates. Knowing what you desire and value, be it educational opportunities and challenge, entertainment activities, sporting events, excellent schools for your children, or other factors, will aid your decision to accept an offered position. Quality of life can be more important than financial gain to some higher education candidates.

Summary

Seeking employment on college and university faculties in education, early childhood education, or another field, requires advanced degrees. Usually candidates for employment are prominent and well-respected in their field of study. Lifelong learning is necessary, and there are different faculty expectations at different colleges. In addition to faculty positions, the text also discussed administrative and classified jobs. Many faculty members are drawn to a college or university because of its reputation for excellence and the quality of life it offers employees.

Helpful Web Sites

Find a Job in Higher Education
　http://www.FindaJob.com
　16,000 jobs listed; resume information for Web site members

Find a Great Teaching Job (a recruitment service)
　http://www.teachers-teachers.com

National Association for the Education of Young Children
　http://www.naeyc.org
　leadership program applications

Oregon State University
　http://www.hhs.oregonstate.edu
　research the model demonstration project—
　Early Childhood Leadership Directions

Teaching Degree Programs
　http://www.teaching-colleges.com

The Center for Early Childhood Leadership
　http://cecl.edu
　training classes in leadership skills

Resources

Bennis, W. (2003). *On becoming a leader.* Cambridge, MA: Perseus.

Maxwell, J. C. (2000). *Developing the leader within you.* Nashville, TN: Nelson.

Rodd, J. (1998). *Leadership in early education: The pathway to professionalism.* New York: Teachers College Press.

References

Arnone, M. (2004, October 29) The malls of academe. *The Chronicle of Higher Education,* LI *(10),* 28–32.

Bloom, P. J., & Bella, J. (2005, January). Investment in leadership training—The payoff for early childhood education. *Young Children,* 60(1), 32–39.

Echaore-McDavid, S. (2001). *Career opportunities in education.* New York: Checkmark Books.

Edelfelt, R. A., & Reiman, A. J. (2004). *Careers in education*. New York: McGraw-Hill.

Fine, J. (2000). *Opportunities in teaching careers*. Lincolnwood, IL: VGH Horizons.

Levine, A. (2004, October 29). Choosing among competing agendas. *The Chronicle of Higher Education, LI* (10) B 10.

Olsen, M., & Hyson, M. (2005, January). Supporting teachers, strengthening families initiative adds a national leadership program for early childhood professionals. *Young Children, 60* (1), 44–55.

Shannon, H. D. (2004, October 29). The biggest challenge for community colleges: Six views on hiring employees and motivating them. *The Chronicle of Higher Education, LI* (10), B12.

Smallwood, S. (2004, October 8). Scrambling for a living: Part-time professors fight for unemployment benefits between low-paying jobs. *The Chronicle of Higher Education, LI* (7), A 10–12.

The Chronicle of Higher Education. (2004, October 29). Community colleges by the numbers, *LI* (10), B46.

The Chronicle of Higher Education. (2002, April 19). Facts and figures: Salaries of professors. *LI* (3), B32. Author.

Zimbleman, D. A. (2004, October 29). A job-hunting guru comes up short. *The Chronicle of Higher Education, LI* (10), B32.

Zimmerman, D. Quoted in Smallwood, S. (2004, October 8). Scrambling for a living: Part-time professors fight for unemployment benefits between low-paying jobs. *The Chronicle of Higher Education. LI* (7) A 10–12.

CHAPTER NINE

Laws Affecting Educators

*Law is order, and good law is
good order.*

Aristotle

A Small Problem

LeNeal was very pleased with his position at a neighborhood center. It was small, well furnished, and the children's curriculum emphasized individual attention to each child's development. Staff seemed to be professional, and the school's owner was supportive of his attempts to add physical sports skills to the center's program of activities. The preschoolers' abilities to kick and throw balls were amazing, and both boys and girls were excited to participate. Also, there were lots of free choice play opportunities scheduled.

LeNeal's pay was above average for a person who had only completed a certificate program in child development. The part of his job that concerned LeNeal happened between 5:30 and 6:15 in the afternoon when the director and the other teacher were off-duty and away from the center. He was the only staff member left. He did have the center director's cell phone number. There were 5 or 6 children who stayed until closing time at 6:15 when he locked the doors.

QUESTIONS TO PONDER

1. Why might this situation happen? What do you suggest LeNeal do?

2. Is it possible that LeNeal has no awareness of licensing law?

3. What could easily occur, if this continues "as is"?

Issues That Impact the New Employee

This chapter starts with law issues that are important or interesting to the new employee. Being knowledgeable about laws that affect educators and their working conditions requires investigation and study. Because laws vary from state to state, this chapter serves as a springboard for your own research. It describes and presents the most common laws related to teaching. You may discover other laws unique to your locality.

Educators entering the caring and giving profession of early childhood expect employers to be ethical and honest. But as with many other fields of work, a few employers may overlook the law that regulates their operation. Informed professionals who know their rights can protect all other professionals by alerting employers to the fact that this career group has become savvy. Educators will advocate changes to promote quality child care, and professionals will also advocate for better working conditions for themselves. Fortunately, most early childhood programs and centers are law abiding. They sincerely attempt to offer quality services to children and families. They seek to establish a working environment that supports those goals.

Credit Reports on Job Applicants and New Employees

Employers must get written consent from a job applicant before requesting a report from a credit reporting agency (Carlson, 1997). By law, *The Fair Credit Reporting Act,* employers must notify an applicant in writing within three days if they asked a credit reporting agency to run a credit report, and employers must also alert applicants to their opportunity to be informed of the nature and scope of the investigation (Joel, 1993). The credit agency's name and address must be given. Applicants have the right to know whether the credit report influenced their job chances. Steingold (1997) believes a credit check is an unnecessary intrusion into employees' private lives and notes some state laws limit the use of credit information in deciding whether to hire.

At-Will Statements

At-will statements on job applications protect employers. It means an employee can be dismissed or disciplined without notice or cause. Steingold (1997) notes some legal experts approach the whole idea of at-will employment with a measure of hostility or skepticism. Judges may disregard even the most carefully worded at-will language on job applications or written job offers because wording seems to contradict employers' oral statements.

Non-Compete Agreements

Employers trying to safeguard business secrets may ask employees to sign a statement to the effect that when leaving employment they will not discuss aspects of the employer's business. Most states require non-compete agreements to be limited to a small geographic area and have time periods (Whitaker, 2004). Experts in the field of employment law suggest having an attorney review such an agreement, and keeping a signed copy to show to the worker's next prospective employer. Do these non-compete agreements exist in education employment? Definitely, especially when a private school wishes to be exclusive and competitive.

References

Your past employer, if used as a reference, can only give truthful, factual, job-related information about you. Steingold (1997) points out that states are starting to pass laws that allow employers to speak more frankly about their former employees. Usually, "acting in bad faith" while providing a past employee's job-related information needs to be proven to collect damages.

Whitaker and Austin (2003), authors of *The Good Girls Guide to Negotiating,* note that a number of American workers have successfully sued former employers for negative references. Many employers stick strictly to dates of employment, job title, and final salary information (Kadaba, 1995). Whitaker and Austin also observe that in some states employers are protected from defamation lawsuits, if their negative comments are truthful. Most early childhood professionals know that not *all* center or school administrators are ethical because they have run into this problem.

By law, disgruntled former employers cannot reveal the confidential contents of personnel files and medical records. Nor can they libel, slander, or give false information or answer questions about age, gender, race, color, national origin, or disabilities.

Employee Personnel Files

Not all states have laws giving employees or former employees access to their own personnel files. Most employers will obtain an employee's consent before sending for their high school or college transcripts and including them in their files. In Iowa, Oregon, Maine, Michigan, Nevada, New Hampshire, Wisconsin, and Alaska, employees have the right to see and make copies of personnel records.

In most states your employer is required to keep the following records concerning your work:

- full name
- Social Security number
- home address
- employee's birth date if younger than 19 years old
- gender and occupation (job title)
- hours: regular time of workday and when workweek begins
- total hours worked each workday and each workweek
- total daily or weekly earnings
- overtime pay for the workweek
- total additions to or deductions from wage for each pay period
- date of pay and the pay period covered by payment
- payroll
- time sheets
- tax information
- safety records

- worker's compensation records
- application forms
- hiring records
- promotion, demotion, transfer, and termination records

Medical Records

The Americans with Disabilities Act (ADA) imposes strict limitations on employers concerning required employee medical examination records. These records must be kept separate from other employee records in a locked area. Employers can inform your work supervisor about necessary restrictions on your work duties, necessary emergency treatment, or evacuation procedures due to your medical condition. In some states, required doctors' examinations are considered an employer expense rather than an employee expense.

Receiving Your First Paycheck

You will be required to fill in a number of tax-related forms and supply your Social Security number before getting a first paycheck. An employer may or may not issue paychecks from which taxes have been withheld. Taxes, if withheld, are paid to the federal government for programs such as Social Security and Medicare. All workers pay taxes on the money they earn. Workers receive a statement of earnings each pay period that reflects their gross amount of earnings.

Federal minimum per hour wage is set by law; however, a number of states have higher state minimum wage laws. A minimum wage that is less than federal or state minimum wage may be paid to apprentices, learners, and certain other workers with the permission of that state's Commissioner of Labor.

If an employer provides housing, meals, transportation to work, and other work-related items, the labor department considers this at a "reasonable cost" (actual cost) to the employer. It can be deemed a partial payment of the employee's minimum wage. The employee must have voluntarily agreed to the arrangement.

Some child center employers may insist that employees sign statements concerning required unpaid additional hours for parent or staff meetings, fundraising events, parent-teacher conferencing, lesson preparation, home visits, training, or even maintenance duties. This is an illegal practice. An employer can't legally ask employees to sign away their rights. Any employer, job-related hour requirement is paid-for hour or overtime pay hour. Errands a child center staff member is required to perform during off-duty hours are paid time under the law.

Any questions workers have about their pay should first be directed to employers. State Department of Labor (Wage and Hour Division) offices can add additional information, helping workers understand whether the employer has correctly figured amounts.

Employers may lawfully deduct money from employee wages for the following reasons:

- legally required federal taxes, state taxes, Social Security, Medicare contributions, and state disability insurance (SDI)
- lateness and absences
- court-ordered child or family support payments
- willful or grossly negligent breakage of equipment

- payments for back taxes the employee owes the government
- payments to retirement plans, medical or insurance plans, charities
- payments the employee has asked the employer to make for union dues, assessments or initiation fees, bank and credit union deposits, and court-ordered debt collection

Antitrust Laws

Individual child care centers and family child care providers cannot join together to agree to charge a certain rate, pay a certain wage, or maintain certain hours of operation according to the antitrust laws of the United States (Bellm & Haack, 2001). This is called "price fixing." Centers and providers can make individual business decisions, but they can't attempt in concert with others to control early childhood worker's salaries. This would be an illegal business practice.

Labor Law: The *Fair Labor Standards Act*

The *Fair Labor Standards Act* (FLSA), which Congress approved in 1938, granted worker protections. It has been amended many times and mandates minimum wage, number of work hours per week, overtime, the employment of minors, and other conditions of employer-employee relations. The law applies to employers engaged in some aspect of interstate commerce (center equipment or supplies that are manufactured in another state). Steingold (1997) notes it is possible but highly unlikely that your employer will be exempt from FLSA law. Almost every work situation is covered by FLSA, but a few employers are exempt from the law's provisions. Church-affiliated school workers need to check with local labor offices concerning FLSA coverage.

The federal law treats executive, administrative, and professional employees differently than blue collar workers. Exempt employees are salaried, management, executive, and supervisory workers who make independent decisions 80 percent of the time and make decisions which 20 percent of the time are approved by someone else.

If you are a certified (credentialed) teacher in a public educational institution, you are considered to be professional. This class of worker is exempt from FLSA wage and hour law. Child center teachers are usually FLSA-covered employees. Independent early childhood contract workers are not.

If you aren't sure which category legally describes your position, call or visit an FLSA office or state labor department. A list of questions is available from FLSA to help to make an assessment.

Another group of workers exempt from FLSA provisions and protections are apprentices, trainees, babysitters, employees in the immediate family of the employer, and persons employed by state, county, and city governments. Penalties (prescribed in FLSA law) exist for employers who categorize workers incorrectly; Figure 9–1. Penalties can be fines, payment of back pay, and employer tax penalties.

The *Fair Labor Standards Act* controls the following areas for full-time and part-time workers:

- minimum wage
- overtime pay

Figure 9–1   Some Teachers May Be Exempt Workers if They Are in Training.

- equal pay for equal work
- compensatory time
- forms of pay
- commissions
- time off
- work hours
- travel time
- on-call pay periods
- meal and rest periods
- record keeping
- child labor
- payroll withholding

Changes in Overtime Pay Rules

A change in overtime pay rules that took place on August 23, 2004 did not affect hourly workers or salaried workers with union contracts that include overtime protections. However, nonunionized salaried workers who used to receive overtime checks could see this extra pay disappear. Updated regulations ensure salaried workers who earn less than $23,660 annually receive overtime pay when they work beyond 40 hours. Previously, only workers who earned less than $8,060 were eligible for overtime pay, regardless of their job title.

The new salary threshold impacts many lower-paid managers (directors and assistant directors). Tessa Barber, an assistant director of a preschool, who earns just under $18,000, was promoted to a director's position at $24,000 annual pay a few months before the new rules took place. She is now just over the legal cutoff to receive overtime pay should she work over 40 hours a week (Dybis & Howard, 2004). Employers are required to pay workers overtime pay if they earn less than the $23,660 amount set by the new laws; employers are not required to cut overtime pay to those currently receiving it, even though the new rules might now categorize those positions as exempt.

The overtime changes are part of the *Fair Labor Standards Act*. The *Act* covers schools, hospitals, and any business with revenues of more than $500,000 annually. Firms below that threshold are covered by state laws. The two Web sites that follow provide additional information:

> http://www.dol.gov
>   U.S. Department of Labor
>
> http://www.aseonline.org
>   American Society of Employers

State Labor Laws

Many states' industrial relations and industrial welfare laws have been drawn from the *Federal Fair Labor Standards Act*. Posters with specific items are, by law, available for reading by employed workers at their work site or central office. Posters specify hours and days, workweek, minimum wage, overtime, age of workers, minors, split shifts, employee records, payment of wages, cash shortage and breakage, uniforms and equipment, meals and lodging, meal periods, rest periods (breaks), room temperature, and inspection and penalties.

Items of great interest to early childhood staff members include rest periods, duty-free meal periods, overtime and compensatory time, workweek agreements, and resting areas. Employee workweek assignments that depend on day-to-day child attendance figures may overlook law stipulations.

State labor law can cover and establish the following policies:

- rest and break policy
- lunch periods
- employee rest areas
- payment of wages due terminated employees
- pre-employment medical exams
- discharge particulars
- a minimum wage that is higher than federal requirements
- additional work-related standards

Most licensed early childhood centers are required to provide constant child supervision and to maintain certain teacher-child ratios set by law. Employers may not wish to hire additional staff for lunch/break periods; doing so can cut employer profits. If a teacher donates 20 minutes without pay each day, considerable pay is lost over a year's time. A California law that applies to most private sector centers specifies a *compensated* 10-minute rest period for every 4-hour work period.

Other Employment Laws

Title VII of the Civil Rights Act of 1964 forbids employment discrimination based on race, color, gender, pregnancy, national origin, or religion. It applies to private employers with more than 15 employees if their business involves interstate commerce. Federal, state, and municipal workers are also covered. Complaints concerning this law are directed to the Equal Opportunity Commission (EEOC), and employers found to be discriminatory can be ordered to pay back wages, reinstate an employee, and pay fees and damages.

Equal Pay Act of 1963 (EPA) requires equal pay to men and women for equal work.

The Family and Medical Leave Act of 1993 (FMLA) stipulates employers of 50 or more individuals provide eligible employees up to 12 weeks unpaid, job-protected leave. Each state differs on family leave law benefits, so an investigation is necessary. Beginning in January 2004, the State of California offers additional benefits that exceed federal law provisions. Family leave law may help families under certain provisions. These include illness, the injury of a worker's family member, the birth of children, adoption and/or foster care provided for a new child.

The Age Discrimination in Employment Act of 1967 (ADEA) forbids employment discrimination and mandatory retirement for most workers above age 40. The law applies to employers with more than 19 employees on staff.

The Immigration Reform and Control Act of 1986 deals with discrimination on the basis of national origin or against non-citizens who may work legally in the United States. Illegal aliens are not protected under this act. Some states have enacted laws requiring that only English is to be spoken in early childhood programs receiving public funds (Clifford, Cochran, & Kagan, 2003).

Occupational Safety and Health Administration Compliance Assistance Authorization Act of 1998 (OSHA). Many states have occupational health and safety agencies whose mission is to make sure employers provide safe and healthful workplaces and working conditions. Laws often require that an effective accident and illness prevention program be in place for employees, which includes lifting procedures, fire protection procedures, and good housekeeping practices. Free informational reading material is available that covers job-related injury or illness from both local, state, and federal offices.

California has passed laws that provide job safety and health protection. Rights provided under this type of law include an employee's right to bring unsafe or unhealthy conditions to an employer's attention and notify state agencies to suggest a work site inspection. Probably the greatest threats to early childhood staff members are upper respiratory illness, childhood diseases, and intestinal illness brought to school by young children. Lack of adequate screening of children upon entrance may constitute a hazard to staff health.

An employee has the right to know about blood borne pathogens and receive training specific to child center settings. This is mandated by the Occupational Safety and Health Administration (OSHA). When worker employment begins, training begins and is conducted on a yearly basis. Some very small centers do not come under OSHA jurisdiction. Early childhood workers are often ignorant of this law's provisions and protections. Hazards do exist for adults in some child centers. Room design and equipment that was primarily planned for children may have overlooked adult safety. In order to prove employer violation of OSHA law, the employer must be out of compliance with adult safety precautions, have recognized the adult hazard, and know there was a likelihood that an employee could be seriously injured. Common jobsite features which can affect worker health or safety are:

- temperature
- lighting
- noise levels
- supplies, art materials, cleaning materials
- walkways, entrances, and exits
- emergency provisions including fire systems, earthquake drill, and training for child emergencies
- first aid supplies including adult protection from blood and body fluids
- training on any potentially hazardous equipment
- waste disposal, child toilet use, and clothing change procedures
- food handling procedures
- floor and ground surface dangers
- children's climbing structures

Employees who eat food prepared and provided as a job benefit will be interested in food service laws. OSHA inspectors have the right to check work places for law compliance. Early childhood employees may need to document requests to supervisors to fix broken equipment, overhanging climbing structures, sandy spots, wet areas, or other features that create hazards for adults in environments designed for children.

The child care industry is exempt from OSHA law requirements concerning the reporting of serious worker injury and illness in many states. This may seem illogical to early childhood workers.

OSHA law protects a worker from retaliation when a worker reports safety and health violations. Because preschools often operate in older buildings, lead contamination from painted surfaces or asbestos exposure can be a valid concern. Other health hazards may exist, for example, in employee rest areas, if smoking is permitted.

An occupational injury is any injury such as a cut, fracture, sprain, or amputation that results from a work-related accident or from exposure involving a single incident in the work environment. An occupational illness is any abnormal condition or disorder, other than one resulting from an occupational injury, caused by exposure to environmental factors associated with employment. Included are acute and chronic illnesses or diseases that may be caused by inhalation, absorption, ingestion, or direct contact with toxic substances or harmful agents.

In addition to making available OSHA poster 2203 (or its state equivalent) at the work site, employers must provide copies of the *Act* and relevant OSHA rules and make these available to employees upon request.

OSHA recognizes the need for safeguards to protect workers against health hazards related to blood borne pathogens (HIV, hepatitis, AIDS). Occupational exposure means reasonably anticipated skin, eye, and mucous membrane contact with blood or other potentially infectious materials that may result from the performance of the employee's duties.

Under OSHA law, each employer must do the following:

- Develop a written exposure control plan.
- Provide personal protective clothing and equipment.
- Give employees information and training.
- Provide vaccine and medical evaluations to an employee exposed to hepatitis at no cost to employee.

The following workers are not covered by OSHA—self-employed persons, workers employed in some federal agencies covered under other federal statutes, and workers employed by some state and local governments.

Early Childhood Workers with HIV or AIDS

Early childhood workers with HIV (human immunodeficiency virus) or AIDS (acquired immunodeficiency syndrome) are protected from discrimination by the *Americans with Disabilities Act* (1990, 1992, 1995). Consequently, job applicants cannot be asked to take diagnostic medical tests. It is illegal for employers to discriminate, refuse to hire, or to restrict contact with children. Under most circumstances, a staff member with HIV or AIDS is considered to pose no threat to children's health or safety under this legislation.

Child program employers who fit the following criteria are required to comply with federal disability discrimination laws.

   1)   all federally funded programs
   2)   employers with 25 or more employees (since July 1992)
   3)   employers of 15 or more (since July 1994)

State and local laws may also require compliance by smaller businesses and child center operators.

Once employed, a staff member with a disability is treated just like other employees. The employer needs to provide reasonable accommodations to allow the disabled employee to continue employment. An employer cannot restrict job duties unless the staff member poses a direct threat to the health and safety of others.

Licensing Law

Every work site has received permission to operate as a service to children and families from some legally authorized authority (granted by law through legislation). Licensing regulations protect the health, safety, and the general welfare of children in group care. Licensing responsibility and regulatory functions are often performed by state welfare, state public health, or state education departments. Federally funded and state funded programs abide by federal or state guidelines and in some states are also licensed. Most programs come under the auspices of a number of regulatory laws.

Licensing laws describe teacher duties and responsibilities. Of particular interest to teachers are sections of law dealing with the following:

- teacher qualifications
- teacher responsibilities in supervising aides and assistants
- ratios of teachers to enrolled children
- disaster plans
- health and safety practices
- screening children daily for illness
- giving children prescribed medications
- supervision and guidance of children
- custodial work unrelated to teaching tasks
- a director's "on site" requirement
- curriculum particulars and recommendations concerning releasing children at pickup times
- heating and lighting

Teacher and staff qualifications can differ greatly from state to state. If one compares publicly and privately funded programs, often qualifications are more stringent when public money is involved. Public money support usually requires a planned developmental offering for each child rather than loosely described program minimums. Schools can, and many schools do, choose to present curriculums that are much more than minimum state licensing requirements.

Some state law and state licensing laws may not forbid corporal punishment such as spanking or paddling. However, most of these states place restrictions on the practice including the admonishment that punishment must be reasonable and not out of proportion to the offense and the child's age. Some states specify that parents must have prior notification and that parental approval must be obtained. Licensing law in many states provides a clear picture of staff disciplinary behavior.

A professional who oversteps legal bounds may face law suits, criminal charges, job discipline, or firing. Early childhood experts and professionals urge all workers to use positive guidance techniques, and they note that corporal punishment is inappropriate for young children in group care. Parents cannot give early childhood staff members permission to break the law.

Facility Requirements

Licensing laws either specifically spell out facility square footage requirements (exteriors, rooms, and playgrounds) or state "sufficient or adequate" when describing space use. The former insures enforceable compliance; the latter can be a disputable value judgement. The following facility particulars are commonly regulated and usually require clearances, periodic inspections, and/or permits issued by planning departments, building inspectors, fire department staff, and public health department evaluators:

- zoning
- building and construction features
- fire safety equipment and building exit features
- health maintenance, furnishings, and food service equipment

Space (square footage) determines the number of children enrolled at any given time. Law provides for a mandatory number of adults with any group of young children (child/adult ratios). All educators working in licensed child care centers and schools should read their state's licensing regulations closely.

Liability

Knowledge of the law is a form of staff protection, as well as child protection. When administrators (directors, owners, principals) are employed in licensed facilities they establish a legal relationship recognized by the courts. Administrators assume responsibility for their school's total operation. When teachers are hired, teachers also assume responsibilities that make them liable for lawsuits. If a teacher or staff member is legally challenged, a suitable explanation must be provided concerning how each job responsibility was met.

In most states, the law clearly stipulates that children must be supervised at all times, Figure 9–2. Job descriptions for teachers include specific references to supervising and/or management of child learning and play. The written policies at child centers often include statements about replacing yourself with another adult before leaving a group of assigned children. If a child is injured because that child was *not* supervised properly by the child's teacher or another qualified adult substitute, the responsible teacher could be proved legally negligent in her responsibilities.

Directors, teachers, and other staff members can obtain insurance to protect themselves from lawsuits involving their work. A clause, or rider, can be added to either their homeowner's, renter's, or car insurance policies. Premiums vary. Negligence and/or failure to perform duties have to be proven in court before an individual or insurance company pays damages.

America has been described as a litigious environment rife with lawsuits. NAEYC (National Association for the Education of Young Children)

Figure 9–2   Children Are Supervised During Mealtimes.

members have been made aware that insurance coverage (up to two million dollars) is available to salaried employees working with educational organizations, and many other insurance companies offer similar insurance.

Professional liability is incurred when certain standards of performance are not maintained or when services are not rendered by individuals with specialized training or experience, and when the person for whom service is rendered has been damaged in some way.

Without liability insurance, an educator's assets such as savings, home, or car may be used to pay damages awarded by courts in some states. Professional liability policies can safeguard assets when educators are sued as a result of an event arising out of their duties. Most employers have liability policies that cover themselves and their employees, but the employer's plans may be inadequate depending on policy limits and exclusions.

Lawsuits against educators have included the following:

- injuries to children under the educator's supervision
- improper instructional methods
- defamation
- violation of children's civil rights
- administrators hiring unqualified workers

Coverage for part-time workers or independent contractors is available at many insurance companies. Contact your insurance agent for information.

Unemployment Insurance (UI)

Employees must contribute to a state unemployment insurance tax fund and also pay a federal unemployment tax. This state-federal partnership pays unemployment benefits to eligible, unemployed workers. An employee who is laid off or fired for a reason other than misconduct may be entitled to unemployment benefits from the state fund.

Worker's Compensation Insurance

Worker's Compensation Insurance is a program established by state law. It provides, at the employer's expense, benefits for workers who have become injured or ill in the course of their employment. Any employee who becomes ill or is injured on the job is automatically entitled to benefits, regardless of negligence or fault. In return, the employee who resides in certain states gives up the right to sue the employer for damages due to injury or illness. In certain instances, a third party (such as manufacturers of equipment) may be sued by the employee.

Some states allow injured employees who have received worker's compensation to bring a suit against an employer who intentionally violated a safety standard or deliberately failed to inform workers about hazardous conditions.

Steingold's (1997) understanding of Worker's Compensation follows:

Workers compensation is a no fault system. The employee is entitled to receive stated benefits whether or not the employer provided a safe workplace and whether or not the worker's own carelessness contributed to the injury or illness.

Insurance rates for employers depend on set rates for child care business owners. The number of claims filed by employees affects the insurance premium. In addition to injuries such as back strain and falls, workers also may be compensated for some illnesses and diseases. These include emotional stress, heart conditions, and stress-related digestive problems, which are increasingly covered by insurance .

Individual states have slightly different laws concerning worker's compensation for on-the-job injury or work-related illness. Worker's compensation laws are enforced and administered by a state's commission or board. Almost all employers in all states except New Jersey, South Carolina, and Texas must purchase worker's compensation insurance for employees. Early childhood educators in Alabama, Arkansas, Georgia, New Mexico, North Carolina, Virginia, Florida, Rhode Island, Mississippi, Missouri, and Tennessee who work in small child care centers with only a few workers should ask questions about coverage. "Non-hazardous" small businesses in these states may not have worker's compensation insurance.

Preschools and child centers that hire staff as independent contractors do not purchase worker's compensation insurance for those workers. Part-time workers in child facilities have worker's compensation insurance coverage if full-time workers have coverage.

Employers obtain worker's compensation insurance from both public and private insurers. Employers are also allowed to self-insure in some states by proving they are able to pay claims and have solvency. If you believe you have suffered a job-related accident or illness, you should do the following:

- Report it to your supervisor, who must then file a report with the insurance carrier.
- See a doctor and make sure that the physician files a report to the workers' compensation insurance carrier or your self-insured employer.
- Consider consulting a worker's compensation attorney in order to make certain you receive the benefits to which you are entitled. Consultation is free.

The Family and Medical Leave Act

Effective August 5, 1993, *The Family and Medical Leave Act* (FMLA) entitles an eligible employee to take up to 12 weeks of unpaid, job-protected leave each year for specified family and medical reasons. Public agency workers (schools) are covered by this legislation as are private sector employees who have worked for employers employing 50 or more employees for at least 20 work weeks in the current or preceding calender year. Special rules apply to temporary employees.

Family leave reasons include childbirth, adoption, and foster care placement. Medical reasons include a seriously ill family member and/or employee illness. Beginning in January 2004, California offers additional benefits that exceed federal law provisions.

Federal legislation guarantees that the employee's job will be available to them when the employee returns to work. The legislation also continues health and other benefits, and protects seniority.

Unlawful Firing

Most early childhood teachers are "at-will" employees who can be fired or leave according to the worker's own decision. Wrongful discharge (discharge in violation of the law) happens when an employer fires an employee for any of the following reasons:

1) on the basis of race, gender, religion, disability, age, marital status, ancestry, or national origin (*Civil Rights Act of 1964, Title VII*)

2) because the employee attempts to organize a union (*National Labor Relations Act*)

3) if the worker asks for lawful wage and hour consideration (*Fair Labor Standards Act*)
4) if the worker complains about safety and employer requirements which the employer is failing to provide (*Occupational Safety and Health Act*)
5) because a worker needs to serve on a jury or answer a summons
6) because a worker refuses to break a public law
7) because the worker refuses to commit perjury on the employer's behalf

Some of these situations deal with "whistle blower" protections found in laws. Before considering whistle blowing actions, Joel (1993) suggests making sure you are *right,* have given the employer time to correct the issue, and the educator has run the complaint by an attorney who specializes in labor law. In any situation, when illegal firing is an issue, legal advice is highly recommended.

Unionization Law

Two large bodies of law affect workers involved in union activities:
1) *The Labor-Management Relations Act* (Taft-Hartley Act) (LMRA)
2) *National Labor Relations Act* (Wagner Act)

Both laws are administered by the National Labor Relations Board (NLRB). About 15 to 18 percent of all workers in the United States are union members. Their unions represent them in negotiations covering most aspects of their jobs and job benefits. Under *Section 7 of the National Labor Relations Act,* employees have the following rights:

- to self-organize
- to form, join, or assist labor organizations
- to bargain collectively through representatives of their own choosing
- to act together for the purpose of collective bargaining or other mutual aid or protection
- to refuse to do any or all of these things

However, the union and employer, in a state where such agreements are permitted, may enter into a lawful union-security agreement requiring employees to pay periodic dues and initiation fees. Non-members who inform the union that they object to the use of their payments for nonrepresentational purposes may be required to pay only their share of the union's costs of representational activities (such as collective bargaining, contract administration, and grievance adjustment).

The agreements worked out between a union and an employer in some states may force a worker to join a union to remain employed. In other instances, union and non-contributing, non-union workers work side-by-side.

Four to five percent of about two million child care and development professionals belong to unions (Corcoran, 2002). Denise Dowell (2002), co-president of United Child Care Union, believes it is going to take a national union of child care workers to improve the quality of jobs and the quality of care. In Philadelphia, union contracts with a large private center and a Head Start center enabled workers to receive guaranteed work hours, paid in-service days, increased paid sick and vacation days, and a 40 percent reduction in employee money expended for health insurance premiums. Union contracts reduced employee turnover and insured pay raises over a five-year period (Corcoran, 2002). Workers paid twenty-five dollars a month in dues.

Bellm and and Haack (2001) state:

Nationally, the unions that have been most active and successful in organizing child care workers are AFSCME (the American Federation of State, County, and Municipal Employees), the NEA (National Education Association), SEIU (Service Employees International Union), and the UAW (United Auto, Aerospace, and Agricultural Implement Workers of America).

More than half of all public school teachers belong to unions—mainly the American Federation of Teachers and the National Education Association. These unions bargain with school systems over wages, hours, and the terms and conditions of employment.

Under the two National Labor Relations laws, union members can recruit and distribute union literature during off-duty hours in nonworking areas. Employers are generally judged to be participating in an unfair labor practice if they increase or promise to increase wages or improve working conditions while a union is trying to organize workers. It is also illegal to decrease or threaten to decrease wages or privileges when a union campaign is in progress (Joel, 1993).

Before becoming involved in union activities, it is wise for any educator to ascertain whether the work site is covered by the National Labor Relations laws! Smaller schools may not be covered; Figure 9–3. Church-affiliated private school staff may not be able to unionize or may not have National Labor Relations Board (NLRB) protections. NLRB field office locations and telephone numbers are available in local telephone books.

The *Employee Retirement Income Security Act* (ERISA)

The *Employee Retirement Income Security Act* (ERISA) recognizes two types of pension plans: traditional "defined benefit" plans and "defined contribution" plans such as a 401(k).

If a worker has questions about the pension plans an employer offers, it is wise to seek information that explains in detail what future benefits are secured and what consequences come to play when an employee terminates employment. Although only a limited number of early childhood employees may have company pension plans as a job benefit, it is important to be aware of laws that protect and affect pensions. For information about the rights of pension plan participants and their survivors under ERISA, contact the following organizations:

Figure 9–3 Teachers in a Small School May Not Be Able to Distribute Union Literature or Organize.

Pension and Welfare Benefit Administration
    U.S. Department of Labor
Pension Benefit Guaranty Corporation
    2020 K Street
    Washington, DC

For more information on tax saving retirement plans (IRAs), contact the Internal Revenue Service or your financial advisor. The *Economic Recovery Tax Act of 1981* established individual retirement accounts (IRAs), which are a widely used and recognized retirement savings plan for many workers. The *Retirement Equity Act of 1984* (REA) affects private pension plans and women's right to receive pension benefits.

Child Abuse Law

Many states require teachers and administrators to report suspected cases of child abuse. Abuse can be defined as cruelty and/or neglect. Teachers often become children's confidants. Disclosing a wide range of feelings, fears, joys, and accomplishments during daily conversations, children cue teachers to important happenings in their lives.

Schools keep growth and weight records, which monitor general health, and schools are in a position to notice subtle changes and trends. Because outer clothing is sometimes removed during rest periods and soiled or wet clothing changed, injuries to the skin may be visible. Speaking to the director or principal about questionable child behaviors, physical conditions, or verbalizations is recommended.

The California Penal Code provides that certain professional and lay persons *must* report suspected abuse to the proper authorities (police or sheriff, county department of children's health or social services, state or local divisions of community care licensing). The following adults are mandated to report child abuse: child custodians (teachers, licensed home care workers, foster parents, social workers) and employees of a child protective agency. Failure to report suspected abuse by a mandated reporter within 36 hours is a misdemeanor punishable by 6 months in jail and/or a fine.

In addition to New York, many states are requiring anyone who works directly with children (teachers, doctors, dentists, etc.) to complete an acceptable or eligible child abuse identification and reporting class designated by state law as part of their initial licensing or renewal of license requirements.

Suspected child abuse or neglect should be reported within 24 to 48 hours in most states. The values and ethnic differences of parents should be considered when making a child abuse report. Recent parent emigres may be unaware of laws.

Social Security

By law, both the employee and employer contribute to the federal Social Security (FICA) program. Tax-exempt organizations can elect to join this program and secure its benefits for employees. FICA contributions are deducted until wages surpass a designated amount. The employee's and employer's matching contributions are forwarded by the employer.

Benefits begin at retirement age or before if a worker is seriously disabled. Payment amounts vary depending on "quarters of coverage" and employees' average earnings over a period of years. The Social Security Administration maintains local offices throughout the country where further information can be obtained. Because private preschool program retirement plans are a rarity, older workers entering the early childhood field may wish to initiate early deductions into plans that supplement Social Security benefits.

Internal Revenue Service

Your federal income taxes are withheld based on your earnings and the number of deductions for dependents. Early childhood professionals' awareness of legal income tax deductions is important. Deductible items can include certain education expenses, certain automobile and travel expenses, professional publications costs, professional membership fees, temporary absence from job expenses, job hunting expenses, partial child care expenses, certain teaching tool and supply expenses, certain clothing expenses, required medical examination fees, home use for work preparation, union dues; tax counsel and assistance, employment agency fees, and certain protective clothing expenses.

Three small publications available at your local U.S. Department of the Treasury or Internal Revenue Service Office are informative and helpful. They are: Miscellaneous Deductions, Educational Expenses, and Child and Disabled Dependent Care.

Summary

State and federal laws affect all workers. They protect children and workers. Laws reviewed included *The Fair Labor Standards Act*, state labor laws, employment law, occupational safety laws, *The Americans with Disabilities Act*, licensing law, family and medical leave law, unionization law, *The Social Security Act*, child abuse law, and federal Internal Revenue Service particulars. Your liability and need of insurance protection was discussed. As your own career manager, this information makes you a more knowledgeable educator.

Abbreviations List

REA	*The Retirement Equity Act*
NLRB	National Labor Relations Board
ADA	*Americans with Disabilities Act*
FUTA	*Federal Unemployment Tax Act*
NCECW	National Center for Early Childhood Workforce
EEOC	Equal Employment Opportunity Commission
SDI	State Disability Insurance
HIV	Human Immunodeficiency Virus
AIDS	Acquired Immune Deficiency Syndrome
FLMA	*Family Medical Leave Act*
FLSA	*The Fair Labor Standards Act*
EPA	*Equal Pay Act of 1963*
ADEA	*The Age Discrimination Act of 1967*
OSHA	Occupational Safety and Health Administration
LMRA	*The Labor-Management Relations Act*
ERISA	*The Employee Retirement Income Security Act*
IRS	Internal Revenue Service
NAEYC	National Association for the Education of Young Children
AFSCME	American Federation of State, County, and Municipal Employees
SEIU	Service Employees International Union
UAW	United Auto Workers
FICA	*Federal Insurance Contribution Act*

Helpful Web Sites

Age Discrimination in Employment Act of 1967
http://www.eeoc.gov

Americans with Disabilities Act
http://www.usdoj.gov

Civil Rights Act of 1964
http://www.eeoc.gov

Equal Pay Act of 1963
http://www.eeoc.gov

Family and Medical Leave Act of 1993
http://www.dol.gov

Federal Laws
http://www4.law.cornell.edu

Minimum Wage
http://www.dol.gov

NAEYC Sponsored Insurance
http://www.ftj.com

OSHA
http://www.osha-slc.gov

U.S. Department of Labor
http://www.dol.gov

Resources

Barrett, E. (2002). *Not another apple for the teacher: Hundreds of fascinating facts from the world of teaching.* York Beach, ME: Conari Press.

Bernback, J. M. (1998). *Job discrimination II: How to fight, how to win.* Englewood Cliffs, NJ: Voir Dire Press.

Repa, B. K. (1999). *Your rights in the workplace.* Berkeley, CA: Nolo Press.

Steingold, F. S. (1997). *The employer's legal handbook: A complete guide to your legal rights and responsibilities.* Berkeley, CA: Nolo Press.

Tobias, P., & Sauter, S. (1997). *Job rights and survival strategies:* A *handbook for terminated employees.* Cincinnati, OH: National Employment Rights Institute.

References

Bellm, D., & Haack, P. (2001) *Working for quality child care: Good child care jobs equals good care for children.* Washington, DC: Center for the Child Care Workforce.

Carlson, B. (1997). Federal law cracks down on using credit history during job screening. *Idaho Business Review.* Vol. XVII (4). 16–18.

Clifford, R. M., Cochran, M., & Kagan, S. L. (2003). Challenges for early childhood education and care policy. In D. Cryer & R. M. Clifford, *Early childhood education and care in the USA* (pp. 191–210). Baltimore, MD: Paul H. Brookes Publishing Company.

Corcoran, K. (2002, November 11). New union targets child care workers. *San Jose Mercury News,* pp. 1B, 3B.

Dowell, D. Quoted in Corcoran, K. (2002, November 11). New union targets child care workers. *San Jose Mercury News,* pp. 1B, 3B.

Dybis, K., & Howard, J. (2004, August 19). Overtime pay rules change Monday. *The Idaho Statesman,* pp. B, 1–2.

Joel, L. G. (1993). *Every employee's guide to the law: Everything you need to know about your rights in the workplace.* New York: Pantheon Books.

Kadaba, L. S. (1995, September 10). Employers fear lawsuits for giving bad references. *San Jose Mercury News,* p. PC.

Steingold, F. S. (1997). *The employer's legal handbook.* Berkeley, CA: Nolo Press.

Whitaker, L. (2004, July 4). Dealing with non-compete clause phobia. *The Idaho Statesman,* p. CB1.

Whitaker, L., & Austin, E. (2003, August 24). If you quit under a cloud, can the cloud follow you? *The Idaho Statesman,* p. CB1.

CHAPTER TEN

Self-Employment

Entrepreneurs share faith in a bright future. They have a clear vision of where they are going and what they are doing, and they have a pressing need to succeed.

—Ronald Reagan

The Book Lover

Analyn went to every booth with children's books in the exhibit hall. The convention drew thousands of reading teachers, so book booths were plentiful. She was looking for books about machines for one of her students. At the next booth the bookseller was very knowledgeable. They discussed Analyn's favorite children's books, books her students liked, authors and illustrators, and newly released titles.

The bookseller, Joe Auberly, mentioned he had just purchased a children's bookstore in a town near Analyn's home. He was impressed by Analyn's love of books and her extensive understanding of book features.

As Analyn filled out a purchase order for the books, Joe asked her if she might be interested in talking to him about employment in the bookstore. Analyn had thought about changing her teaching hours, job sharing, and cutting back somehow. She had been writing children's books for a few years, and no longer needed to work full-time. She saw Joe's offer as a way to do what she loved to do—be immersed in children's books. Her teaching career was fulfilling, but Analyn believed a second career was possible.

QUESTIONS TO PONDER

1. What should Analyn do? Why?

2. What are the chances for Analyn to be a success in a second career?

3. Would becoming a reading specialist be another option Analyn should consider?

Nationally 48 percent of all businesses are at least half-owned by a woman, and 1 out of every 11 adult women in the United States owns a business (Estrella, 2004). Men, of course, own or half-own the rest. States differ widely in the growth of women-owned businesses with Utah, Nevada, Idaho, Kentucky, New Mexico, South Carolina, North Carolina, Arkansas, and Oregon recognized among the top ten states (Center for Women's Business Research, 2004). Women-owned businesses grew 17 percent between 1997 and 2004, and employment at these firms increased 24 percent nationwide according to U.S. Census Bureau data (Estrella, 2004).

Winik (2003) offers the following statistics concerning self-employment:

> *When it comes to money, self-employed independent workers average $58,000 a year, compared to $45,000 for those with regular wage jobs. But the self-employed are less likely to have health insurance for themselves and their families. Small business owners are often the most successful, averaging more than $110,000 a year, and they report more job creativity and satisfaction in life. But they also put in much longer hours (38 percent of them work more than 50 hours a week).*

The number of women-owned businesses continues to grow at twice the rate of all U.S. firms, with an expected 6.2 million such businesses in 2002 (Costco Connection, 2002). Some of the fastest growing metropolitan areas for business growth include Salt Lake City and Ogden, Utah; Las Vegas, Nevada; Phoenix and Mesa, Arizona; Kansas City and St. Louis, Missouri.

The University of Dayton has over 100 students concentrating in entrepreneurship, the most students since it introduced the curriculum in 1999 (Regan, 2004).

To be a successful entrepreneur, you need a killer idea, and you need to know that you won't be the first to have the idea (Jordan, 2004). J. Foster, author of *How To Get Ideas* (1996), a volume that promotes thinking about a business venture, believes "All you have to do is take some ingredients you already know about and combine them in a new way."

Ideas might come out of the blue but most often they grow out of a recognition of an unmet need, human desire, or opportunity. Hobbies often turn into businesses. Recognizing you have a passion for some aspect of education can lead to developing a business venture. Edwards and Edwards (2003) believe about one in four people who choose self-employment do so to pursue "a fire in the belly," a passion for doing something that they love to do. Awareness of trends, fads, or what real estate agents call "recognizing the path of progress" may be motivational. Dreams can be an escape from current reality or a foundation for a new reality.

Innovative job creation and self-employment offers considerable appeal to educators who may feel they do not receive the compensation they are worth. Certain features of operating a business may be appealing. See Figure 10–1.

> *What motivates people to choose self-employment?*
>
> *More than 24 million Americans have decided to become their own bosses and to create their own jobs, so they can live the lives they want and do the kind of work they want to do. For many, this has become the New American Dream. For some, it took a crisis, a traumatic, life-changing event, to force them into finding some new way to hold on to their dreams. For others, it was a conscious choice; they decided there had to be a better way, and they set out to create one. Still others simply stumbled quite by chance onto some new opportunity and eagerly seized the moment to give their dreams a chance (Edwards & Edwards, 2003).*

Employed by Others	Self-Employed (excluding contractors)
There is a specified beginning, lunch time, break time, and ending time.	self-choice
Work schedule is fixed.	self-choice
Daily workload is similar each day.	self-choice
Job location is identified.	self-choice or business site
Job description and tasks are identified.	set by self
Work taken home is paid if required by boss.	yes, paid by business income
Work demeanor is expected.	businesslike
Dress is specified.	self-choice
Duties are fixed.	duties vary
Pay increases are tied to negotiation, collective bargaining, or a developed pay salary scale.	depends on success
Pay has a top level.	no top or bottom limit
Performance reviews are fixed.	self-evaluation
"At will" employees have little job security.	security depends on success
Tenured employees have greater job security.	does not apply

Figure 10–1 Contrasting Two Forms of Employment.

One enterprising early childhood educator approached a sub-acute rehabilitation center for senior citizens and convinced administrators to open an adjacent child development center to benefit both age groups (Corcoran, 2002). Another newly graduated teacher hollowed out a large bus and refurbished it as a preschool. She drives to neighborhoods where "child enrichment and play" sessions are offered. Jane Zaccaria opened Tiddlywink and Scallywags, a children's clothing store, just west of Chicago. She believes "clothes seem too grown-up for little girls these days" (Flurry, 2003). Her children's clothing features sweet, colorful self-designed dresses and other clothing with a European, particularly English, flair. Whimsical trims and pom-pom fringe are her signature accents. You can't help but admire these entrepreneurs and another educator whose love of teddy bears led to the successful development of nationwide mall stores. These stores have the goods and equipment necessary for the construction of personalized teddy bears. Children select their size, shape, form, and dress and then take home their unique creations. If you haven't seen these mall stores, visit one and watch children's excitement and delight.

Jacquelyn Aven started a business manufacturing personalized doctor's scrubs for children (Torres, 2004). Her idea came to her as she watched a sick child on television. She believed a hospitalized child dressed in his/her own medical uniform would feel better by looking like one of the medical team. Another innovator, A. Krilov, a man of Russian heritage, and J. Butler, partners and manufacturers of traditional nesting dolls with the likenesses of sports and entertainment celebrities, noticed individuals collected these dolls. Their sales have totaled over $1 million a year (Torres, 2004). In considering opening a business to create self-employment, remember that risks are plentiful; failure stories are as abundant as success stories.

Self-employment can involve direct or indirect services. Tom Brownlee, an early childhood major with handyman skills, observed centers needed help with the repair and replacement of play yard equipment. He started a part-time business while still in school.

He plans a career that includes creating and designing "far from traditional" play areas and equipment. Figure 10–2 describes a wide variety of other education and childhood-related business ventures. Your placement site, past school observations, and individual teaching philosophy may give clues and ideas for a business enterprise.

- emergency care provider
- ski lodge child care
- tennis or health club provider
- weekend and overnight provider
- parent magazine or newsletter publisher
- teacher identity item manufacturer (apron, jewelry, etc.)
- children's film and audiovisual rental service
- children's photography service
- advertising/promotion, fundrasing service
- bulk food service supplier
- food service
- scrap item supplier
- teaching aid manufacturer (puppets, toys, equipment, etc.)
- curriculum idea book publisher
- private school tax consultant
- field trip coordinator
- visiting teacher, speaker service
- industry child care consultant/specialist
- testing service
- substitute teacher service
- child and family lobbyist
- workshop and in-service training service
- specialty teacher (dance, foreign language, gymnastics, science etc.)
- family day care respite service
- child home safety consultant
- nanny service provider
- Saturday fathers activity service
- preschool backpack manufacturer
- surveillance services to parents wishing to monitor sitters in their own home
- parent educator service
- school auditor, accountant, payroll, or collection service
- online parent advisor
- overnight preschool care service
- soccer camp for preschoolers

Figure 10–2   Samples of Self-Employment Businesses and Services.

- children's song writer
- children's stamp set manufacturer
- princess party organizer
- ethnic storyteller
- nature docent
- flannel board set designer and manufacturer
- gingerbread "create and decorate your own cookie or house" bakery
- paint-and-take ceramics center
- toy store owner
- children's hairdresser on wheels
- toy exchange store
- nanny and au pair agency

Figure 10–2 *(Continued)*

Note: This is not intended to be a complete list.

Creating and building self-employment means gaining a heightened awareness of trends and making a careful examination of unmet services plus innovative thinking. It will be helpful to ask yourself the following:

- Is there a service you can perform that will enhance the quality of children's lives or programs?
- What kinds of direct or support services for children and parents do not exist?

Thinking along the lines of discovery of unmet needs, do the following exercise. You will need a pencil or pen, and paper. Look at the following categories of family life and brainstorm self-employment ventures that would help the family with a family task, desire, or goal. Don't worry about a parent's economics; we'll cover that later. Just think of businesses that might offer services or products.

1) *family routines* such as food shopping, cooking, driving, and cleaning
2) *parenting routines* such as helping children organize their rooms, children's bath, bedtime, and reading to children
3) *child routines* such as washing, brushing teeth, dressing, eating, resting, going to school, and doctor's and dentist's visits
4) *play activities* such as games, interactive toys, drawing, other art pursuits, and computer use
5) *children's physical play* (indoors and outdoors) such as sports, games, and play
6) *family entertainment* such as watching, dancing, singing, musical instruments, card games, projects, and traveling
7) *family celebrations* such as holidays, parties, birthday, and decorating
8) *socialization activities* such as picnics, visiting, joining, and guests
9) *gardening activities* such as watering, cutting, planting, growing, and preserving

What might families pay for? Rate each of your ideas—(1) only a few parents could afford, (2) some parents might be interested and could probably afford, (3) many parents would be able to afford this product or service. This is the kind of thinking that uncovers self-employment opportunities and helps with writing a business plan.

Figure 10–3 Developing Toys Has Led to Self-Employment.

Trends to Consider

Educational toys and media businesses are expected to grow 50 percent in the next few years (Silver, 2002); Figure 10–3. Parents want the toy world to keep up with today's technology (della Cava, 2002). Baby Einstein, a successful homegrown phenomenon, helped ignite the infant-through-toddler video market. It is a business that earns $1 billion per year. Classical tunes and vivid colorful imagery are Baby Einstein's trademark. Parents who believe the early childhood years are a prime time for learning and language are the video's major purchasers. Julie Aigner-Clark, the president of Baby Einstein and a former English teacher, is credited with the creative idea. She states, "It's hard to believe what this has turned into in 5 short years." She adds, "This was never about making your baby into Einstein, Mozart, or Beethoven, but about exposing them to these wonderful geniuses of the adult world" (Aigner-Clark, 2002).

A *USA Today*'s online survey for *Parent*'s magazine reports that when parents were asked whether they were inclined to purchase a brain-boosting video or toy, 69 percent responded "somewhat" or "very likely" (della Cava, 2002).

Clarifying a Business Idea

Abrams (2004b), writer of a successful business strategies column and publisher of books and tools for business planning, suggests the following when thinking about a business venture:

But where do we start? How do we learn to recognize an opportunity when it comes our way?

Make a plan. *Form a vision of what you want to achieve, then develop a plan of how to make that vision a reality. To judge whether an opportunity is one to seize or let pass you need to understand whether it fits your goals.*

Get accustomed to making choices. *Moving forward means seizing some opportunities but allowing others to pass by.*

Recognize that the perfect solution is never going to come along. *Life doesn't offer perfection: it offers chances. Looking for perfection is a way of avoiding making choices.*

Get out of your comfort zone. *Sure, you're comfortable doing what you're doing. But if it's not bringing the results you want, you have to change.*

Make a commitment. *Get used to saying no. Get used to saying yes. But whatever you do, do it with commitment and conviction.*

If you have an idea for a product or service, Gage and Gore (2004) have questions that help analyze whether the idea is viable.

1) Has it been done before? If so, can one improve upon it?
2) How big is your target market? A very small niche market will produce limited sales, and one will have to sell at higher prices to make a profit. (With

Tom Brownlee's handyman business mentioned earlier there had to be many schools needing his services.)

3) Who is your target market? Think about gender, age, demographics, and geographic location. (With the teddy bear mall stores idea the target market was the parents of children who love teddy bears, and the appeal of creating a unique, one-of-a-kind, take-home toy. In some economically depressed areas this may not have been a viable business idea.)

4) Who is the competition? (If a large toy manufacturer like Disney was already producing sports figures or movie character nesting dolls, a small nesting doll business probably couldn't compete.)

5) What's unique about your idea? A product or service that is unique may have an edge.

6) Has the idea been protected legally? Your idea may have already been patented or copyrighted.

You have to check with local town, city, and county offices for business license, permits, and tax information. State business filing may also be necessary. Requirements depend on the type of business operated. Insurance availability and costs also should be researched. Gage and Gore (2004) remind entrepreneurs that there is always a cost to doing business, and market testing an idea may save you both time and money. Market testing is described as the first step in finding a small segment of the market that you ultimately want to be your customers. You can start out with 50 or 100 people from your target market. Ask these people to look at what you're offering. Would they buy your product or service, and how much would they spend? If they wouldn't buy it, ask why. Try to determine if people feel that what you are providing would satisfy their needs, and to what extent. The feedback you receive can help refine ideas and convince you either to push ahead or pursue a different direction. In self-employment it is wise to have one-year and five-year action plans along with monthly plans to track progress. Identifying resources and supportive assistance including family members is also important. See Figure 10–4 for advice from successful entrepreneurs.

"You should only start a business if you have more energy than the average person." (Dion, 2003)

"One of the joys of being an entrepreneur is when you have satisfied customers." (Dion, 2003)

"The ups and downs of the economy offer ongoing challenges." (Dion, 2003)

"You need to be persistent, inquisitive, and not afraid to take chances." (Dion, 2003)

"Owning your own business is a double-edged sword." (Doherty, 2003)

"The many hats an entrepreneur must wear can make life stressful." (Doherty, 2003)

"An entrepreneur is someone that is willing to take some well-calculated risks." (Doherty, 2003)

"Being a business owner is what I always wanted to do." (Elcox, 2003)

"I think in my industry women do well because women are caregivers—they're more patient." (Elcox, 2003)

"It's okay to sweat, but it's not okay to let them see you sweat. Walk in confidence—like you own the place." (Elcox, 2003)

"You have to accept change, embrace it, and move forward." (Elmore-Yalch, 2003)

Figure 10–4 Advice and Comments from Successful Entrepreneurs.

"Every day is a challenge, but the biggest challenge is managing growth." (Elmore-Yalch, 2003)
"You have to be willing to take risks with a lot of money and still be able to sleep at night." (Elmore-
    Yalch, 2003)
"I know where we are, where we're going and what pitfalls to watch out for." (Lemas, 2003)
"If I make my business the best it can be, everything else will fall into place." (Olson, 2003)
"Make a list of your abilities and interests. Of course, you'll need a business plan, but most people
    block their creativity initially with negativity when starting out." (Nathanson, 2003)
"What I didn't know was that I wasn't going to make any money the first few years." (Martin, 2004)
"You have to be able to withstand the hours and drudgery. If you're not a high-energy person, you
    should go work for somebody else." (Martin, 2004)

Figure 10–4   *(Continued)*

Time Management

Effective time management skills and techniques are indispensable for the self-employed. These include prioritizing tasks in order of importance, scheduling daily activities, making to-do lists and calendars, protecting health, minimizing interruptions, breaking tasks into segments, delegating or outsourcing, using technology, managing stress, and resolving conflicts.

A Preschool Venture

If you are considering owning, administering, and/or managing your own early childhood-related (particularly a preschool) business, Farr and Ludden (2003) suggest assessing your skills and understandings in the following areas:

customer service
human behavior
parenting styles
learning theory
curriculum development
English language proficiency
business and management principles
resource allocation
leadership techniques
coordination of people and resources

Following are examples of schools that offer special services to busy parents:

- **Bright Horizons Family Solutions** (more than 400 centers in the U.S. and Canada) These centers provide ready-to-heat dinners for purchase nightly and after-school programs for elementary school-aged family members.
- **Creme de la Creme Atlanta** (5 centers in Georgia) These centers offer extra free dry cleaning drop-off and pickup and free parent-education nights with speakers and parenting experts.
- **Little Leprechaun Academy** (2 centers in Ohio) Two Fridays a month, the centers stay open at no cost until midnight so parents are free to do other activities. Inexpensive haircuts for children are available once a month.

- **Primrose Schools** (110 schools in the South and West) These centers host a free dinner on-site for the whole family once a month. Throughout December, centers stay open late so parents can do holiday tasks (Stevens, 2003).

Franchise Preschools and Mall Businesses

Investing in a franchise is a quick and easy way to become self-employed. This takes lots of investigation and perhaps a lot of money. Here's how to recognize a good franchise business opportunity:

offers a secured investment
earns a return on investment
has an infrastructure of support and guidance
offers corporate guidance, investment, and growth
builds equity that can be sold
provides self-employment

Don DeBolt, (2004) President of the International Franchise Association, notes that in the United States franchising is a $1.53 trillion business annually that generates 18 million jobs. Franchising allows individuals to be in business for themselves but not *by* themselves. Certain federal and state laws require franchise companies to comply to federal and state regulations. DeBolt warns that operating a franchised small business doesn't guarantee success. He acknowledges that many are profitable. A thorough investigation and evaluation of the marketplace is suggested. See Figure 10–5.

A Web search in June of 2004 using key words "early childhood franchises" turned up 33,700 items on the Web site. Mentioned were My Gym Children's Fitness Center, Rainbow Years Preschool, Primrose School, KinderCare Learning Centers, Gymbaroo, FasTrackKids, and Grade A Learning Centers. Other franchise opportunities and links to sites offering information related to early childhood education franchises were also found.

Consult professionals including the International Franchise Association (IFA), a business lawyer, and an accountant, and all advisors that can help you.

Read the Uniform Franchise Offering Circular available from the IFA.

Check the history and experience of franchise officers and managers.

Check stock market record and record of others in the same industry.

Check public trends affecting the franchise operation.

Talk to as many franchisees as possible.

Ask lots of questions; do extensive research.

Don't hurry or over-extend finances. Plan for more expenses than you think will be necessary.

Talk to other franchise groups.

Evaluate yourself and your comfort level in doing what the business requires.

Figure 10–5 Franchise Hints and Tips.

Women's Business Centers

Women's business centers offer the latest business information, training, best business practices know-how, computer and Internet counseling, plus access to the Small Business Administration (SBA) programs and services. What else is offered at the 90 women's business centers? Courses, workshops, seminars, instruction in various languages, child care during classes at some locations, and in some areas a computer-equipped van brings programs to neighborhoods.

Women's business centers work closely with Small Business Association offices and the Service Corps of Retired Executives (SCORE). Many classes are free, others require a small fee. Guides to local resources, chat rooms, and bulletin boards are usually available and provide users with valuable links to other business resources.

Small Business Administration (SBA)

SBA offices are located in all 50 states, the District of Columbia, Puerto Rico, the Virgin Islands, and Guam. Look in your local telephone directory for local offices or call 1-800 U ASK SBA. The Small Business Administration made more than 4,600 investments worth $5.6 billion through its venture capital program and provided more than 28,000 loans totaling nearly $1 billion to business disaster victims and others in 2003 (USSBA, 2003). Technical assistance was provided to 1.23 billion entrepreneurs, and $18 billion was devoted to the financing of America's small businesses. Stamler (2003), an SBA spokesman, notes the SBA can help you write a business plan and apply for a loan.

Writing a Business Plan

When investigating the wisdom of starting a business, writing a business plan is a necessity. Without a business plan, you leave things to chance. Pakroo (2003) explains:

> *A business plan describes key features of your business including how it will operate, what will give it an edge over competition, market research and marketing strategies, and several financial forecasts.*

You increase odds for success with a well-written plan. An effective plan estimates whether a good profit can be made. A good business plan also estimates start-up costs, indicates funds necessary and where they will come from, convinces investors and lenders, estimates revenue, defines your market, identifies your customers, designs an effective marketing strategy, analyzes the competition, and anticipates possible problems.

Reading

To be successfully self-employed, follow Edwards and Edward's (2003) advice:

> *Read everything you can that will provide you with the information you need at each step of the way. Go to the nearest bookstore or library and surf the net. Head for the career and business sections. Take courses on becoming self-employed.*

Financing

Individuals have been successful in raising start-up money for their new business in many ways including bank loans, **venture capital investors**, life insurance policy loans, stock sales, house mortgages, IRA accounts, relative loans, and angel investors.

The Center for Venture Research estimates there are 400,000 active individual or "angel" investors who invest in more than 50,000 businesses each year (Worrell, 2004). Worrell suggests a quick search will help one find a local angel group, and most CPAs and business lawyers will know what is available in your area.

Assets

Assets can be defined as something you own or any personal quality that you possess that has value. You can have the power to use, control, or develop an asset. Individuals can use these "givens" or assets to their vocational advantage. If you inherit a commercial piece of property and you are an early childhood educator, you could possibly think of establishing a preschool. Using other assets to further a self-employment endeavor might not be seen as readily. Take a piece of paper and list your assets. Include natural gifts, talents, developed skills along with property, other things of monetary value, possessions, hobbies, or anything else you can think of that might be viewed as a positive asset. If your father is an accountant or your uncle is a banker, consider those facts an asset. In a previous job if you did secretarial work, that is also an asset.

SCORE

If you are looking for no fee small business advice, the Service Corps of Retired Executives (SCORE) is the place to turn for confidential, professional business counseling. E-mail advice, one-to-one counseling, and business workshops are usually available. Check http://www.svscore.org for locations or your local telephone directory.

State Loan Programs

Many states have loan programs to stimulate and support state-run commerce. Any bank loan made in these states may qualify for a state business loan. Each state has loan terms and maximum loan amounts. State loan programs usually issue loans to individuals wishing to start a new business, expand or modernize a facility, purchase equipment and fixtures, increase inventory and working capital, acquire an existing business or franchise, refinance existing debt, or construct or purchase commercial buildings.

What do banks look for in borrowers? They consider management ability and experience in an industry, adequate investment by the borrower, ability to repay the loan, and a satisfactory personal and business credit history.

What does the bank usually require of borrowers? The following items are commonplace—a statement of purpose, a business plan, a past and current investment in business history, description of collateral, income projections, expenses, cash flow data, signed personal financial statements, personal tax returns, a resume, incorporation papers, by-laws, partnership agreements, franchise agreements, and other papers as appropriate. If you apply for a loan after a business has been successfully started, you are required to submit full business records as well.

Additional Training

An advanced degree may be necessary for many self-employment ventures. You can enroll in administrative or director coursework at most community colleges. Business management and principles, marketing, accounting, and other similar coursework is offered. Distance learning opportunities are also available through institutions of higher learning. Apprenticing and volunteering are other routes to gaining skills. Working in an early childhood service industry job and learning the ropes firsthand provides an intimate knowledge of some business operations.

It is a good idea to self-assess and to develop plans to acquire skills if you don't already have them. As your own career manager, no one can do this for you.

Training for Women Small Business Owners

Through the cooperative efforts of the Office of Women's Business Ownership (SBA), the Women's Business Centers, the Small Business Development Center program, and the Service Corps of Retired Executives, the WNET (Television Channel 13 of Public Broadcasting System), Roundtable was established to give counseling, training, and technical assistance to new women business owners. It is called a "mentoring program" and hundreds of WNET roundtables meet nationwide. Seasoned advice from experienced women business owners is available. Through regular, informal meetings, you can benefit from the personal support extended from other group members who understand the ups and downs of self-employment (SBA, 2003).

Other Resources for Self-Employment Information

Business information centers. Many metropolitan areas have business information centers that have libraries with start-up information, how-to books, free counseling, idea books, and other supportive resources. Most are funded by local companies and organizations with a common interest in stimulating business formation and success in their particular city or state. Other sources of information include:

Professional associations. Many early childhood professional associations offer publications helpful to entrepreneurs. Exhibit halls at major national and state conferences offer a wealth of innovative and creative business ventures started by other educators.

Other owners of early childhood-related businesses. If you plan to open a business similar to other businesses in your area, Fairbrother (2003) suggests asking noncompetitive business owners in other towns and cities for the five best and five worst things they did when they started their business.

Business Insurance

Insurance protects an owner's personal assets. Childcare Choice from THOMCO, an insurance program for the child care industry, is endorsed by the National Child Care Association. It provides automobile, child abuse, property, general liability, umbrella policies, child accident coverages, equipment breakdown coverage, and other business-related coverages. Other insurance firms do likewise.

Joining an Association of "Like" Businesses

Abrams (2004a) believes whether you run the smallest home-based business or the largest multinational corporation, you should look for and join a group of colleagues in the same field. You can find industry associations or professional societies in most locales. Most offer information, education, and marketing opportunities. Many people think that these trade groups' sole function is to lobby for legislation that is favorable or protects their industry. Most trade groups do so on a state, local, and national level. They also are an opportunity for networking and skill improvement. Keeping abreast of your industry happenings is important to your success.

Self-Employed Contract Employees

In Chapter 9, contract work was mentioned. Contract workers are self-employed workers. Your own attorney should approve an offered contract before you sign. See Figure 10–6 for the duties and responsibilities of an independent contractor.

Independent contractors have to pay their own Social Security taxes, and estimated income taxes may need to be filed. If business expenses are claimed, complete records must be kept. Independent contractors should seek competent tax advice.

A growing number of large preschools, large private corporations, and church-affiliated preschools and centers offer employment contracts rather than hourly wages to employees. A contract is a formal agreement between two parties defining mutual obligations and responsibilities for a specific period of time.

Negotiated Contracts

Most public elementary, middle, and secondary school teachers have negotiated contracts agreed upon through a bargaining process involving teacher representatives and their school

---

The major difference between an independent contractor and an employee is that one is self-employed, the other is not.

You agree to job specifications in a contract.
You obtain your own training and skills.
You hire and supervise yourself and your staff.
You make independent decisions.
Your services are available to the general public.
You develop your own work schedule, or it is specified in a contract.
You furnish your own materials.
You pay business expenses.
You can subcontract work depending on contract terms.
You provide services when and where the contract stipulates.
You work at regular intervals.
You can work part-time.
Your pay is stated in a contract.
You have an investment in your business.
You can work anywhere you choose and when you choose if the contract does not specify.
You agree to perform tasks over a period of time.
You report work progress as goals of the contract are met.
You work under a legal contract and can be sued for nonperformance of duties.

Figure 10–6 Characteristics of an Independent Contractor.

boards. A bargaining agent or union negotiator may represent the employees during contract discussions. Individual and group negotiated contracts with both public and private schools may include but not be limited to base salary, specific salary increments, fringe benefits, number of working days, polices regarding leaves for personal illness and emergencies, evaluation procedures, termination guidelines, and renewability for both parties. But these workers are employed educators rather than self-employed contract workers.

Family Care Providers

Bush (2001), the author of *Dollars and Sense*, promotes professionalism and urges home providers to commit to the following goals:

- I will consider myself a professional, and I will expect appropriate work conditions and compensation.
- I will use basic practices common to small businesses (written contract and policies, record keeping system, cash flow plan, competitive pricing, and marketing.)
- I will improve my communication with parents about my professional role as caregiver, my philosophy of quality child care, and my business policies.
- I will increase my understanding of parent concerns, enforce my policies assertively, and treat parents with compassion and professionalism.

Although most states license family child care homes or require voluntary registration, many homes remain unlicensed and unregulated. Family day care homes accredited by the National Association for the Education of Young Children (NAEYC) are growing in number as more owner-providers voluntarily undertake the accreditation process.

Family day care homes are defined as child care that takes place in the home of a non-relative for up to 12 hours a day or 5 or more days a week. As was mentioned in Chapter 1, two-thirds of all workers in the early childhood education field are self-employed, and the majority of these are family day care providers (Krantz, 2000).

Caruso and Fawcett (1999) describe the varied backgrounds and other additional characteristics of family child care providers:

- Almost all are women.
- 75 percent are married.
- Median age is about 41.
- About 12 to 13 percent have college degrees.
- About 11 percent have not graduated from high school.
- Most work to supplement family income.
- One-half periodically meet with other providers or join affiliates of the National Association for Family Child Care.

Trawick-Smith & Lambert (1995) believe family care providers generally must struggle with an image problem. When it is asserted that any kind, warm person can care for children, the status of the profession suffers. Family child care providers may be the least respected of all educators.

A business plan outline for family child care business is included in Bush's *Dollars and Sense* (2001). A resource booklist at the end of this chapter has readings concerned with family child care businesses.

Redleaf National Institute is a national center devoted to those who are in the business of family child care. Information concerning training, workshops, books, assistance, and membership particulars are available on it's Web site (http://www.redleafinstitute.org).

Summary

Self-employment is an option for educators. Women-owned businesses are growing in number, and male educators can also follow this career path. Many educators choose self-employment out of necessity, a passion to do something they love, and for other factors including becoming aware of an opportunity. Examples of successful operations and entrepreneurial advice were included, as well as cautions and recognition of risk. You were made aware of funding possibilities, business plans, and resources for professional help. The personal abilities and business skills that promote success were listed. Contract work was also described.

Helpful Web Sites

Building Child Care
http://www.buildingchildcare.org
a California Department of Education collaboration helping child care providers find financing

Computertots
http://www.computertots.com
offers an education-based technology program, trains or provides skilled on-site teachers

Costco and American Express OPEN: The Small Business Network
http://www.costco.com
click "Services," then click on small business loans and lines of credit

Entrepreneur Magazine
http://www.entrepreneur.com

Families and Work Institute
http://www.familiesandwork.org
statistics on family care providers

Internal Revenue Service
http://www.irs.gov
selected excerpts of IRS publications for family child care providers

National Association for Family Child Care
http://www.assoc-mgmt.com
information on accredited family child care homes

National Federation for Women Business Owners
http://www.nfwbo.org

Playground Design Companies
http://www.groundsforplay.com

Small Business Association (SBA)
http://www.business.gov
legal information for small businesses

School Supply Companies
http://www.angeles-group.com

THOMCO
http://www.thomcoins.com
insurance for child facilities

U.S. Census Bureau "American Community Survey"
http://www.census.gov
an ongoing nationwide survey

Women's Business Centers
http://www.womensbusinesscenter.org
http://www.onlinewbc.org

Women's Network for Entrepreneurial Training
http://www.onlinwbc.gov

Resources

Daily, F. (2001). *Tax savvy for small business*. Berkeley, CA: Nolo Press.

McKeever, M. (2004). *How to write a business plan*. Berkeley, CA: Nolo Press.

Pakroo, P. (2003). *Business planpro 2003*. Berkeley, CA: Nolo Press.

Steingold, F., & Portman, J. (2000). *Leasing spaces for your small business*. Berkeley, CA: Nolo Press.

Steingold, F. (2000). *Legal guide for starting and running a small business*. Berkeley, CA: Nolo Press.

The Children's Foundation. (2001). *2001 family child care licensing study*. Washington, DC: Author.

Whitely, K., Elliott, K., & Duckworth, C. (2003). *The old girl's network: Insider advice for women building businesses in a man's world*. New York: Perseus Publishing.

Family Child Care Provider Resource List

Bush, J. (2001). *Dollars and sense: Planning for profit in your child care business*. Clifton Park, NY: Thomson Delmar Learning.

Copeland, T. (1997). *Family child care contracts and policies: How to be businesslike in a caring profession* (2nd ed.). St. Paul: Redleaf Press.

Copeland, T. (1999). *The 1999 family child care tax workbook*. St. Paul: Redleaf Press.

Ferrar, H. M. (1996). *Places for growing: How to improve your family child care home*. Princeton: Mathematica Policy Research, Inc. Rockefeller Foundation.

Neugebauer, B., & Neugebauer, R. (1996). *On-target marketing: Promotion strategies for child care centers*. Redmond, WA: Child Care Information Exchange.

Pruissen, C. M. (1998). *Start and run a profitable home day care: Your step-by-step business plan*. North Vancouver: Self Counsel Press.

References

Abrams, R. (2004a, August 19). Joining association can boost your business. *The Idaho Statesman*, p. B1.

Abrams, R. (2004b, April). Fresh views: Brain food for the entrepreneur—don't wait for rescue. *The Costco Connection, 19* (4), 11.

Aigner-Clark, J. Quoted in della Cava, M. R. (2002, July 23). Building a brainier baby. *The Idaho Statesman*, pp. 1L, 3L.

Bush, J. (2001). *Dollars and sense: Planning for profit in your child care business*. Clifton Park, NY: Thomson Delmar Learning.

Caruso, J. J., & Fawcett, M. T. (1999). *Supervision in early childhood education: A developmental perspective.* New York: Teachers College Press.

Center for Women's Business Research (2004). *Women owned businesses: Growth study.* Washington, DC: Author.

Corcoran, K. (2002, November 18). Nursing home nursery school. *San Jose Mercury News,* pp. 1A, 16A.

Costco Connection. (2002, March). Women-owned firms growing. *17* (3) 9. Author.

DeBolt, D. (2004, July 7). Considering a franchise? Then do your homework. *USA Today,* p. 7B.

della Cava, M. R. (2002, July 23). Building a brainier baby. *The Idaho Statesman,* pp. 1L, 3L.

Dion, K. Quoted in Martin, S. (2003, September 15). Being in the right place at the right time leads Dion down the road to entrepreneurial success. *Idaho Business Review,* pp. 4–5.

Doherty, K. Quoted in Martin, S. (2003, September 15). Doherty finds niche in civil engineering field. *Idaho Business Review,* pp. 6–7.

Edwards, P., & Edwards, S. (2003). *Finding your perfect work: The new career guide to making a living, creating a life.* New York: Penguin Putnam Inc.

Elcox, J. Quoted in Martin, S. (2003, September 15). Early determination to excel leads Elcox to success. *Idaho Business Review,* pp. 8–9.

Elmore-Yalch, R. Quoted in Martin, S. (2003, September 15). Thirst for knowledge drives Elmore-Yalch. *Idaho Business Review,* pp. 10–11.

Estrella, J. (2004, June 6). I'll get paid what I'm worth: Idaho ranks fourth in the nation in growth of female-owned firms. *The Idaho Statesman,* p. 1B.

Farr, M., & Ludden, L. (2003). *300 best jobs without a four-year degree.* Indianapolis, IN: JIST Publishing, Inc.

Flurry, A (2003, April). A British import near Chicago. *Family Circle, 16* (3), 13.

Fairbrother, C. Quoted in Kalish, N. (2003, January). Do the things you love—now. *Reader's Digest,* p. 125.

Foster, J. (1996). *How to get ideas.* San Francisco: Berrett-Koehler Publisher.

Gage, C., & Gore, S. (2004, July). Bring your products or services to market. *Memphis Woman, 12* (6) 40–41.

Jordan, L. Quoted in Howard, J. (2004, May 22). Seminar focus on ways to support entrepreneurship. *The Idaho Statesman,* p. 1B.

Krantz, L. (2000). *Jobs rated almanac.* (5th ed.). New York: St Martin's Press.

Lemas, N. Quoted in Martin, S. (2003, September 15). Commercial real estate proves perfect fit for optimist Lemas. *Idaho Business Review,* p. 1b.

Martin, E. Quoted in Estrella, J. (2004, June 6). I'll get paid what I'm worth: Idaho ranks fourth in the nation in growth of female-owned firms. *The Idaho Statesman,* p. 1B.

Nathanson, C. (2003, October 14). Q & A with the vocational coach. *Career Source,* p. 18.

Olson, S. Quoted in Martin, S. (2003, September 15), A new business. *Idaho Business Review,* pp. 12–13.

Pakroo, P. (2003). *Business planpro 2003.* Berkeley, CA: Nolo Press.

Regan, M. (2004, September 16). Experts: Majors, not schools, determine grad's starting pay. *The Idaho Statesman,* p. M5.

Silver, J. Quoted in della Cava, M. R. (2002, July 23). Building a brainier baby. *The Idaho Statesman,* pp. 1L, 3L.

Small Business Administration. (2003). [Brochure.] The facts about ... WNET roundtable: The small business mentoring program for women.

Stamler, M. Quoted in Kalish, N. (2003, January). Do the thing you love—now. *Reader's Digest,* p. 125.

Stevens, L. R. (2003, December). Day care perks parents love. *Parents,* p. 59.

Torres, N.L. (2004, July). What's up doc? *Entrepreneur,* p. 104.

Trawick-Smith, J., & Lambert, L. (1995, March). The unique challenges of the family child care provider. Implications for professional development. *Young Children, 50* (3), 25–32.

Winik, L.W. (2003, October 26). What you may not know about workers in America today. *San Jose Mercury News*, p. 4.

Worrell, D. (2004, July). The other colors of money. *Entrepreneur*, pp. 65–67.

CHAPTER ELEVEN

Advocacy Never Ends

The time is always right to do what is right.

—Martin Luther King Jr.

The Park

Emma was in the coffee shop on a Friday after school when she noticed a group of people with signs and banners walking across the town square. When she finished her latte, she went to see what was happening. She recognized a neighbor and talked with her. The city council was considering closing a children's park and turning it into a commercial area. "Not that beautiful little park on Washington Street," she thought. That was the area where traffic was heavy and children had few places to play on grass or in the shade. Some of her first-graders lived there. She debated whether as a teacher, she should get involved. She knew there were many people in town who supported the project because it would bring jobs.

QUESTIONS TO PONDER

1. If I were Emma I would... .

2. Can teachers in a small town be politically active?

3. Is advocating for teachers' salaries, benefits, and working conditions a self-serving act? Or does it benefit children and families, too? If so how?

There are so many children's stories emphasizing that just one individual can make a difference by standing up for what is right. Every professional educator sees "standing-up-for" as part of their job. Educators need to believe they can influence others by small acts, one at a time, and by participating in larger group actions. Robinson and Stark (2002) believe advocacy is every educator's responsibility:

> As teachers, families, policy makers, community leaders, and concerned adults, we all share responsibility for making sure young children get the most out of the opportunities of their early years. It's up to all of us to make the early years count! An important step in improving opportunities for all young children is getting more people involved and encouraging them to raise their voices in support of high-quality childhood education.

The goal of advocacy is to educate policy makers and the general public concerning the importance of children's education and families' health, educational opportunity, and economic stability. Educators work toward a sensitized public view that is reflected in government, state, and local budgetary priorities which determine public investment. Robinson and Stark (2002) point out that although nearly two-thirds of states now fund at least one program that targets infants and toddlers and at least one aimed at preschoolers, five states do not (Alabama, Mississippi, South Dakota, Utah, and Wyoming) fund any child development or family support programs for young children and families.

Following are some secrets to success in advocacy:

- working individually to provide quality developmental care
- working individually to understand types and the strategies of advocacy
- actively communicating a clear message
- understanding in what ways others have successfully advocated
- working with advocacy group efforts
- never giving up

Because this book's focus is on career management, Chapter 1 delved into the realities of work in education. Many dedicated professionals are not receiving wages equal to their contribution to our society or equal to their background or training. Consequently, a "revolving door" exists in many early childhood centers as teachers come and go. This negatively affects young children. Educators need to advocate for themselves. It may appear to

---

Question: It is estimated that teachers spend an average of $589–$700 a year for classroom supplies not provided by their school districts (Singletary, 2004). Should Congress give teachers a tax credit or deduction for their out-of-pocket donations?

Answer: Congress passed a bill in 2002 for a federal $250 tax deduction for eligible educators, but the bill expired at the end of 2003. This is a legitimate advocacy issue. *The Teacher's Act* is still being considered by federal representatives. Go to http://www.house.gov to identify a congressman/woman to send a message. To find a senator go to http://www.senate.gov.

be promoting self-interest, which it is, but research consistently points out that better educated, better paid, better benefitted educators provide higher quality services to children and families and achieve better results in child learning!

Robinson and Stark (2002) suggest an answer to the question "How long will early childhood educators have to advocate?":

> *Until all children in America have access to high-quality, developmentally appropriate early childhood and early grade experiences, and until all early childhood providers and teachers are able to receive the training and financial support they require to keep them in the field and ensure their commitment and competence, early childhood educators should continue their advocacy efforts.*

Ways to Advocate

You can participate in advocacy activities daily by speaking out and expressing your personal concern for the care and welfare of young children and their families. Your belief that young children flourish when quality developmental care is provided by well-trained, well-paid professionals should enter conversations and influence listeners. Mention the role of early childhood educators in extending professional supportive assistance to parents as well. Public investment in young children and families is an investment in America's future. This is an important point.

Advocating publicly to change public policies, priorities, and practices for the benefit of children and families is another activity professional educators pursue. Realizing that policy makers at local, state, and federal levels have the power to enhance quality and educational opportunity, educators call attention to problems, necessary changes, and then propose answers, solutions, and legislative actions. This is usually done through a group effort, but individual advocacy counts, too.

A lot of public attention has been given to "leaving no child behind" and the federal legislation aimed at increasing children's academic skills. Early childhood experiences are viewed as crucial. Young (2004) describes the present situation in the following statement:

> *Want to know why Johnny and Susie can't read, don't graduate, and wind up losers? In part it's because 34 percent of children enter kindergarten without knowing their letters, and 42 percent can't count to 20. States and the federal government spend about $10 billion annually on early education, but the average U.S. preschool doesn't even get a "good" rating on a scale used by teachers worldwide.*

In this same article, Young provides quotations from Amy Wilkins, Executive Director of the nonpartisan Trust for Early Education, who is speaking about funding:

> *It's not at a level that's detrimental to children—their brains aren't melting—but it doesn't assure kids are cared for in an optimal way (Wilkins, 2004).*

The article goes on to describe Georgia's funded universal preschool program and notes that experts give the program solid marks (Young, 2004).

Wilkins (2004) explains the crux of the national problem:

> *Good preschool isn't cheap though. There is no point in subsidizing low-quality programs. Because we haven't invested in quality, we haven't got the returns we want.*

The message is clear here. Wilkins is advocating for additional funding. Funding is necessary for providing quality, developmental care by well-trained and fairly compensated professionals.

Local efforts can include advocating for supportive family assistance and/or child safety with business leaders, manufacturers, developers, builders, and others in private industry. An advocacy example here might be as simple as promoting nonsmoking areas in the local businesses that young children frequent, or as controversial as proposing lowering mandated child-adult ratios in preschools or infant-toddler centers.

Robinson and Stark (2002) believe effective advocacy groups have four components.

1) They are *intentional* with actions and plans based on a clear goal(s).
2) They are *strategic* for the political climate, the group's financial and emotional resources, and its ability to progress to a conclusion has been considered.
3) They are *flexible,* having the ability to adjust plans, secure the necessary tools, and take actions that are needed.
4) They are *organized* with succinctly identified issues for the intended audience(s), and they have the created materials necessary to inform, they have proposed solutions, and have the ability to organize the advocacy group and others around advocacy purposes and goals.

Kamerman and Gatenio (2003) clarify how each early childhood career worker's advocacy efforts help change early childhood education and care policy. These authors note the "hundred and even perhaps thousands" of advocacy institutions including private advocacy, think tank, research, outreach, university, foundation, and public policy institutions that advocate and influence policy decisions involving families and preparing children to succeed in primary school. They also point out that more policy-making responsibilities have shifted to state level. Although early childhood workers who join advocacy activities may not see immediate pay-offs for their efforts, policy makers do notice and are responsive to those who work on the front lines. They also notice large group efforts.

Educating Yourself

Adams (2001) suggests that child care advocates are made, not born. Learning about what to do about advocacy issues may not come easily. It takes time, effort, practice, and attention when you already have a busy schedule. With practice, skills develop making you ready for the next round.

There is no way to develop advocacy skill and become knowledgeable about advocacy group efforts except to jump in and do it. Keeping abreast of local and state efforts takes a willingness and a personal commitment to do work after working all day. Some of the terms you'll become familiar with follow:

coalition	regulatory implementation
proactive agenda	task force
forum	referendum
partnerships	lobbying
legislative process	grassroots network
appropriations	action alerts
amendments and passages	media releases

A great way to start advocacy efforts is by joining a local chapter of a professional association or the NEA (National Education Association). NAEYC (National Association for the Education of Young Children) has an advocacy history, and they recently revised standards for college and university programs that prepare early childhood teachers. The NAEYC's leaders and members are attempting to raise the quality of all programs for all young children by improving the preparation of early childhood teachers in colleges and universities. The Appendix contains a list of other early childhood associations and advocacy groups.

An Author's Aside

One of the authors of this book has had a long career as an early childhood community college instructor. Many of her students proposed the same solution to the issue of low pay. "What if every graduating early childhood teacher refused to work for centers and schools that did not offer equitable pay for their services, experience, and education?" Equitable pay, they felt, was salary and benefits equal to the pay received by publicly funded early childhood teachers with the same qualifications in their community or state. Their rationale was that *all* young children deserve well-paid early childhood teachers not just young children who are at-risk because they happen to live in lower income or single parent families, and not just children whose families have the economic resources to pay higher fees that in turn pay for higher teacher salaries in some private schools. These students also felt that more graduates should combine their resources and efforts and open schools themselves so that they could control teacher pay. They hoped communities would promote their self-employment attempts with tax relief, waived fees, and other incentives. The solution here was to cut profit-taking that keeps teachers' pay low, and to put the business of child care into professionals' hands rather than corporate hands. If schools and centers had to close because they can't offer equitable pay, so be it, students in training said. New self-employed owner schools could take their place. The students sincerely believed that a lot of individual new teachers could help all teachers by refusing to be exploited.

Summary   Advocacy involves working to promote and assure quality education and care for America's children. This is accomplished through individual and group efforts that gain public support and funding at an adequate level. It includes advocating for proper educational facilities, educational materials, well-trained and compensated teachers, and many other issues that affect children and family welfare. It is every dedicated educator's professional responsibility. Advocacy, like an educator's lifelong learning, never ends.

Abbreviations

AACC	The American Association of Community Colleges
ACEI	The Association for Childhood Education International (birth through adolescence)
AFSCME	The American Federation of State, County, and Municipal Employees
CCR&R	The Child Care Resource and Referral (agency)
CDA	Child Development Associate
ESL	English as a Second Language
NACCP	The National Association of Child Care Professionals
NACCRRA	The National Association of Child Care Resource and Referral Agencies

NACCTEP	The National Association for Community College Teacher Education Programs
NACTC	The National Alliance of Community and Technical Colleges
NAECTE	The National Association of Early Childhood Teacher Educators
NAEYC	The National Association for the Education of Young Children
NAFCC	The National Association for Family Child Care
NCCA	The National Child Care Association
NCCCC	The National Coalition for Campus Children's Centers
NCES	The National Center for Education Statistics, U.S. Department of Education
NCLBA	*The No Child Left Behind Act*
NCTE	The National Council of Teachers of English
NIEER	The National Institute for Early Education Research
NSACA	The National School Age Care Alliance

Helpful Web Sites

Center for the Early Childhood Workforce
http://www.ccw.org

Families and Work
http://www.familiesandwork.org

NAEYC (The National Association for the Education of Young Children)
http://www.naeyc.org

National Black Child Development Institute
http://www.ncdi.org

National Latino Children's Institute
http://www.nici.org

Stand for Children
http://www.stand.org

The Children's Defense Fund
http://www.childrensdefense.org

ZERO TO THREE
http://www.zerotothree.org

Resources

Bellm, D, Burton, A., Shukla, R., & Whitebook, M. (1997). *Making work pay in the child care industry: Promising practices for improving compensation.* Washington, DC: Center for the Child Care Workforce.

Center for the Child Care Workforce. (1998, 1999). *Creating better child care jobs: Model work standard for teaching staff in center-based child care.* Washington, DC: Center for the Child Care Workforce.

Center for the Child Care Workforce. (1999). *Creating better family child care jobs: Model work standards.* Washington, DC: Center for the Child Care Workforce.

Lombardi, J., & Goffin, S. G. (1998). *Speaking out: Early childhood advocacy.* Washington, DC: National Association for the Education of Young Children.

Moss, P. (2000). Training of early childhood education and care staff. *International Journal of Educational Research 33* (2000), 31–35.

Rodd, J. (1994). *Leadership in early childhood: The pathway to professionalism.* New York: Teachers College Press.

Shields, K. (1994). *In the tiger's mouth: An empowerment guide for social action.* Gabriola Island, BC: New Society Publishers.

Whitebook, M., Howes, C., & Phillips, D. A. (1998). *Who cares? Child care teachers and the quality of care in America.* Final Report of the National Child Care Staffing Study. Washington, DC: Center for the Child Care Workforce.

References

Adams, D. Quoted in Bellm, D., and Haack, P. (2001). *Working for quality child care: Good child care jobs equals good care for children.* Washington, DC: Center for the Early Childhood Workforce.

Kamerman, S. B., & Gatenio, S. (2003). Overview of the current policy context. In D. Cryer & R. M Clifford (Eds.) *Early childhood education and care in the USA* (pp. 1–30). Baltimore, MD: Paul H. Brookes Publishing Co.

Robinson, A., & Stark, D. (2002). *Advocates in action: Making a difference for young children.* Washington, DC: National Association for the Education of Young Children.

Singletary, M. (2004, September 5). Congress should give teachers a tax break. *The Idaho Statesman,* p. B1.

Wilkins, A. Quoted in Young, J. (2004, January). Wouldn't it be great if.... *Reader's Digest,* pp. 91–95.

Young, J. (2004, January). Wouldn't it be great if.... *Reader's Digest,* pp. 91–95.

Appendix

Chapter 1

Self-Aptitude Exercise

Respond to the following using one or two short sentences.

1. Your old deaf cat sleeps in the sun on your neighbor's driveway, making your neighbor get out of the car before driving in. This neighbor's dog uses your yard as his bathroom. You'd

   _____ .

2. A young child nervously looks both ways at the curb. You need to cross the street. No one else is around. You'd

   _____ .

3. At a party with strangers I'd

   _____ .

4. A friend without money needs money to correct a disfigurement. You'd

   _____ .

5. Two small boys are fighting in the park. Their parents are looking the other way. You'd

   _____ .

6. A child under your supervision is rude and discourteous during dinner at a restaurant to the waiter. You'd

   _____ .

7. What family situations seem to promote continually unhappy children?

   _____ .

8. Your sister is upset at your mother and comes to you. You'd

   _____ .

9. A work associate is goofing off and making more work for you. You'd

   _____ .

10. A lot of people don't really understand teenagers' behavior because teenagers are

   _____ .

11. Your nephew is having trouble tying his shoe. You'd

   _____ .

12. Your brother-in-law thinks it is funny to push others in the swimming pool. He is walking toward you. You'd

   _____ .

13. The outside lights in your condominium complex don't work. Your neighbors grouse about it, but so far the condo managers have not fixed the lights. You'd

   _____ .

14. Your second grade child seems stuck in her artwork. She always draws the same picture—a house with smoke coming out of the chimney. You'd

   _____ .

15. Most teachers who know what they are doing have classrooms that

   _____ .

16. What are a few characteristics of people who like people?

   _____ .

17. If you had to plan a wedding in a week, how would you accomplish this with your family members?

   _____ .

18. You are the principal of an elementary school. One teacher drops by daily with flowers for your office, another has good suggestions and contributes at staff meetings, another complains that parents don't understand her. You'd suspect what about each teacher, and do what?

   _____ .

19. What type of parents seem to push their child, as quickly as possible, into academic pursuits and demand high grades?

   _____ .

20. If you were choosing people to work in your newly formed consulting business, what personality traits would you prefer? List five in priority order.

   _____ .

Analyzing Your Answer

Give yourself a point if your answer involves _____ .
1. helping
2. recognizing, facing, or attempting to solve a personal problem
3. extending advice to another
4. guiding another's behavior in a positive way
5. delegating tasks
6. motivating yourself or another
7. showing flexibility
8. displaying compassion
9. an observational skill
10. communicating to solve a problem

This exercise attempted to probe the following.

- people skills (social, interpersonal, etc.)
- motivational aptitude
- communication skills
- organizational skills
- counseling aptitude
- problem-solving orientation

   Anonymously give your point score to your instructor who will develop a range-of-scores graph.

Note: This assessment is slanted toward the assessment of aptitudes for teaching careers rather than those of other specialties or other positions within the field of education.

Chapter 1

Early Childhood Teaching Skills

Do You Have Skills in These Areas?

Ask yourself the following questions. Rate yourself using a 1 to 5 scale, 5 meaning "I absolutely possess this skill," and 1 meaning "I need to work on this."

- Do I respect, nurture, and challenge children?
- Do I present ongoing opportunities for children to learn important skills, knowledge, and dispositions when in my care?
- Am I able to let children make meaningful decisions throughout the day?
- Do I respect, appreciate, and include children's home language and culture in the classroom?
- Do I plan individual, small-group, and large-group activities?
- Do I work toward promoting the skills necessary for children's future academic success?
- Do children have the opportunity to learn basic kindergarten readiness skills in my classroom?
- Do I use children's natural curiosity as a motivator?
- Are children provided variety in their daily schedule in my classroom?
- Do I include families as partners in all aspects of the educational program?
- Are family members welcome to observe and participate in activities?
- Do I promote parenting skills?
- Do I routinely share information about each child's progress?
- Do parents have opportunities to contribute to the policies and program in my classroom?
- Are the children's home cultures and languages respected and appreciated?
- Am I able to guide and manage children's behavior effectively?
- Can I plan and offer activities for intellectual, social-emotional, physical and creative growth and development?
- Am I able to offer a developmentally appropriate program?
- Am I aware of children's learning styles?
- Can I teach important concepts such as mathematics and early literacy through projects, everyday experiences, and collaborative activities?
- Can I assess each child's progress and make adjustments as necessary?
- Do I refer children who may have special learning needs for evaluation and diagnosis?
- Do I maintain a respectful, collaborative relationship with other staff, parents, and professionals?
- Can I plan a curriculum with specified goals and offer planned activities and experiences to reach those goals?
- Can I prepare and design an inviting, developmentally appropriate, and well-equipped classroom?
- Am I able to develop individual learning plans for individual children?

Chapter 3

Professional Associations and Organizations

American Association of Higher Education (AAHE)
One Dupont Circle, Suite 360
Washington, DC 20036
http://www.aahe.org

American Association for Employment in Education (AAEE)
3040 Riverside Drive Suite 125
Columbus, OH 43221-2550
http://www.aaee.org

American Association of Christian Schools (AACS)
P. O. Box 1097
Independence, MO 64051-0597
http://www.aacs.org

American Association of Colleges for Teacher Education (AACTE)
1307 New York Avenue NW, Suite 300
Washington, DC 20005
http://www.aacte.org

American Association of State Colleges and Universities (AASCU)
    1307 New York Avenue NW, Fifth Floor
    Washington, DC 20005-1701
    http://www.aascu.org

American Association of Community Colleges (AACC)
    One Dupont Circle NW, Suite 410
    Washington, DC 20036
    aacc.nche.edu

American Association of University Professors (AAUP)
    1012 Fourteenth Street NW, Suite 500
    Washington, DC 20005
    http://www.aaup.org

American Federation of Teachers (AFT)
    555 New Jersey Avenue NW
    Washington, DC 20001
    http://www.aft.org

Association for Childhood Education International (ACEI)
    17904 Georgia Avenue Suite 215
    Olney, MD 20832
    http://www.udel.edu

Association of American Colleges and Universities (AAC&U)
    1818 R Street NW
    Washington, DC 20009
    http://www.aacu.org

Association of American Universities (AAU)
    1200 New York Avenue NW, Suite 550
    Washington, DC 20005
    http://www.aau.edu

Distance Education and Training Council (DETC)
    1601 18th Street NW
    Washington, DC 20009
    http://www.detc.org

Institute of International Education (IIE)
    809 United Nations Plaza
    New York, NY 10017-3580
    http://www.iie.org

International Reading Association (IRA)
    800 Barksdale Road
    P. O. Box 8139
    Newark, DE 19714-8139
    http://www.reading.org

National Association of Family Child Care Providers (NAFCC)
    5202 Pinemont Drive
    Salt Lake City, UT 84123
    http://www.nafcc.org

National Association for Gifted Children (NAGC)
    1707 L Street NW, Suite 550
    Washington, DC 20036
    http://www.nagc.org

National Association of Independent Colleges and Universities (NAICU)
    1025 Connecticut Avenue NW, Suite 700
    Washington, DC 20036
    http://www.anicu.edu

National Association of Independent Schools (NAIS)
    1620 L Street NW, Suite 1100
    Washington, DC 20036-5695
    http://www.nais.org

National Center for Education Statistics (NCES)
    U.S. Department of Education
    1990 K Street NW
    Washington, DC 20006
    http://www.nces.ed.gov

National Education Association (NEA)
    Teaching and Learning
    1201 16th Street NW
    Washington, DC 20036-3290
    http://www.nea.org

Recruiting New Teachers, Inc. (RNT)
    385 Concord Avenue, Suite 103
    Belmont, MA 02478
    http://www.rnt.org

Note: This is not a complete list of professional educator associations.

Chapter 3

Self-Awareness: What Stereotypes Have Been Attached to You?

Fill in the blanks.

1. _____ is a person who _____
   (your name)   _____
                 _____ .

2. _____ has the following strengths: _____
   (your name)   _____ .

3. _____ has the following weaknesses: _____
   (your name)   _____ .

4. _____ won't seek higher education because _____
   (your name)   _____
                 _____ .

5. _____ should work as a _____ or a _____
   (your name)   _____
   Stereotypes can be limiting and can be replaced by _____
                 _____
                 _____
                 _____
                 _____
                 _____ .

Chapter 4

Examples of Education Job-Related Advertisements and Possible Job Ideas in Metropolitan "Free" Magazines

- child home safety consultant and house proofing service
- children's shoe store
- child psychologist
- child dentistry
- in-home tutoring service
- personalized puzzle designers
- chess instruction and tutor
- child party planners
- children's physician
- mothers' child clothing exchange store
- pick your own fruit and vegetables patch with kids
- children's photographers
- art and drawing classes center
- tennis instructor (child's)
- educational therapy and consultant service (assessment and remedial treatment)
- child gymnastics instruction
- child motor development instruction
- child cheerleading instruction
- child violin instruction
- kindermusik summer camp
- child ballet instruction
- children's clothing store (bring last year's clothes for credit or cash)
- children's aquatics instruction
- children's portrait studio
- drama school
- girls' self-esteem classes (9–12)
- social etiquette instruction

- academic tutor
- karate for kids classes
- skating classes
- Girl Scouts
- ice skating classes
- Suzuki institute
- child orthopaedics center
- Irish dance instruction
- positive parenting instruction
- customized birth announcement service
- family first referral service (resource and referral agency)
- child ski instruction
- center for stepfamily development
- rainy day resources (babysitting and child care referral services)
- sympathy and support foundation (loss of child service)
- babysitting safety classes for babysitters (11–13)
- mother's nonprofit support group
- bookstore story hours
- new parent support group
- yoga for youth classes
- Boy Scouts
- early pregnancy classes
- environmental awareness classes for children
- kid's cooking classes
- zoo programs for children
- fossil find day camp (Grades 1–6)
- weekend fathers' classes
- sibling preparation classes (for child expecting a new sibling)
- bookstore book club for children
- botanical garden's bug day classes
- Lego lab for children
- future community leaders class for middle and secondary school students
- marvelous multiples classes (for multiple birth famlies)
- sunset nature hike classes
- family art courses
- miraculous bodies class (parents and preteen girls discussion of puberty issues)
- choosing a child care provider class
- nurturing fathers classes
- parent's toddler understanding class
- family services mental health clinic
- art museum classes for children
- gym and swim parties and service
- ceramic painting parties for children service
- overnight child care service
- independent storyteller consultants and party service
- organizing service (children's room and other home areas)
- YMCA classes for children
- children's athletic training center
- special needs early childhood program
- developmental disabilities community agency
- migrant child care agency
- grandparents as parents support group
- children's shelter home
- fetal photos service
- horseback riding instruction
- magic birthday party bus and party presenters service
- creative memories scrapbook store and classes
- early childhood clearinghouse service (parent information)
- backseat child entertainment and education kit manufacturers

Chapter 6

Sample Application Form

I. PERSONAL DATA

Name _____   Desired Position _____

Present Address _____   Until _____
        (Street)   (City)   (Date)

_____   Telephone _____
        (State)   (Zip)

E-mail _____   FAX _____

Social Security No. _____

Permanent Address _____   Telephone _____
    (Street) (City) (State) (Zip)

II. PREPARATION FOR TEACHING

	Schools Attended	Dates Attended	Diploma or Degree
A. College or University	_____	_____	_____
	_____	_____	_____
	_____	_____	_____
	_____	_____	_____
	_____	_____	_____
	_____	_____	_____

B.A. Major _____   Minor _____

M.A. Major _____   Minor _____

Other _____

B. College Work

Total number of semester hours or credits you have in professional education courses _____

Student teaching _____

What is your college grade point average? _____

What languages do you speak? _____

   List five courses (including three education courses) you have taken that you think will be valuable to you as a teacher.

1. _____
2. _____
3. _____
4. _____
5. _____

Check areas of special training

Music _____   Children's literature _____

Child growth/development _____   Storytelling _____

Physical education _____   Arts and crafts _____

Guidance/counseling _____   Nutrition _____

Second language _____   Language development _____

Science and math _____   Multicultural _____

Other _____

C. Extracurricular Activities. List activities you have participated in and feel able to direct (parent counseling, first aid, etc.).

_____

_____

_____

D. Certificate or Credential
Name(s) of certificate/credential _____

_____ Issued in the state of _____

III. TEACHING EXPERIENCE

Years (from–to)	Type of school	Location	Grades of subject
_____	_____	_____	_____
_____	_____	_____	_____
_____	_____	_____	_____

IV. WORK EXPERIENCE OTHER THAN TEACHING

Years (from–to)	Employer and location	Type of work and/or position
_____	_____	_____
_____	_____	_____
_____	_____	_____

V. REFERENCES (administrators or supervisors with whom you have worked)

Name	Position/Occupation	Address
_____	_____	_____
_____	_____	_____
_____	_____	_____

VI. OTHER INFORMATION List participation within the last two years in any professional activity for the improvement of the school or schools where you have been employed.

_____

_____

_____

Do you have specific talents outside your teaching specialty? Do you play a musical instrument?

_____

_____

VII. CANDIDATE'S SPACE Write any information, which has not already been covered, that you feel may be helpful and pertinent to your possible employment.

_____

_____

_____

Date _____

_____

Signature of Applicant

Chapter 6

Application Screening Form

Applicant's Name: _____ Date:_____

Position: _____

_____

	Scale
	1 5
	acceptable unacceptable

1. Application complete   _____

   What's needed? _____

   _____

   _____

2. Education requirement satisfied?   _____

   What's needed? _____

   _____

   Strengths: _____

   _____

3. Experience requirements satisfied?   _____

   Strengths _____

   _____

   _____

4. Past work experience complete?   _____

   What's needed? _____

   _____

   Strengths _____

   _____

   _____

5. Reference information complete?   _____

   What's needed? _____

   _____

   _____

6. Recommended references contact?   _____

   If unacceptable, list reasons _____

   _____

   _____

   _____

Glossary Terms

career manager   one who guides and directs another toward career goals; may offer training in assessment, communication, finance, interpersonal relationships, leadership, or other skills and educational topics.

diversity   refers to the influence of age, class culture, language, gender, ethnicity, race, disability, sexual orientation, family structure, and religion

early childhood   refers to children birth through age eight; includes terms such as infant, toddler, preschool, pre-kindergarten, and school-aged children

mean   a quantity having a value intermediate between the values of other quantities; an average

middle school   refers to grades 7, 8, and 9 in most states; sometimes described as a junior high.

practicum   placement or work in a facility such as one that involves children or families, where one performs a direct or indirect service or a job under the supervision of a training supervisor; student teaching is a practicum

prekindergarten   programs offered for children prior to attending kindergarten

secondary   refers to high school

teacher certification   a process by which a state's department of education qualifies individuals for teaching positions in the public school system

tenure   a status granted to an employee indicating that the position or employment is permanent.

venture capital investors   individuals or companies that invest in promising businesses

Index